KAREN BROWN'S
California
Charming Inns & Itineraries

Written by

CLARE BROWN   JUNE BROWN   KAREN BROWN

Illustrations by Barbara Tapp

Cover Painting by Jann Pollard

Travel Press
Karen Brown's Country Inn Series

Karen Brown Titles

Austria: Charming Inns & Itineraries

California: Charming Inns & Itineraries

England: Charming Bed & Breakfasts

England, Wales & Scotland: Charming Hotels & Itineraries

France: Charming Bed & Breakfasts

France: Charming Inns & Itineraries

Germany: Charming Inns & Itineraries

Ireland: Charming Inns & Itineraries

Italy: Charming Bed & Breakfasts

Italy: Charming Inns & Itineraries

Spain: Charming Inns & Itineraries

Switzerland: Charming Inns & Itineraries

Karen Brown's Guides
Post Office Box 70
San Mateo, California 94401, USA
Tel: (415) 342-9117   Fax: (415) 342-9153
e-mail: karen@karenbrown.com

Dear Friends:

Thank you for your many letters. They help to keep us current on the over 1,600 properties in our guides. Although we personally inspect (without exception) every accommodation we recommend, places change from one visit to the next. Sometimes they improve dramatically. Sometimes they go downhill. With this in mind, we eagerly read what you, our "inspectors on the road," have to say about your personal experiences. We often receive mixed reviews—some of you rave about a property, while others have complaints. When this happens, we weigh all comments and try to make a balanced judgment—and target the property for another inspection.

Thanks too for the many spectacular discoveries you have shared with us. Many of the finest places in our guides are those you have found. Please drop us a line when you come across a real "winner." Tell us why you think it's special and if possible include a photo or a brochure.

We value all your fine letters. Please keep them coming.

Warm personal regards,

Karen   Clare   June

Editors: Clare Brown, Karen Brown, June Brown, Iris Sandilands
Technical support: William H. Brown III; Aide-de-camp: William H. Brown
Illustrations: Barbara Tapp; Cover painting: Jann Pollard; Cover design: Tara Brassil
Maps: Susanne Lau Alloway—Greenleaf Design & Graphics; Cover photo: William H. Brown
Written in cooperation with Carlson Wagonlit/Town & Country Travel, San Mateo, CA 94401, USA
Distributed USA & Canada: The Globe Pequot Press, Box 833, Old Saybrook, CT 06475, USA
Tel: (860) 395-0440, fax: (860) 395-0312
Distributed Australia & New Zealand: Little Hills Press Pty. Ltd., 1st Floor, Regent House
37–43 Alexander Street, Crows Nest NSW 2065, Australia, tel: (02) 437-6995, fax: (02) 438-5762
Distributed UK & Europe: Hi Marketing, 38 Carver Road, London SE24 9LT, England
Tel: (0171) 738-7751, fax: (0171) 274-9160
A catalog record for this book is available from the British Library

Library of Congress Cataloging-in-Publication Data

Brown, Clare.
    Karen Brown's California charming inns & itineraries / written by
Clare Brown, June Brown , Karen Brown. – Totally rev. 5th ed.
      p. cm. -- (Karen Brown's country inn series)
    Includes index.
    ISBN 0-930328-42-6 (pbk)
    1.   Bed and breakfast accommodations--California--Guidebooks.
2. Hotels--California--Guidebooks. 3. California--Guidebooks.
I. Brown, June, 1949- . II. Brown, Karen, 1956- . III. Title.
IV. Series.
TX907.3.C2B756   1997
647.94794'01- - dc20

                                                    96-22792
                                                      CIP

Dedicated with Love and Hugs

To

Our Little Ones

Who are so quickly growing up

Clare, Alexandra, Richard, Georgia, & Claire

Check out Karen Brown's Web Site at
http://www.karenbrown.com

With the click of a button you can:

Research accommodations

Select hotels by region and review color photos and information on individual properties—an excellent way to visualize and compare your choices

Make on-line reservations

Make on-line reservations at a selection of our recommended properties, as well as at other hotels around the world

Review itineraries

Investigate recommended countryside itineraries and personalized countryside mini-tours designed by Karen Brown

Connect to Karen Brown Travel Services

Just fill out our web page form or send an e-mail to Karen Brown Travel Services to book a mini-tour or to make air, car and hotel reservations

Contents

Introduction

San Francisco Cable Car

California, the Golden State, is a fascinating region of dramatic scenery, exciting places to visit, and appealing places to stay. There is almost too much—it can be confusing to decide the most important sights to see and the most special inns to choose. This book is written to help you through the maze: we have done your homework for you. The first section of the book presents five detailed driving itineraries that spider-web across the state. The second section features our personal recommendations of places to stay, written with the sincere belief that where you lay your head each night makes the difference between a good and a great vacation. Every inn in this guide is one we have seen and enjoyed—no inn ever pays to be included.

About Driving Itineraries

Five driving itineraries map a route through the various regions of California so that you can choose one that includes the area you have your heart set on visiting. Each itinerary is preceded by a map that shows the routing and all the towns in which we have a recommended inn. Each routing can easily be tailored to meet your own specific needs by leaving out some sightseeing if time is limited, or linking several itineraries together if you wish to enjoy a longer vacation.

CAR RENTAL

The itineraries are designed for travel by automobile. If you are staying in San Francisco at the beginning of your trip, it is not necessary to pick up a rental car until you leave the city since the public transportation system is so convenient and this is a wonderful town for walking. However, if your vacation begins in Los Angeles, you will need a car within the city to get from place to place and should pick it up on arrival at the airport.

DRIVING TIMES

California is a large state, approximately 1,000 miles from tip to toe. If you stay on the freeways, you can quickly cover large areas of territory, but if you choose to savor the beauty of the coast along California's sensational Highway 1 or dip into the countryside along scenic back roads, plan on traveling about 30 miles in an hour and remember to allow extra time for stopping to enjoy countryside vistas.

MAPS

Each itinerary has a map outlining the suggested routing and detailing sightseeing and overnight stops. Alternate places to stay are also marked. The maps are an artist's renderings and do not show every road and highway—you need to supplement them with more comprehensive commercial maps.

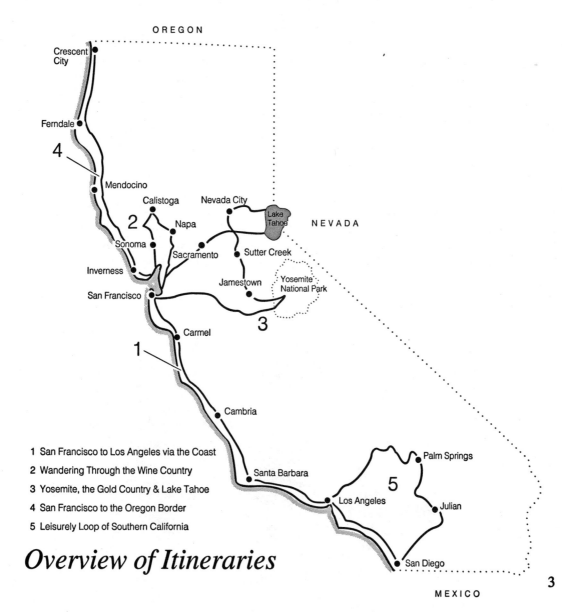

OREGON

Crescent City

Ferndale

4

Mendocino

Calistoga

Nevada City

Napa

Lake Tahoe

NEVADA

Sonoma

2

Sacramento

Sutter Creek

Inverness

Jamestown

Yosemite National Park

San Francisco

3

Carmel

1

Cambria

1 San Francisco to Los Angeles via the Coast

2 Wandering Through the Wine Country

3 Yosemite, the Gold Country & Lake Tahoe

4 San Francisco to the Oregon Border

5 Leisurely Loop of Southern California

Palm Springs

Santa Barbara

5

Los Angeles

Julian

San Diego

Overview of Itineraries

MEXICO

3

PACING

At the beginning of each itinerary we suggest our recommended pacing to help you decide the amount of time to allocate to each one. The suggested time frame reflects how much there is to see and do. Use our recommendation as a guideline only, and choreograph your own itinerary based on how much leisure time you have and whether your preference is to move on to a new destination each day or settle in and use a particular inn as base.

WEATHER

At the beginning of each itinerary a brief note is given on what you can expect to encounter weather-wise in the various regions. In California a whole new climate emerges in just a short distance. The idea that the entire state is sunny and warm year-round can all too quickly be dispelled when the summer fog rolls into San Francisco or 3 feet of winter snow falls in the High Sierras.

Introduction—About Driving Itineraries

About Inn Travel

We use the term "inn" to cover everything from a simple bed and breakfast to a sophisticated resort. A wide range of inns is included in this guide: some are great bargains, others very costly; some are in cities, others in remote locations; some are quite sophisticated, others extremely simple; some are decorated with opulent antiques, others with furniture from grandma's attic; some are large hotels, others have only a few rooms. The common denominator is that each place has some special quality that makes it appealing. The individual descriptions are intended to give you an honest appraisal of each property so that you can select accommodation based on personal preferences. To help you appreciate and understand what to expect when traveling the "inn way," the following pointers are given:

BATHROOMS

It is not standard that every inn recommended in this book has a bathroom for each bedroom. Some inns will offer guestrooms that share a bath with other guestrooms, or rooms that have private baths down the hall. We specify under each description how many of the guestrooms have private bathrooms. We do not detail whether the bath is equipped with shower, tub-shower, tub, or Jacuzzi. Inquire as to what the term "with bathroom" means when making your reservation.

BREAKFAST

A welcome feature and trademark of many inns is their morning repast—many cookbooks have been authored and inspired by innkeepers. Breakfast is almost always included in the room rate, but we definitely mention if it is NOT. Although most innkeepers take great pride in their delectable morning offerings, know that breakfast can

range from a gourmet "waddle away" feast (as proudly described by one innkeeper-chef) to muffins and coffee. Sometimes breakfast is limited to a Continental in the privacy of your room or a hot breakfast with others in the dining room, and sometimes both. Breakfast times vary as well—some innkeepers serve a hot breakfast at a specified time, while others replenish a buffet on a more leisurely schedule. Breakfasts are as individual as the inns themselves and are something to look forward to.

CANCELLATION POLICIES

Although policies vary, inns, by necessity, are usually more stringent than large chain hotels in their cancellation policies: understand their terms when securing a reservation.

CHARM

It is very important to us that an inn has charm—ideally an inn should be a historic building, beautifully decorated, lovingly managed, and in a wonderful location. Few inns meet every criterion, but all our selections have something that makes them special and are situated in enjoyable surroundings—we have had to reject several lovely inns because of a poor location. Many are in historic buildings, but remember that California is a relatively young state, so anything over 50 years in age is considered old—few inns date back further than the mid-19th century and many are new or reproduction-old buildings. Small inns are usually our favorites, but size alone did not dictate whether or not a hostelry was chosen. Most are small (a few have only three guestrooms), but because California offers some splendid larger establishments of great character and charm (one has 700 guestrooms), a few of these are also included.

CHECK-IN

Inns are usually very specific about check-in time—generally between 3 and 6 pm. Let the inn know if you are going to arrive late and the innkeeper will make special arrangements for you, such as leaving you a door key under a potted plant along with a note on how to find your room. Also, for those who might arrive early, note that some inns close their doors between check-out and check-in times. Inns are often frequently staffed only by the owners themselves and that window of time between check-out and check-in is often the one opportunity to shop for those wonderful breakfasts they prepare in addition to running their own personal errands.

CHILDREN

Many places in this guide do not welcome children. They cannot legally refuse accommodation to children, but, as parents, we really want to know and want to stay where our children are genuinely welcome. Under each description we have indicated the general policy of each inn, i.e., whether it is, or is not appropriate for children—but these are only guidelines. Many places will accept children with certain stipulations such as if they have the proper room available, if the children are of a certain age, if other families are going to be in residence, or if it is a slow period.

COMFORT

As influential as charm, comfort plays a deciding role in the selection of inns recommended. Firm mattresses, a quiet setting, good lighting, fresh towels, scrubbed bathrooms—we do our best to remember the basics when considering inns—the charming decor and innkeeper will soon be forgotten if you do not have a good night's sleep and comfortable stay. Also, do remember, however, that parts of California can be hot during the summer months and that many inns are in older buildings and do not have the luxury of air conditioning.

CREDIT CARDS

Whether or not an establishment accepts credit cards is indicated at the bottom of each description—AX (American Express), MC (MasterCard), VS (Visa), all major, or none accepted. Even if an inn does not accept plastic payment, it will perhaps take your credit card number as a guarantee of arrival.

FOOD

The majority of places featured in this guide do not have restaurants but innkeepers are usually very knowledgeable and happy to recommend local favorites. However, almost all of the inns do serve breakfast: quite often a sumptuous one. Frequently, in addition to breakfast, tea or wine and hors d'oeuvres are served in the afternoon. Sometimes, if you request in advance, a picnic lunch can also be prepared.

If you have any special dietary requirements most innkeepers will gladly try to accommodate your needs. Not having the stock a restaurant would have, innkeepers usually plan a menu that features one entree and have those ingredients on hand. Therefore, it is best to mention any special requests at the time of making your reservation both as a courtesy and from a practical point of view so that they can have items such as special low-fat dairy products, egg substitutions, sugar-free syrups, etc.

PROFESSIONALISM

All the inns we selected are run by professional innkeepers. There are many homes that rent out extra bedrooms to paying guests but this was not what we were looking for and they are not included in our guide. We have recommended only inns that have privacy for the guests and where you do not have to climb over a tricycle to reach the bathroom.

RESERVATIONS

The best way to make a reservation is to just pick up your phone and call. It is very satisfactory and helpful to be able to personally discuss the various differences in available accommodation and policies of the inn. As a courtesy to the innkeepers, however, keep in mind that staff is often limited, and during certain periods of the day, such as the breakfast hour, they are busier than others—flipping pancakes, checking out guests, helping plan activities. Also, inns are often homes, and you might be waking up the innkeeper if you call late evenings or early mornings. Another convenient and efficient way to request a reservation is by fax: if the inn has a fax, we have noted the number in the information line next to the telephone number. Also quickly becoming a widely accepted and inexpensive means of communicating is by computer modem and the use of e-mail—where only local, rather than long-distance phone charges are incurred. For the computer-savvy, included in this 1977 edition are e-mail addresses whenever available for the individual inns. As a final note: When planning your trip be aware that the majority of inns in this guide require a two-night stay on weekends and over holidays.

RESPONSIBILITY

Our goal is to outline itineraries in regions that we consider of prime interest to our readers and to recommend inns that we think are outstanding. All of the inns featured have been visited and selected solely on their merits. Our judgments are made on the charm of the inn, its setting, cleanliness, and, above all, the warmth of welcome. No inn ever pays to be included. Each property has its own appeal, and we try to present you with a very honest appraisal. However, no matter how careful we are, sometimes we misjudge an inn's merits, or the ownership changes, or unfortunately sometimes inns just do not maintain their standards. If you find an inn is not as we have indicated, please let us know, and accept our sincere apologies.

ROOM RATES

It seems that many inns play musical rates, with high-season, low-season, midweek, weekend, and holiday rates. We have quoted the 1997 high season, general range of rates from the lowest-priced bedroom for two people (singles usually receive a very small discount) to the most expensive suite, including breakfast. The rates given are those quoted to us by the inn. Please use these figures as a guideline and be certain to ask at the time of booking what the rates are and what they include.

We have not given prices for "special" rooms such as those that can accommodate three people traveling together. Discuss with the innkeeper rooms and rates available before making your selection. Please be aware that taxes are not included in the rates quoted and usually inn taxes are very high—frequently over 10%. Of course, several inns are exceptions to our guidelines and whenever this is the case we mention the special situation (such as breakfast not being included in the rate).

SMOKING

Most inns have extremely strict non-smoking policies, while a few permit smoking in restricted public areas or outside. Ask about smoking policies—it is best to be forewarned.

SOCIALIZING

Inns usually offer a conviviality rarely found in a "standard" hotel. The gamut runs all the way from playing "cozy family" around the kitchen table to sharing a sophisticated, elegant cocktail hour in the parlor. Breakfast may be a formal meal served at a set hour when the guests gather around the dining-room table, or it may be served buffet-style over several hours where guests have the option of either sitting down to eat alone or joining other guests at a larger table.

Then again, some inns will bring a breakfast tray to your room, or perhaps breakfast in the room is the only option. After check-in, many inns offer an afternoon refreshment, such as tea and cakes or wine and hors d'oeuvres which may be seen as another social opportunity. Some inns set out a buffet where guests are invited to meander in and out mixing or not mixing with other guests as they choose and then others orchestrate a more structured gathering, often a social hour, with the innkeeper presiding. What you need to do is choose the inn that seems to offer the degree of togetherness or privacy that you desire.

TELEPHONES

California attracts not only a lot of visitors but people who decide to settle here as well—evidenced by the fact that as this edition of the book goes to press, we have just learned that certain area codes will be changed in 1997 to accommodate the increasing population. Actually in the next five years, thirteen new area codes will be introduced in California, doubling the current count.

Telephone numbers referenced throughout this guide, both for sightseeing and hotel contacts, reflect the current (i.e., 1996) area codes. Although there will be a six-month permissive dialing period where both the old and the new area codes will operate, and afterwards a recording to advise customers of the reassignment, we thought it best to bring the fact that the numbers will change to your attention.

New area codes that have been announced thus far include:

Parts of (310)—Eastern Los Angeles, will change to (562) on January 25,1997

Parts of (619)—Portions of San Diego, Imperial, Riverside, San Bernardino, Mono, Kern and Inyo, will change to (760) on March 22, 1997

Parts of (818)—Northern Los Angeles County will change to (626) on June 14, 1997

Parts of (415)—San Francisco Bay Area will change to (650) on August 1, 1997

Parts of (916)—Sacramento area will change to (530) on November 1, 1997

Introduction—About Inn Travel

San Francisco to Los Angeles via the Coast

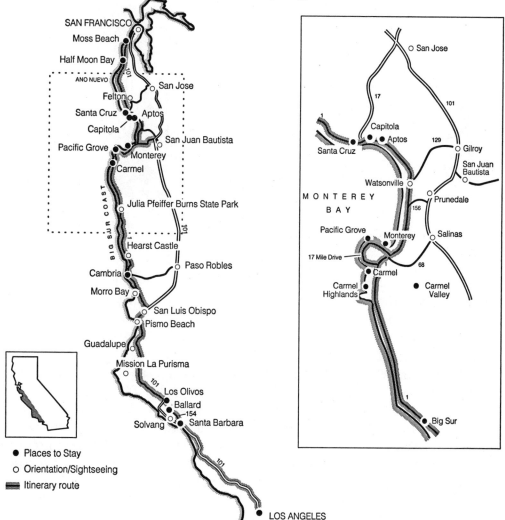

SAN FRANCISCO
Moss Beach
Half Moon Bay
ANO NUEVO
Felton
Santa Cruz — Aptos
Capitola
Pacific Grove
Monterey
Carmel
San Jose
San Juan Bautista

BIG SUR COAST

Julia Pfeiffer Burns State Park

Hearst Castle
Paso Robles
Cambria
Morro Bay
San Luis Obispo
Pismo Beach
Guadalupe
Mission La Purisma
Los Olivos
Ballard
154
Solvang — Santa Barbara

LOS ANGELES

San Jose
17
101
Santa Cruz
Capitola
Aptos
129
Gilroy
San Juan Bautista
Watsonville
MONTEREY BAY
Prunedale
156
Pacific Grove
Salinas
17 Mile Drive
Monterey
Carmel
68
Carmel Highlands
Carmel Valley
1
Big Sur

● Places to Stay
○ Orientation/Sightseeing
▨ Itinerary route

13

San Francisco to Los Angeles via the Coast

Golden Gate Bridge

You can drive between San Francisco and Los Angeles in a day or fly in an hour. But rather than rushing down the freeway or hopping aboard an airplane, drive leisurely along the coast between these two metropolises and enjoy the quaintness of Carmel, the charm of Santa Barbara, the splendor of the Big Sur coastline, the opulence of William Randolph Hearst's hilltop castle, and the fun of experiencing a bit of Denmark in Solvang. Also intertwined in this itinerary are stops to appreciate a piece of California's colorful heritage—her Spanish missions. This routing roughly follows the footsteps of the Spanish padres who, in the 1700s, built a string of missions (about a day's journey on horseback apart) along the coast of California from the Mexican border to just north of San Francisco. Today many of these beautiful adobe churches and their surrounding settlements have been reconstructed and are open as museums, capturing a glimpse of life as it was lived by the Spaniards and the Indians in the early days of colonization.

Recommended Pacing: We recommend a minimum stay of two or three nights in San Francisco, affording two full days for a quick introduction to the city, and definitely more time if your schedule allows. San Francisco is a beautiful city and there is much to explore and enjoy. From San Francisco, if you take the direct route, you can easily drive to Carmel in about three hours. However, located just south of San Francisco is the Año Nuevo Reserve, where you can observe the enormous elephant seals in their natural habitat. It takes several hours to walk around the secluded beaches where the seals congregate, so if you want to visit the reserve en route to Carmel, we recommend an early start from the city. Plan on at least two to three nights (or again, if possible, more) in the Carmel, Pacific Grove, or Monterey area. One day can easily be devoured exploring the Monterey Bay Aquarium, Cannery Row, and the wharf. Another full day is needed to drive the gorgeous 17-Mile Drive, walk the spectacular Point Lobos State Park, visit the beautiful Carmel Mission—and we have yet to even discuss shopping in downtown Carmel. From Carmel, you can drive the dramatic coastline of Big Sur and on to Santa Barbara in four to five hours, but plan to overnight in Cambria if you want to include even just one of the tours of Hearst Castle and visit the cute artist's town of Cambria—it's too much to do in one day. Santa Barbara is a beautiful, charming city with an expanse of lovely beach. You'd be disappointed if you didn't plan at least two nights in the area before continuing on to Los Angeles.

Weather Wise: San Francisco and the coast are often foggy during June, July, and August. The farther south you go, the earlier in the day the fog burns off. The northern California coast is cool and rainy during the winter. In southern California the weather is warmer year-round and traditionally less rain falls during the winter. Smog is a problem in certain parts of the Los Angeles area during the summer.

When you ask travelers around the world, "What is your favorite city?" many times the answer is "San Francisco." And it is no wonder: **San Francisco** really is very special, a magical town of unsurpassed beauty—spectacular when glistening in the sunlight, equally enchanting when wrapped in fog. But the beauty is more than skin deep: San

Francisco offers a wealth of sightseeing, fabulous restaurants, splendid shopping, and a refreshing climate.

There are many large, super-deluxe hotels in San Francisco and we recommend a marvelous selection of small, intimate inns. Study our various recommendations to see what most fits your personality and pocketbook. Be advised that hotel space is frequently tight, so make reservations as far in advance as possible.

A good way to orient yourself in San Francisco is to take a half-day city sightseeing tour (brochures on these tours should be available at your hotel) and then return to the destinations that most catch your fancy. If you like to study before you arrive, there are entire guidebooks devoted to San Francisco and the Visitors' Bureau will send you an information packet on what to see and do. San Francisco Visitors' Bureau, P.O. Box 6977, San Francisco, CA 94101, (415) 391-2000. To keep you on the right track the following is an alphabetical listing of some of our favorite sights:

Alcatraz: A visit to the abandoned prison island in the middle of San Francisco Bay is a fascinating excursion and affords a magnificent view of the city skyline—if you don't have a friend with a yacht, this is the next best thing! The lonely, concrete, fortress-like structure of Alcatraz was deemed escape-proof until a couple of prisoners (yet to be found) dug their way out with a spoon. The tour of the prison involves lots of walking, so be sure to wear sturdy, comfortable shoes and don't forget your camera or woolly sweater because the views are gorgeous and it is cold on this windswept rocky island. This excursion is very popular. For further information call: (415) 546-2700.

California Palace of The Legion of Honor: Without a doubt, this is our favorite museum in San Francisco—we just love the exhibits and the spectacular setting on a bluff in Lincoln Park overlooking the ocean. The original of Rodin's famous Thinker welcomes you to the San Francisco replica of the Palais de la Légion d'Honneur in Paris where Napoleon first established his new government. A self-guided audio tour is available to steer you through the galleries which include one devoted to medieval art (there's a ceiling from a 15th-century Spanish palace), a British gallery with paintings by Gainsborough and Constable, and 19th- and 20th-century galleries with their popular works by Monet, Renoir, and Picasso. For more information call (415) 750-3600.

Cable Cars: You cannot leave San Francisco without riding one of the colorful little trolleys that make their way up and down the breathtakingly steep city hills. Rather than touring by cab or bus, plan your sightseeing around hopping on and off cable cars. You can travel easily from the shopping district of Union Square past Chinatown and the "crookedest street in the world"—Lombard, and on to the Ghiradelli Square-Fisherman's Wharf area. For a behind-the-scenes look at this charmingly antiquated transit system visit the Cable Car Museum at the corner of Washington and Mason Streets. Here you can view the huge cables that pull the cars from below the streets and a historical display that includes the first cable car.

Chinatown: Just a few short blocks from Union Square enter beneath the dragon arch (at the corner of Bush Street and Grant Avenue) into another world with street signs in Chinese characters, tiny grocery stores displaying Chinese vegetables and delicacies, apothecary shops selling unusual remedies, spicy aromas drifting from colorful restaurants, older women bustling about in traditional dress, and the surrounding hum of unfamiliar phrases. Of course the streets are jammed with tourists and locals and there is a plethora of rather tacky, but fun-to-explore souvenir shops. Don't limit your exploration of Chinatown to the main thoroughfare of Grant Avenue: poke down the intriguing little alleys and side streets. Plan a visit to 56 Ross Alley, the Golden Gate Fortune Cookie Factory. Down another alley, at 17 Adler Place, is the Chinese Historical Society of America—a small museum portraying the story of the Chinese immigration. The Chinese Cultural Center, housed in the Holiday Inn at Kearny and Washington streets, offers fascinating docent-led heritage and culinary walks affording a glimpse of the "real Chinatown." For information call (415) 986-1822. The Cultural Center also has a wonderful small museum which offers an ever-changing schedule of exhibits.

Coit Tower: Coit Tower, located at the top of Telegraph Hill, is a relic of old San Francisco and fun to visit—not only because of the great view, but because its story is so very "San Francisco." The money to construct the watch tower, which resembles the nozzle of a fire hose, was willed to the city by the wealthy Lillie Hitchcock Coit, a volunteer fireman (or should we say firewoman) who dearly loved to rush to every blaze wearing her diamond-encrusted fire badge. A mural on the ground floor provides a vivid depiction of early California life.

Fisherman's Wharf to Ghiradelli Square: This portion of the waterfront is very popular with tourists. **Pier 39** is lined with New England-style shops; nothing authentic, but a popular shopping and restaurant arcade complete with street performers and a beautiful two-tier carousel. Pier 39 is also home to a new aquarium (in our opinion not worth the money) and some very boisterous and amusing sea lions. (415) 981-7437. Pier 41 is where you purchase tickets for the popular excursion to Alcatraz (see listing). **Fisherman's Wharf** where fishermen haul in their daily catch, has long been a favorite with tourists. It is difficult to find even the heart of Fisherman's Wharf behind all the trinket-filled souvenir shops and tourist arcades, but look carefully and sure enough, you will see the colorful fishing boats bobbing about in the water at the waterfront between Jones and Taylor Streets. Nearby, Fish Alley, a small pier extending out into the harbor, affords a good view of the fishing fleet and the aroma of fresh fish mingling with the salty air. At the corner of Leavenworth and Jefferson **The Cannery**, formerly a fruit cannery, is today an attractive shopping complex. At the foot of Hyde Street **Hyde Street Pier** is home to the Maritime Museum's fleet of historic ships, several of which can be boarded and explored. Our favorite is the *Balclutha* (1886) a three-masted merchant ship typical of the hundreds that came round the Horn to San Francisco. Inspect the comfortable captain's quarters and cramped crew's quarters and exhibits of nautical gear. (415) 556-3002. Just beyond the **Hyde Street cable car turnaround** lies **Ghiradelli Square,** a lovely brick building that used to house the Ghiradelli chocolate factory, now a complex of attractive stores and restaurants. The ship-shaped building in

Aquatic Park (in front of Ghiradelli Square) is the land base of the **Maritime Museum,** full of displays on the history of water transportation from the 1800s to the present, including some marvelous photos of old San Francisco. (415) 556-3002.

Golden Gate Bridge and **Fort Point:** San Francisco's symbol is the Golden Gate Bridge with its graceful orange arches. The visitors' viewing area on the San Francisco side offers stunning views (if the fog is not in) and access to the pedestrian walkway that enables a walk across the bridge (2½ miles round trip, wear warm clothing). At the base of the Golden Gate Bridge's south pier, Fort Point, built in 1861 as one of the west coast's principal points of defense, provides a fascinating insight into military life during that period. (415) 556-1693.

Golden Gate Park: You will need to take a bus or taxi to Golden Gate Park, but don't miss it. The park encompasses over 1,000 acres, so large you really cannot hope to see it all, but many attractions are located near each other. Wander through the traditional **Japanese Tea Garden** and enjoy tea and cookies Japanese-style at the tea house. (415) 666-7024. The **De Young Museum** is primarily devoted to American art while the adjacent **Asian Art Museum** contains one of America's finest collections of Asian art. (415) 750-3600. The **Museum of Natural History** offers dioramas of wildlife from African to Californian (along with an impressive collection of gems and minerals), while the neighboring **Steinhart Aquarium** has all things fishy from a tropical swamp with alligators and turtles to a fish roundabout—an enormous donut-shaped fish tank. (415) 750-7145. Just a short walk from the museums lies the **Conservatory of Flowers,** an immense Victorian wooden greenhouse full of plant life varying from a humid rain forest to colorful displays of seasonal flowers. (415) 666-7024.

Lombard Street: Lombard is an ordinary city street—except for one lone, brick-paved block between Hyde and Leavenworth where the street goes crazy and makes a series of hairpin turns as it twists down the hill. Pretty houses border each side of the street, and banks of hydrangeas add color. Start at the top and go down what must be the crookedest

Lombard Street

street in the world: it is lots of fun. The Hyde Street cable car makes a stop at the top of the hill and from here you can easily walk down to Fisherman's Wharf.

Mission San Francisco De Assisi: This mission at Dolores and 16th Streets is frequently referred to as the Mission Dolores. If you are interested in Californian missions, you will find a visit here worthwhile. It was on this spot that San Francisco was born when Father Francisco Palou founded his mission here in 1776. At one time this was a large complex of warehouses, workshops, granaries, a tannery, soap shop, corrals, Indian dwellings, and even an aqueduct. Today, all that is left is the chapel and next to it the garden where gravestones attest to the fragility of life. Although small, the chapel is beautiful in its simplicity with 4-foot-thick adobe walls and massive redwood timbers. Tel: (415) 621-8203.

Museum of Modern Art (MOMA): A cylindrical, striped turret rising from blocks of red bricks gives a hint of what lies within this futuristic building at 151 Third Street. To help you appreciate the exhibits, an audio cassette can be rented in the lobby to guide you through the museum's permanent collection of abstract expressionistic paintings and avant-garde photography. Even if you are not a fan of modern art, you will be awed by the building's interior: the space soars upwards from the lobby for seven stories to a broad catwalk that runs below the cylindrical glass skylight. (415) 357-4000. Just across the street from the MOMA lie the **Yerba Buena Gardens and Galleries**. The gardens are an oasis of tranquillity where a broad expanse of grass leads to a cascading sheet of water—a perfect place to relax and people-watch. The galleries offer changing exhibits that showcase the San Francisco Bay Area's cultural diversity. Just round the corner (678 Mission Street) a turn-of-the-century hardware store houses the **California Historical Society** with its bookstore and changing exhibits of photographs, paintings, and objects documenting California's growth and change. (415) 357-1848.

Sausalito and **Tiburon:** An enjoyable excursion is to take the ferry from Pier 43½ in San Francisco to Sausalito or Tiburon, small towns just across the bay full of intriguing shops, art galleries, and wonderful restaurants. As a bonus, en route you enjoy wonderful vistas of San Francisco and the Golden Gate Bridge. For information call the Red and White Fleet at (415) 546-2815.

Theater: For theater buffs, San Francisco offers an excellent variety of entertainment. Most theaters are located in the heart of San Francisco within walking distance of Union Square. In addition, San Francisco has fine opera and ballet. The San Francisco Visitors' Bureau, (415) 391-2000, can send you a packet with information on what is going on in the city. You can also call the "hot line" at (415) 391-2001 for a recording of all current events.

Union Square: In the center of the city sits Union Square, hallmarked by a small park around which tower deluxe hotels and fancy department stores. Do not tarry too long at the "biggies" because just beyond the square lies every specialty shop imaginable from FAO Schwartz's toy emporium to any number of "designer" boutiques. San Francisco's own exclusive and elegant Gumps at 135 Post Street merits a visit. The Crocker Galleria at 50 Post houses collections from top names in international design and many fine specialty stores and restaurants.

Union Street: Union Street (between Laguna and Steiner), lined with lovely restored Victorian houses, offers a wonderful variety of quaint gift shops, elegant boutiques, beautiful antique stores, small art galleries, excellent restaurants, and a multitude of intriguing little shops hidden down tiny brick-paved lanes.

It's a 3 hour drive south from San Francisco to Carmel taking the scenic Highway 280 to San Jose and Highways 17 and 1 on to Carmel. But rather than head directly to Carmel, we suggest you meander down the coast, enjoying a number of sights en route—a journey that will deserve a couple of days.

Leave San Francisco to the south on 19th Avenue to Highway 280 and take Highway 1 through Pacifica where the freeway ends and the road narrows to meander around the precipitous rocky promontory known as Devil's Slide. Just south of Devil's Slide is **Moss Beach,** a suburban coastal town home to Karen Brown and her inn, **Seal Cove,** named after the nearby crescent of golden sand. Seal Cove Inn and the colorful restaurant, the **Moss Beach Distillery,** (415) 728-5595, known for its ghosts and beautiful ocean setting, are neighbors to the **Fitzgerald Marine Reserve** and park, where you can walk along the bluffs and investigate the tidepools at low tide. (415) 728-3584.

Just to the south of Moss Beach, **Princeton harbor,** with its mass of fishing vessels and sailboats, is one of California's last true commercial fishing harbors. Sport-fishing and whale-watching boats leave early mornings from Princeton. Bookings can be made through Huck Finn Sport Fishing, (415) 726-7133.

Detour off the Coastal Highway to the east at Highway 92 and take it for one block, making a right on **Half Moon Bay's** Main Street. Park just across the bridge and visit **Half Moon Bay Feed and Fuel,** an authentic country store that sells saddles, rabbits, chickens, animal feed, and farm implements. Poke your head in the various shops and businesses that line Main Street: you find excellent casual clothing at **Buffalo Shirt**

Company, a marvelous Italian restaurant, **Pasta Moon**, (415) 726-5125, and art galleries aplenty. (Another detour, traveling past Main Street farther east on Highway 92, is to the **Half Moon Bay Nursery**, nestled off the road just before it begins its climb up the mountain. An attraction in its own right with its wood-burning fireplace and classical music, the nursery also offers a bounty of reasonably priced plants.) Leaving Half Moon Bay, continue down Main Street to rejoin Highway 1 to the south of town.

Lengthy expanses of sandy beach are accessible from the many state parks along the coastline. **Pigeon Point Lighthouse** is one of the tallest lighthouses on the west coast. Tours are given only on Sundays between 10 am and 3 pm.

Thirty miles south of Half Moon Bay is the **Año Nuevo State Reserve**, home to elephant seals whose huge males with their trunk-like snouts reach a whopping 6,000 pounds. From mid-December to the end of March docents conduct a 3-mile round-trip hike to the breeding grounds of these car-size mammals. Reservation lines open in October for the following season: (800) 444-7275. If you are not able to book several months in advance, call the park directly, (415) 879-2025, and they may be able to advise you if last-minute tickets are available. We have, in the past, secured tickets by arriving at 8:30 am and queuing at the entrance booth for tickets for tours that day. Outside of the breeding season obtaining permits to view the seals (there are often also a great many sea lions in residence) is not a problem: tickets are issued on arrival and you follow the well-marked path out to the distant beach where the seals are found. The best time to visit outside of the breeding season is during July and August when the males return for their summer molt.

Ten miles to the south of Año Nuevo you come to the cluster of houses that makes up the town of **Davenport**. Fronting Highway 1 is the **New Davenport Cash Store** which sells everything from handmade jewelry to local pottery and whose restaurant offers a varied and healthful menu with excellent soups and tasty vegetarian dishes. Tel: (408) 426-4122.

Downtown **Santa Cruz**, 11 miles south of Davenport, was badly damaged in the 1989 earthquake, but a newly revived Pacific Avenue demonstrates all the laid-back charm the town is noted for, with outdoor cafés, a variety of shops and galleries, and numerous street performers. Years ago this busy seaside town, with its bustling **boardwalk** and amusement park bordering a broad stretch of white sand beach, was a popular day trip for workers in San Francisco. In recent years the rides and attractions have received a face-lift, making it a pleasure to visit, particularly since it is so clean and well maintained. The rides include a heart-stopping wooden roller coaster and a wonderful old-fashioned carousel. An effort is being made to make the adjacent fishing pier attractive with restaurants and shops. If you enjoy riding trains, you may want to take the old-fashioned diesel that departs from the boardwalk twice a day during the summer months for the 60-minute ride to Felton to board an old stream train of the **Roaring Camp Railroad**, a train that winds along narrow-gauge tracks up into a redwood forest. The train leaves several times a day from its main station in **Felton** (except Christmas) along narrow-gauge tracks built to carry lumber out of the forest. The conductor tells stories of the old days as the train circles up through the trees, making a brief stop at the "cathedral," a beautiful ring of redwoods that form a natural outdoor church, before heading back to the

Roaring Camp Railroad, Felton

depot. It is possible to take a picnic with you, alight at the top, and take the next train back. Call for departure times and directions: (408) 335-4400.

Leaving Santa Cruz, take Highway 1 south for about 20 miles to Highway 129 where you head east. Continue on the 129 for approximately 16 miles through small farms and rolling hills to **San Juan Bautista** and its most attractive **mission**. There is far more to see here than just an old church, for an area of the town has been restored to the way it was 150 years ago with the mission as its focus. Facing the square is the restored Plaza Hotel, now a museum where tickets are sold for admission to the attractions in the park. The focal point of the sightseeing is, of course, the mission, but do not end your touring there. Directly across from the mission is a most interesting house, nicely restored, and furnished as it must have looked many years ago. Adjacent to this is a blacksmith's shop and stables where there is a colorful display of old coaches. Next door to the Plaza Hotel is another home now open as a museum with period furnishings. Also, be sure not to miss San Juan Bautista which still maintains its 19th-century, small-town ambiance.

Follow Highway 156 west for a couple of miles until it merges with Highway 101 going south to the Monterey Peninsula. As you pass through Prunedale, begin to watch for signs indicating a sharp right-hand turn on Highway 156 west to the Monterey Peninsula. Along the way, fields of artichokes dominate the landscape as you near Castroville, the artichoke capital of the world. When you begin to smell the sea air, stay in the left lane following signs for Highway 1 south to the Monterey Peninsula. As you approach Monterey, dunes lining the sweep of the bay come into view.

The main sightseeing attractions in **Monterey** are in two areas: old town and the marina, and Cannery Row and the Monterey Bay Aquarium. A bayside walking and biking path runs from the Marina beside Cannery Row to the Aquarium and beyond to the adjoining town of Pacific Grove. A fun way to explore Monterey is to rent a side-by-side tricycle near the aquarium and pedal to the Marina.

In **Old Town** a 3-mile walking tour links the restored buildings of early Monterey. The old adobes are interesting and a sharp contrast to the bustle of nearby **Fisherman's Wharf,** a quaint wooden fishing pier lined with shops and restaurants. At the end of the pier huge sea lions vie for the fish cast off the fishing boats.

Cannery Row, once the center of this area's thriving sardine industry (the fish are long gone), and brought vividly to life by John Steinbeck in his novels featuring Doc and the boys, is now filled with small stores and tucked into an old warehouse are some outlet stores. The premier attraction in Monterey is the adjacent **Monterey Bay Aquarium**. The centerpieces of the Aquarium are the huge glass tanks that showcase the underwater world of the local offshore marine habitat from the diverse tidepools to the multitude of life in the Monterey Bay: one tank is populated by huge sharks and colorful schools of fish while another contains a mature kelp forest teeming with fish. Opened last year, the Outer Bay exhibit, a vast tank of water representative of the outer ocean, brings a new dimension to the Aquarium and leaves the visitor with a memorable impression of just how little is known about that massive body of water. For information call (408) 648-4888.

Monterey is all hustle and bustle (especially in summer) and it is quite a relief to continue to the neighboring, much quieter town of **Pacific Grove**. To reach Pacific Grove, follow the road in front of the Aquarium up the hill and make a right turn onto Ocean View Boulevard, a lovely drive lined on one side with gracious Victorian homes and splendid views of the sea on the other. Besides being an affluent residential community, Pacific Grove is famous for the Monarch butterflies that return each October and cluster in the grove of trees next to Butterfly Grove Inn on Lighthouse Avenue. The butterflies return faithfully every year.

Carmel lies just a few miles beyond Pacific Grove and there is no more perfect way to arrive than along the famous Seventeen-Mile Drive which meanders around the Monterey Peninsula coastline between the two towns. The route is easy to find as the road that leads to the "drive" intersects Lighthouse Avenue and is appropriately called Seventeen-Mile Drive.

The **Seventeen-Mile Drive** loops through an exclusive residential area of multi-million-dollar estates and gorgeous golf courses. Because the land is private, $5 per car is levied at the entrance gate, where you'll receive a map indicating points of interest along the way. The scenic drive traces the low-lying shore, passes rocky coves where kelp beds are home to sea lions, sea otters, cormorants, and gulls (remember to bring your binoculars), and

Carmel

meanders through woodlands where Monterey pines gnarled by the wind stand sentinel on lonely headlands. Along the drive is the famous **Pebble Beach Golf Course**, site of the National Pro-Am Golf Championship each January.

Carmel—filled with Hansel-and-Gretel-style cottages nestled under pines and surrounded by flower-filled gardens—is one of California's most appealing towns. Tourists throng the streets lined with enticing boutiques, attractive art galleries, pretty gift stores, appetizing sweet shops, beckoning bakeries, and a wonderful selection of restaurants. The picturesque combination of fairy-tale cottages and a sparkling blue bay makes Carmel so very special. Its main street slopes gently down the hill to a glorious white sand beach crested by windswept sand dunes.

Just south of town is the **Carmel Mission**, established in 1770 by Father Junipero Serra. Beautifully restored and fronted by a pretty garden, the mission was Father Serra's headquarters. It is from here that the stalwart little priest set out to expand the chain of missions. A small museum shows the simple cell in which Father Serra slept on a hard wooden bed. The church itself, with its Moorish tower, star-shaped window, and profusion of surrounding flowers, has a most romantic appearance.

Located just south of Carmel on Highway 1, **Point Lobos State Reserve** is, in our estimation, the premier place to enjoy the California coast. A small admission fee entitles you to day use of the park. Walk along the coastal trails and venture down wooden steps to secluded sandy beaches. Rocky coves are home to sea lions, harbor seals, and sea otters. Between December and May migrating gray whales surface and dive offshore. Bring your binoculars and head for Sea Lion Point and the headland on Cypress Grove Trail, the best places to see the whales. Walking trails and picnic areas are well marked and the times of guided nature walks are posted at the entrance gate. (408) 624-4909.

Believe everything you ever read about the beauties of the **Big Sur** coastline: it is truly sensational. However, hope for clear weather, because on foggy or rainy days an endless picture of stunning seascapes becomes a tortuous drive around precipitous cliff roads. (If the weather is inclement, you may wish to take the inland route to Cambria by following the picturesque Carmel Valley road east to Highway 101 where you then head south. When you come to Highway 46, turn west. The road intersects with coastal Highway 1 just south of Cambria.) As you drive south on Highway 1, you have an indication that you are approaching Big Sur when you see the road sign "Hill Curves—63 miles," which is exactly what the road does as it clings precipitously to the edge of the cliff. While the road is quite narrow, there are plenty of turnouts for photo-taking.

The highway passes over the much-photographed, long concrete span of Bixby Creek bridge. A few miles later the rocky volcanic outcrop topped by the Point Sur lighthouse appears. About 40 miles south of Carmel is the **Pfeiffer Big Sur State Park** with its camping facilities and many miles of hiking trails among coastal redwood groves.

If you choose only one place to stop along the Big Sur drive, make it **Nepenthe**, about 3 miles south of the entrance to Pfeiffer Big Sur State Park. Nepenthe is a casual restaurant, with a 60s-style decor, perched on a cliff high above the ocean offering unsurpassed views (on a clear day) of the coast to the south. (408) 667-2345. Below Nepenthe, **The Phoenix Shop** has a wonderful offering of clothes, artwork, books and gifts. (408) 667-2347. Interestingly, at the heart of the complex is a cottage that Orson Welles bought for his then wife, Rita Hayworth.

Another stop along the way where you can gain a closer view of this magnificent coastline is at the **Julia Pfeiffer Burns State Park**. The parking area is to the left of the road. Leave your car and take the short walk leading under the highway and round the face of the cliff that overlooks a superb small cove with emerald-green water and a white sand beach. From the rocky bluff a waterfall drops directly into the ocean and the restless sea beats against a craggy point. After you pass the Ragged Point Inn, the bends become less frequent, and as the cliffs give way to the coastal plain, the driving becomes far less arduous.

After the road begins to flatten out, watch for **Hearst Castle** impressively crowning the coastal hills. In 1919, William Randolph Hearst commissioned California's famous architect Julia Morgan to design a simple vacation home atop a hill on his estate overlooking the California coastline. Twenty-eight years and $10,000,000 later, his 100-room retreat, La Cuesta Encantada (the enchanted hill), was complete. Now more commonly known as Hearst Castle, the enchanted hill continues to delight its millions of visitors. Next to Disneyland, Hearst Castle is the most popular visitor attraction in California.

The number of visitors allowed on the hill during any one day is limited, so it is essential that you make reservations in advance. Hearst Castle is open every day except Thanksgiving, Christmas, and New Year's Day. Several different one-hour and forty-five-minute tours are available. On certain days an evening tour that combines the highlights of the castle is offered—this tour is tremendously popular and must be booked well in advance. Tickets for all tours are available for purchase eight weeks in advance by calling (800) 444-4445. Plan on arriving at the visitors' center at the foot of the hill at least half an hour before your scheduled departure, as the tours depart with clockwork-like precision and do not wait for stragglers. If you arrive early, you can browse through the small museum located next to the departure depot where groups assemble by number for their turn to be taken up the hill by bus.

Tour 1, the overview of the castle, is the one recommended for first-time visitors. You walk through the gardens to the main house, La Casa Grande, to tour the rooms on the lower level. The sheer size and elaborate decor of the assembly room where Hearst gathered with his guests before dinner sets the opulent mood of this elegant establishment.

In the adjoining refectory Hearst and his guests dined in a re-created medieval banquet hall—the bottles of Hearst's favorite ketchup on the table seem rather out of place. In the theater a short home movie of Hearst and some of his celebrity friends gives you an idea of life at the castle during the 1930s. A feeling for the opulence of the guest accommodation is given as you tour the bedrooms of the guesthouse, Casa del Sol. The indoor Roman pool has over half a million Italian mosaic tiles, vast amounts of gold leaf, and took over five years to complete. Tour 2 views suites of bedrooms, the kitchen, and the swimming pools. Tour 3 shows you the guest wing of the castle, a guesthouse, and the pools. Tour 4, offered only in summer, does not go into the main house, but focuses on the gardens.

From the Hearst-San Simeon State Historical Monument it is just an 8-mile drive south to Cambria. **Cambria** was once a whaling station and a dairy town that shipped butter

Hearst Castle

and cheese to San Francisco. Now the main town lies away from the coast and encompasses two streets of art galleries, gift shops, antique stores, and restaurants.

Leave Cambria on Highway 1 going south. The road leaves the coast and travels through low-lying hills to **San Luis Obispo**, merging with Highway 101 traveling south. If you want to visit every mission en route, when you reach San Luis Obispo take the Broad Street exit and follow signs to the **mission** which lies at the heart of this busy town. (Although it is an interesting mission, the setting does not compare in beauty with others included in this itinerary.)

About 10 miles south of San Luis Obispo Highway 101 returns to the coast at Pismo Beach where you take the exit for Highway 1 and **Pismo Beach**, a 12-mile arc of white-sand beach backed in part by dunes. This is the home of the famous Pismo clam which has unfortunately in recent years become rather scarce. As you travel south on Highway 1, views of the beach are blocked by apartments and motels, but do not despair: 2 miles south of town, leave the freeway by turning right into **Pismo Beach State Park**. After paying the entrance fee, pass quickly over the soft sand. Once your tires hit the well-packed, damp sand, your way feels more secure as you drive along the beach, paralleling the crashing waves. From this vantage point you can really appreciate the beautiful sweep of this white-sand bay. While it is possible to drive about 5 miles south on the beach, the auto exit ramp lies 1 mile to the south.

Leaving Pismo Beach, follow Highway 1 south, passing flat wide fields of vegetables and eucalyptus groves through Guadalupe, a rather poor agricultural town. The road becomes a divided two-lane highway as Highways 135 and 1 merge. After passing the gates of Vandenburg Air Force Base (on the approach to Lompoc), take a left turn onto Mission Purisma Road which leads to **Mission La Purisma Concepcion** founded in 1787 and now carefully restored and maintained by the state park system. A self-guided tour offers you the opportunity to see how the Indians practiced mission crafts such as leather working, candle making, and building. The simply decorated church with its sparse furnishings, rough floors, and stenciled walls is typical of Spanish and Mexican churches of the period. One of the nicest aspects of La Purisma Concepcion Mission is its lovely setting—far in the countryside amidst rolling hills and meadows filled with flowers.

Leaving the mission, follow signs for **Buelleton** which has the redoubtable fame of being the home of split-pea soup—you come to **Andersen's Pea Soup Restaurant** just before Highway 246 crosses Highway 101. The menu has more to offer than soup, but it is still possible to sample a bowl of the food that put this little community on the map.

From Buelleton it is just a short drive into **Solvang,** a town settled originally by Danish immigrants which has now become a rather Disneyfied version of how the perfect Danish village should look—a profusion of thatch-like roofs, painted towers, gaily colored windmills, and cobblestoned courtyards. The shops house a plethora of calorific bakeries and fudge and candy stores interspersed with lots of nifty-gifty Scandinavian craft shops. Interestingly enough, a large

Solvang

portion of the town's residents truly are of Danish descent. Even if you are not in the mood for shopping, the town merits a bakery stop.

Leaving Solvang, rejoin Highway 246 and follow signs for Santa Barbara. Just outside Santa Inez, Highway 246 merges with Highway 154 and the lush green valley gives way to hills as the road climbs through the mountains up the San Marcos Pass. Rounding the crest of the pass, you see **Santa Barbara** stretched out below, hemmed between the mountains and the sea. The red-tile roofs and abundance of palm trees add an affluent look to this prosperous town.

Santa Barbara is one of California's loveliest cities. The homes and public buildings show a decidedly Spanish influence and make such a pretty picture—splashes of whitewashed walls, red-tiled roofs, and palm trees snuggled against the Santa Ynez mountains to the east and stretching to the brilliant blue waters of the Pacific to the west.

A pleasant introduction to Santa Barbara is to follow the scenic driving tour that is outlined in the brochure published by the Chamber of Commerce. You can probably pick up a brochure at your hotel or by calling the Chamber of Commerce at (805) 965-3023. The route is well marked and gives you an overall glimpse of the city as you drive by beaches, the wharf, the old downtown area, and affluent suburbs. The brochure also outlines what is called the "Red-Tile Walking Tour" which guides you through the beautiful streets of Santa Barbara. It will take discipline to stay on the path as you pass the multitude of shops filled with so many tempting things to buy, but do continue on, because Santa Barbara is a beautiful city whose public buildings are lovely. The highlight of the tour is the **Santa Barbara County Courthouse**, a magnificent adobe structure with a Moorish accent.

You definitely must not leave town without visiting the splendid **Mission Santa Barbara** which is located at the rise of the hill on the northern edge of town. This beautiful church with two bell towers faces a large park laced with rose gardens. As in many of the other missions, although the church's main purpose is for religious services, a museum is incorporated into the complex with examples of how life was lived when the Spaniards first settled in California.

When your allotted stay in Santa Barbara draws to a close, it is a little less than a 100-mile drive to the Greater Los Angeles area. The vast, often smog-filled **Los Angeles** basin is criss crossed by a mind-boggling network of freeways which confuses all but the resident Southern Californian. Frustrating traffic jams during the morning and afternoon rush hours are a way of life. Therefore, plot the quickest freeway route to your destination and try to travel during the middle of the day in order to avoid the worst traffic. Los Angeles does not offer a wide selection of inns, but there are many attractive, modern hotels where you can stay. The Greater Los Angeles area has an incredible wealth of places to visit and things to do—something to suit every taste. Sightseeing suggestions are described in the *Leisurely Loop of Southern California* itinerary.

Wandering through the Wine Country

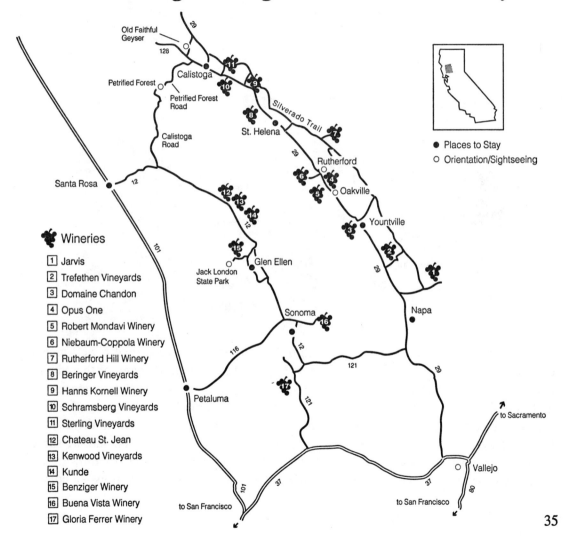

Old Faithful Geyser

128

Petrified Forest

Calistoga

Petrified Forest Road

Calistoga Road

Silverado Trail

29

St. Helena

Rutherford

Oakville

Yountville

Santa Rosa

12

101

Glen Ellen

Jack London State Park

Napa

Sonoma

Petaluma

116

12

121

121

to Sacramento

37

101

37

Vallejo

80

to San Francisco

to San Francisco

● Places to Stay
○ Orientation/Sightseeing

Wineries

1. Jarvis
2. Trefethen Vineyards
3. Domaine Chandon
4. Opus One
5. Robert Mondavi Winery
6. Niebaum-Coppola Winery
7. Rutherford Hill Winery
8. Beringer Vineyards
9. Hanns Kornell Winery
10. Schramsberg Vineyards
11. Sterling Vineyards
12. Chateau St. Jean
13. Kenwood Vineyards
14. Kunde
15. Benziger Winery
16. Buena Vista Winery
17. Gloria Ferrer Winery

35

Wandering through the Wine Country

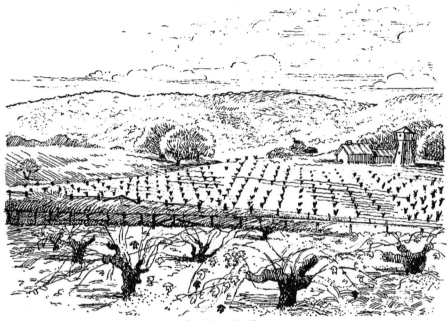

The Napa Valley

The Napa and Sonoma Valleys, just north of San Francisco, have earned a well-merited reputation for the excellence of their wines. Happily for the tourist, many of the wineries are open to the public for tours and tasting. But it is not only visiting the wineries that makes this area so special—these valleys are also memorable for their beauty. A visit to the wine country makes a pleasant excursion any time of year. In summer the days are long and warm, perfect for bike rides, picnics, music festivals, concerts, and art shows. As summer days give way to the cooler afternoons and crisp evenings of fall, the lush foliage on the thousands of acres of grapevines turns to red, gold, and yellow—a colorful reminder that it is time for harvest. You can sense the energy of the crush as vintners work against the clock and weather to pick grapes at their prime. In winter, cool days are often washed by rain, but this is also an excellent time to visit since this is "off season" and the winery tours will be almost private as you travel from one winery to the next. Spring is glorious: mustard blossoms paint the valley yellow, contrasting dramatically with the dark bark of the vines laced with the delicate green of new leaves.

Recommended Pacing: The Napa and Sonoma wine regions can possibly be squeezed into a day's journey from San Francisco with time to visit one or two wineries. It requires only about an hour to drive from San Francisco to the southern boundaries of either valley. Running north and south, Napa Valley spans a territory of approximately 35 miles while the Sonoma Valley stretches about 17 miles. However, since the primary attraction in either valley happens to be its vineyards, and wine tasting is offered at almost every one, it is most restful to investigate a few in an afternoon's time, sample their wines and then incorporate a nap or a laze by a pool into the day's schedule. Since the prospect of returning to San Francisco and battling traffic at rush hour is not a welcome notion, we recommend that you plan to leisurely spend a minimum of one to two nights in the Napa Valley and one to two nights in the Sonoma Valley. With the distance between the valleys being only about 10 to 12 miles, you can also use either valley as a base from which to explore both wine regions.

Weather Wise: The Napa and Sonoma Valleys have a very similar climate. Summer days can be scorching hot and roads are often clogged with visitors. Autumn gives way to mild, sunny days, cooler afternoons, and crisp evenings. From autumn to spring you can expect some rain although many days will be sunny. In winter temperatures are mild yet several degrees cooler than in the nearby San Francisco Bay Area.

Note: We have tried to be as accurate as possible when giving information about touring wineries, but things change, so be certain to give each winery a call in advance to see whether or not they are open and whether you need an appointment for a tour or tasting.

This itinerary which wends up the Napa Valley and down the Sonoma Valley is an introduction and a sampling of what the wine country has to offer. This itinerary is not intended to be strictly adhered to in its exact routing. Rather, it is meant as an overall master plan from which you can pick and choose what sounds most interesting to you. Use it as a framework to plan your own holiday, taking various segments as they fit in with your time frame. The featured wineries have been chosen for a variety of reasons such as their historical interest, the excellence of their wines, the appeal of their tour, and their special ambiance. Some wineries offer wine tasting free of charge, others charge a fee.

From San Francisco, travel east on Highway 80 across the San Francisco-Oakland Bay Bridge. After crossing the bridge, stay in the left-hand lane and follow signs for Highway 80 in the direction of Sacramento. Approximately 5 miles after crossing the Carquinez Bridge, watch for the Marine World Parkway (Highway 37) turnoff. Take the Parkway that takes you right past the exit to **Marine World, Africa USA**, a wonderful park and family attraction. If traveling with children you might want to allocate a day here. On an expanse of 160 acres, there are numerous theaters that stage a multitude of shows to include both marine and African life: tigers, elephants, lions, killer whales, dolphins, seals, and sharks, to name a few. Admission to the park covers the cost of all shows and attractions. Shows are staggered throughout the day and it is feasible to see them all if you want to. Food service is available throughout the park, but you can also pack a picnic and enjoy the expanse of tables set under trees next to the children's playground. For additional information and their calendar, telephone (707) 643-6722.

After Marine World, continue on the parkway for 2 miles and turn north on Highway 29 which travels in the direction of Napa. The road widens and the scenery improves dramatically as the road nears the base of the Napa Valley. There are two parallel roads that stretch the length of the valley—Highway 29 and the Silverado Trail. Highway 29 is the busier road and the address for many of the valley's larger wineries and all the towns. The Silverado Trail, the more scenic, less commercial route, hugs the eastern hills, and twists and winds amongst smaller vineyards, often offering a welcome escape from the summer crowds and traffic. This itinerary suggests a route north through the Napa Valley, criss crossing back and forth between Highway 29 and the Silverado Trail, and then travels west to follow a route south through the Sonoma Wine Valley.

For our first suggested winery stop, the Jarvis Winery, continue on Highway 29. When the road divides, take the east (right) fork, Highway 121, which goes to Napa and on to Lake Berryessa. To reach the Jarvis Winery, stay on Highway 121, continuing to follow signs to Lake Berryessa. When Highway 121 makes a turn to the east and leaves the valley floor, it begins to climb into the wooded hills and assumes the name Monticello Road. After the turnoff, continue toward Lake Berryessa for about 4 miles. Watch for a gate on the left marking the Jarvis entrance at 2970 Monticello Road. The gates will automatically open after you give your name and say you have a reservation for the tour.

A tour of the **Jarvis Winery** necessitates a reservation well in advance. If you are watching your pennies, you can bypass this tour (which costs $10 per person) and proceed on to the next stop. However, the structure of the Jarvis Winery is different than any other winery you will see in the Napa Valley. It also produces excellent wines (Cabernet Franc, Cabernet Sauvignon, Chardonnay, and Merlot) and offers a fun tour. All you see as you approach are two massive doors built into the hillside—it looks like an entrance into a bunker. But inside, another world opens up as you find yourself in a giant cave. Tour groups are limited to a very small number, which makes the tour very personal. You follow a path that forms a loop around the cave, passing by an underground stream and a waterfall, and visiting the Crystal Chamber, a grand reception hall. The tour ends in an intimate room where guests sample fine wines at a small table surrounded by gilded chairs with blue velvet upholstery. Tours are offered six days a week at 1:30 pm and an additional 3:30 pm tour is offered based on demand. For reservations call (707) 255-5280.

Leaving the Jarvis Winery, retrace your route back down the hill until Highway 121 (Monticello Road) intersects the Silverado Trail. Turn right (north) on the Silverado Trail until you come to Oak Knoll Avenue. Turn west on Oak Knoll, a beautiful drive bounded by walnut trees and vineyards, and watch for a small signpost on your right marking the entrance of **Trefethen Vineyards** at 1160 Oak Knoll Avenue. Surrounded by its own grapevines, Trefethen Vineyards is housed in the oldest wooden winery in the Napa Valley. Pumpkin in color with a brown roof, this handsome complex recently celebrated its one hundredth birthday and there was much reason to celebrate, as the Trefethen family fortunately rescued and lovingly restored the property. This wonderful old winery was designed by the same architect responsible for the Niebaum-Coppola and Beaulieu wineries. Trefethen Vineyards is a delightful small winery, family-owned and operated, which has proved that size is in no way a factor in excellence. The Trefethens have converted a bulk winery to the production of fine estate-grown Chardonnay, Riesling, Cabernet Sauvignon, and proprietary wines under the Eshcol label. Trefethen wines are featured in some of the finest restaurants. Old farming implements border the parking area and a brick walk encircles a handsome oak in front of the winery where you can sample the wines. The winery is open to the public and tours are available each day at 10:30 am and 2:30 pm, but you must make an appointment: call (707) 255-7700.

After a visit to the Trefethen Vineyards, continue west on Oak Knoll Avenue and in a few minutes you come to highway 29 where you turn right and continue north up the valley. When you come to the small town of **Yountville**, take the first exit, keep to your right, then turn left at the first street which is Washington. You will see on your left **Vintage 1870**, a wonderful complex of 40 shops and restaurants housed in a quaint old brick winery. Even non-shoppers will enjoy a stroll through this lovely building: the old brick, heavy beams, and tiled and cobbled floors are dramatic against a meticulously groomed backdrop of green lawn and flowers. A variety of specialty shops make any purchase possible: toys, antiques, handmade sweaters, books, kitchenware, jewelry, or art. An assortment of restaurants will appease most appetites whether you desire a gourmet salad, pastries, or simply a refreshing ice cream cone. You can also arrange for an early-morning balloon ride—the office for **Adventures Aloft** is located in Vintage 1870, next to the Vintage Café. The telephone number is (707) 255-8688. Departures are at sunrise, the best possible time as the winds are gentle and the air is cool. The flights are expensive, but memorable.

Drive south from Yountville on California Drive, crossing under Highway 29 in the direction of the Veterans' Home. Just after passing under the freeway, turn right onto the property of **Domaine Chandon** at One California Drive. When the proprietors of Moët & Chandon first came to the valley with the intention of making sparkling wine following the principles and rigid process of true French champagne, *methode champenoise*, they contracted to use Trefethen Vineyards. Successful in their venture, their sparkling wine was well received and they moved to the present location and established their own winery, Domaine Chandon. Roses front the vineyards, a French tradition, copied both for its practicality as well as for its aesthetic value. The roses add a grace and beauty to the planted fields, but they are also susceptible to the same root diseases and insect problems. If the roses are blemished, vintners know to investigate the vines closely.

Although the winery is relatively new, mature oak trees shade a lovely lawn and a series of terraced ponds with fountains. A wooden footbridge spans the creek-fed ponds to the stone winery tucked back into the hillside. Tours are offered daily on the hour between 11 am and 5 pm. The visitors' center is closed on Mondays and Tuesdays from November to April: for further information call (707) 944-2280. The tours are hosted by courteous guides who are well informed about the aspects of *methode champenoise*. Visitors see first the traditional storage of the wine in polished stainless-steel tanks and then continue on to observe the additional steps involved in making champagne. In the cellar, bottles of sparkling wine are aged and riddled (turned). In the bottling room you see the process of freezing then disgorging the sediment, corking, cleaning, and labeling the bottles. After the tour visitors are invited back to the salon where Domaine

Chandon's sparkling wines may be purchased by the glass. From the salon it is possible to view through a glass partition Domaine Chandon's elegant restaurant. A visit to Domaine Chandon shows French and Californian vintners sharing expertise and working side by side.

From Domaine Chandon, return to Highway 29 heading north a few miles to the roadside town of **Oakville**. A few buildings comprise this town, the principal one being the original **Oakville Grocery**. If you plan to picnic, stop here for supplies and gourmet treats to accompany your wine-tasting purchases.

Just to the north of Oakville, on the right of Highway 29 you soon come to **Opus One** (the address is 7900 Saint Helena Road, Highway 29). This winery is a masterpiece which is the showplace of Robert Mondavi and the Rothschild family. The purpose of their joint venture was to combine the talents of the best French wine-makers with the know-how of California's Mondavi family to produce some of the world's finest wines. The gleaming white, circular structure looks a bit like a luxurious, futuristic, coliseum— it is totally different in ambiance from the typical Napa Valley winery. It certainly makes a statement, which is just want the owners wanted to do. As you enter the impressive building, it is immediately obvious that no expense was spared: everything is of the finest quality. Visitors are treated as honored guests and wait in an elegant lounge before the tour begins. You must sign up in advance for Opus One's complimentary tour. The tasting of premium wines costs $12. The telephone number is (707) 944-9442.

Your next stop, the **Robert Mondavi Winery** (the same Robert Mondavi who is a partner in the Opus One which you have just visited), is just a little bit farther north, on the left side of the highway (7801 Saint Helena Road, Highway 29). This modern winery with an original Bufano statue of Saint Francis at its entrance was styled after the Franciscan missions, with an open-arched entry framing an idyllic view of vineyards. The one-hour tour is extensive, extremely informative, and provides a good general introduction to the essence of wine making. By special arrangement, you can also make reservations for an advanced wine growing tour ($15 per person), touring the fields and studying the grapes as well as the winery. After each tour guests are invited into the tasting room to sample the wines. The lovely lawn at the back is the site of summer concerts and art shows. Reservations are advisable. For further information call (707) 259-9463.

After visiting the Robert Mondavi Winery, your next stop is another real winner, the **Niebaum-Coppola Winery**. Continue north on Highway 29 for a few miles beyond the Robert Mondavi winery. Just past Niebaum Lane on the left, you will see the entrance to the winery. In the late 1870s a Finnish sea captain, Gustave Niebaum, retired from shipping to invest his fortune in the Napa Valley, envisioning a winery that would produce magnificent wines, even surpassing the finest French wines. After his death, Niebaum's property was divided, but in 1995 the Coppola family (owners of the Niebaum-Coppola Winery since 1975) purchased the adjacent Inglenook château and its vineyards, thus uniting once again the original historic estate. Francis Ford Coppola (world-renowned movie director) and his wife, Eleanor, have great respect for wine and the enormous potential of the land. They carry on the Niebaum tradition by growing, producing, and bottling all on the estate—a rare occurrence in today's viticultural world. Niebaum-Coppola is a handsome winery which enjoys a superb setting nestled against the western foothills of the Napa Valley. Since the winery dates back to the 19th century, it is able to offer what the valley's new wineries cannot—character achieved with age and time. A tour planned for 1977 will take visitors on a walk through the original stone aging cellar containing some magnificent large German oak casks. Reservations will be required and there will be a $5 charge for tasting of five wines. For further information call (707) 967-3450. Note: As we go to press, even grander dreams are in the making. The original château is being restored to its original splendor and a museum both to commemorate Gustave Niebaum and to explore the creative workings of film and the work of Francis Ford Coppola is under way. By the time you visit, this lavish project might be completed.

Niebaum-Coppola Winery

From Niebaum-Coppola cross over Highway 29 to Rutherford Road, directly opposite. On the corner is a clustering of buildings forming **Beaulieu Vineyards**. Referred to as BV, Beaulieu is known for some excellent wine and now offers both a tour and wine tasting. The tour is free. Wine tastings feature four to six reserve wines at a flat rate of $10. For additional information call (707) 967-5200.

Rutherford Road affords a scenic drive shaded by an archway of oak trees. Travel the short distance to its end, past the Louis Honig Winery, and then turn north on Conn Creek Road which then intersects with the Silverado Trail. Turn north on the Silverado Trail, but drive slowly as you want to take the first right turn onto Rutherford Hill Road which winds up past the Auberge du Soleil, to the Rutherford Hill Winery.

Although relatively new, the **Rutherford Hill Winery** is housed in a stunning building of weathered redwood in the shape of a chalet-barn, draped with Virginia creeper and wisteria and bounded by grass and flowers. The winery crowns a plateau and enjoys a spectacular valley view. Paths lead down the hillside to picnic tables set under olive trees where the views will tempt you to wile away an afternoon. Rutherford Hill is the dream of a number of independent vintners who together purchased what was once the Souverain Winery (now located in the Sonoma Valley) in order to process and control the production of their limited quantities of grapes into wine. By now, Rutherford Hill Winery is widely considered the leading producer of Merlot in the Napa Valley. The owners also constructed what was at the time the largest expanse of underground caves in the valley—these maintain a constant natural temperature of 58 degrees, minimizing evaporation far more successfully than when temperatures are controlled by air conditioning. The tour of Rutherford Hill includes a visit to these caves and a sample from a barrel. Guides at Rutherford Hill are friendly and quite proud of (as well as knowledgeable about) the winery and visitors are encouraged to ask questions. Although all wine-making procedures are basically the same, Rutherford Hill is a small winery and the guide's explanation of the step-by-step process seems easier to understand than the same explanation at a much grander winery. Wine tasting is $3 per glass. Advance reservations are not needed. For more information call (707) 963-7194.

From Rutherford traveling north on Highway 29 it is just a few miles to **Saint Helena**. Highway 29 becomes this lovely town's Main Street, lined with elegant stores, boutiques, and restaurants. Detour east two blocks off Main Street via Adams Street to Saint Helena's **Library and Museum**. The library has a very interesting section on wine and one wing of the museum is dedicated to Robert Louis Stevenson, the great Scotsman who settled with his new bride in an old miner's shack northeast of Calistoga. It was here that he wrote *Silverado Squatters*, a book romantically promoting the beauty of the Napa Valley. Stevenson buffs can also visit the **Robert Louis Stevenson Park** on Highway 29 between Calistoga and Middletown and also make an appointment to tour Schramsburg Vineyards, the winery Stevenson featured in his chronicles of the wine country.

Also in Saint Helena, at 2555 Main Street (which is also named Highway 29), is the **Culinary Institute of America**, a fascinating place for either lunch or dinner. The prestigious institute, which opened in the fall of 1995, is housed in what has long been a landmark of the Napa Valley—the Christian Brothers Winery. On the second floor of the right wing of the massive old winery is the **Greystone Restaurant**, a super place to eat lunch or dinner. The culinary team is made up entirely of Culinary Institute graduates or advanced students who display their skills at an open-to-view kitchen, set center stage in the room. Greystone's own organic gardens inspire the menu which mingles Mediterranean flavors and textures with the culinary aesthetics of Northern California. The food is delicious and the price is an excellent value. Lunch is served from 11:30 am to 3 pm, a light "tasting" menu from 3 to 5:30 pm, and dinner from 5:30 to 9 pm every day except Tuesday. For reservations call (707) 967-1010. In the left wing of the Culinary Institute is a museum where you can see many antique tools used for wine making and an extensive display of antique corkscrews.

Before leaving Saint Helena visit the **V. Sattui Winery**, at 1111 White Lane Street. Sattui wine-making history dates back to 1885 when Vittorio Sattui founded the winery in the North Beach district of San Francisco. Great-grandson Daryl Sattui revived the family tradition in 1973 by moving the winery to Saint Helena. Currently 15 vintage-dated wines are produced, all of which are sold exclusively at the winery or by mail order. V. Sattui wines are not available in any stores, wine shops, or restaurants. With a lovely garden setting, this is an attractive winery where you can also purchase picnic supplies—such as over 200 different kinds of cheeses, homemade salads, patés, breads, and desserts. The winery has a wonderful picnic spot with tables set on the lawn beneath shady trees. Tours are self-guided and tasting is complimentary. For further information call (707) 963-7774.

As Highway 29 leaves the commercial district of Saint Helena and enters a very exclusive residential district on its northern borders, watch carefully for the gated entry to **Beringer Vineyards** (2000 Main Street, Highway 29), set on a knoll, surrounded by beautifully landscaped grounds of mature trees, lawns, and gardens. What was once the home of the founding Beringer family now houses a wine and gift shop. Reflecting its heritage and standing as a tribute to one of the valley's founding wineries, the dramatic stone and half-timbered building with a slate roof was one of two family homes built as a replica of the German home that Frederick and his brother Jacob left behind when they emigrated. The second house (which is smaller) is currently under restoration. Half-hour tours are offered every day between 9:30 am and 5 pm and availability is on a first-come basis. Tours emphasize the historical aspect of the winery and include a memorable visit through the tunnels and caverns where the wine is aged in barrels. For information call (707) 963-4812.

From Beringer head north another 4 miles and then turn right on Larkmead Lane. The **Hanns Kornell Winery,** a name synonymous with fine champagne, is located at 1091 Larkmead Lane. Hanns Kornell is devoted entirely to the production of traditional, bottle-fermented sparkling wines. Visitors are welcome and tours are informal and personalized to suit the group and the production activities of any particular day or hour. The tour is more informative than visual: an in-depth, detailed explanation is offered about the traditional methods of making sparkling wine. For further information call (707) 942-0859.

Schramsberg Vineyards, which offers tours by appointment, (707) 942-4558, is tucked in the western foothills of the Napa Valley just off Highway 29 to the south of Calistoga at 1400 Schramsberg Road. Over 2 miles of tunnels are devoted to the production of sparkling wine in this historic winery. Wine tasting is offered only in conjunction with the tour.

Beyond the Schramsberg Vineyards, a large sign on Highway 29 instructs you to turn just a few miles farther north on Highway 29 at Dunaweal Lane to visit **Sterling Vineyards**. Reminiscent of a Moorish castle, Sterling Vineyards enjoys a crowning position on a hill idyllically set in the middle of the valley. From the winery you can savor panoramic views looking down through tall pines to a checkerboard of vineyards. Access to Sterling is possible only by small gondolas. For a fee of $6 (the fee is $3 for children under 18 which includes juice at the top) you can ride the aerial tramway from the parking lot to the winery and back (first tram 10:30 am, last 4:30 pm). Arrows and detailed signs direct you on an informative, but impersonal, self-guided tour through the maze of rooms that comprise the winery. By appointment, group tours are available Monday to Friday: call (707) 942-3359. At the end of the tour, a flight of steps leads up to a tasting room with disappointedly limited rather than panoramic views of the valley. However the wines are lovely, and another inviting feature about Sterling is the wonderful melodic sound of bells that ring out every quarter-hour. These bells once hung in London's Saint Dunstan's-in-the-East Church.

The delightful town of **Calistoga** is just a few miles north from Sterling Vineyards at the intersection of Highway 29 and Highway 128. Bounded by rugged foothills and vineyards, Calistoga is an attractive town servicing local residents and tourists alike. Its main street, Lincoln Avenue, is lined on both sides by attractive shops and numerous restaurants. This charming town has been famous ever since Spanish explorers arrived in 1823 and observed Indians taking mud baths in steamy marshes. Sam Brannan, who purchased a square mile of land at the foot of Mount Saint Helena, gave the town its name: he wanted the place to be the "Saratoga of California" and so called it Calistoga. He bought the land in the early 1860s and by 1866 was ready to open his resort of a few cottages and palm trees. The oldest surviving railroad depot in California, now serving as a quaint and historic shopping mall, received its first train-load of passengers when they came to Calistoga for the much-publicized opening of Sam Brannan's resort. For more than a hundred years, Calistoga has attracted visitors from all over the world, primarily for its hot springs and spas. People came in search of its glorious, healing waters long before the region became a popular destination for its wineries.

There are many spa facilities to choose from—at the eastern end of town look for the **Calistoga Spa and Hot Springs**, 1006 Washington Street 94515. (707) 942-6269. Their facilities are newly renovated, expansive, and modern and the attendants are professional and very nice. Offered are volcanic-ash mud baths, mineral baths, steam baths, blanket wraps, and massage. The entire package, "the works," takes almost two hours and their rates are very competitive.

If you are feeling adventurous, You can take a balloon flight with **American Balloon Adventures**. A sunrise launch is arranged from a selection of wineries. This one-hour balloon fantasy voyage includes a gourmet brunch. For further information call (707) 942-6546. Another adventure is the **Calistoga Gliders**, located at 1546 Lincoln Avenue. To arrange for a glider ride, call (707) 942-5592.

If you have never seen a geyser, travel a few miles farther north from Calistoga on Highway 128 in the direction of Lakeport to Tubbs Lane. Turn right onto Tubbs Lane and in half a mile you see the entrance to the **Old Faithful Geyser** on the left. Old Faithful, one of only three such regularly erupting geysers in the world, erupts at intervals of every 50 minutes with a spume of about 4,000 gallons of water reaching more than 60 feet into the air. This is certainly an interesting phenomenon, although the staging is a bit honky-tonk.

Leaving Calistoga, take the Petrified Forest Road west in the direction of Santa Rosa, forsaking the Napa Valley for the neighboring Sonoma Wine Valley. The road climbs and winds a scenic 10 miles through forest and past pastures where cattle graze next to neighboring vineyards and orchards of apples and almonds. You may wish to stop at the rather commercial **California Petrified Forest**, a grove of redwoods that was petrified by ash from the volcanic eruption of Mount Saint Helena over 6,000,000 years ago. It is this same ash that is responsible for fertile wine-valley soil.

On the residential outskirts of Santa Rosa Petrified Forest Road merges with Highway 12 and you turn south (left) toward Sonoma. This highway travels down the center of Sonoma Valley, often referred to as the "Valley of the Moon" after Jack London's famous novel of the same name. London fell in love with Sonoma Valley's magnificent landscape—a wondrous mix of high hills, oak-covered knolls, open pastures, forests of oaks, madrones, fir, and redwood trees, grassy fields, and streams. The author chose the valley as his home—"a quiet place in the country to write and loaf in and get out of nature that something which we all need, only most of us don't know it."

Your first destination in this lovely valley, **Château Saint Jean**, lies about 7 miles south of Santa Rosa on the left, at 8555 Sonoma Highway 12. An extremely pretty road winds up through the vineyards to the strikingly beautiful winery and main house surrounded by lush lawns. With the exception of its mock tower, Château Saint Jean is Mediterranean French in its architecture, its red-tile roofs and arched entries stunning against a backdrop of green hills. The estate is dedicated exclusively to the production of premium wines, but as a visitor you will feel that the winery's chief concern is making visitors feel welcome by outlining a very comprehensive self-guided tour of the wine-making process. After the tour you cross the courtyard to the original "château" for tasting. Questions you have will be answered graciously. For additional information call (707) 833-4134.

Your next stop, **Kenwood Vineyards,** is just beyond Château Saint Jean, but completely different in character. Kenwood occupies an attractive complex of old wooden barns where wine is produced, stored, and tasted. Mini-tours of this small winery are offered by request, daily between 10 am and 4:30 pm. (707) 833-5891.

The next winery you come to (just beyond Kenwood Winery on the same side of the road) is the **Kunde Winery** at 9592 Sonoma Highway 12. The founder, Louis Kunde, settled in the Sonoma Valley in 1904. The present-day winery, which re-creates an 1883 barn that previously stood on the same site, houses a reception area with wine tasting and a small shop where you can find attractive, wine-oriented gift items. In addition to wine tasting, tours are available of the caves which feature half a mile of interconnecting tunnels. For further information call (707) 833-5501.

As you travel south on Highway 12, take a turnoff to the right marked to Glen Ellen. Travel this main road through Glen Ellen, following signs for Jack London State Park. Before you reach the park, stop to visit the Benziger Winery, which you will see on your right.

The **Benziger Winery** is family-run in the truest sense of the word—signs warn to watch for children at play. From babies to Goober, the family dog and "official reception committee," everyone at Benziger is warm and friendly. The Benziger family were wine importers in New York before moving to the Sonoma Valley to produce their own wines. If it's close to lunch time, take advantage of picnic tables set under redwood trees. The tasting room is quite a hike from the parking lot, so if someone in your party has difficulty with a hilly driveway, continue on to the handicapped area, or circle round to drop them off in the front. The tour here is truly a treat: guests climb onto a trolley, pulled by a cheerful bright red tractor, for a tour of the vineyards. The day we took the tour, Goober climbed aboard and sat on the bench next to the other guests, happily wagging his tail as the tram moved through the fields. Stops are made en route where a guide explains the production of wines. Appointments are not necessary, but space on the trolley is limited, so arrive early. Weather permitting, the tours are at 12:30 pm, 2 pm, and 3:30 pm. After the tour, visit the gift shop and stay to taste some of the excellent wines. For further information call (707) 935-3000 or (800) 989-8890.

Trolley at Benziger Winery

Continue on to **Jack London State Park** where Jack London is buried. This is a lovely wooded park, established as a tribute to the famous author who has had such an impact on the Sonoma Valley. This strikingly handsome man lived a life of rugged adventure and wrote passionately about life's struggles and how to survive them with integrity. In the 16 years prior to his death at age 40, he wrote 50 novels which were immensely popular and are today considered classics. Two of his more renowned novels are *Call of* *the Wild* and *Sea Wolf.* This park offers a fitting tribute to Jack London, a courageous, dynamic man, full of life and concern for others. Open all year, admission is $5 per vehicle—for information call (707) 938-5216.

In the park you can visit the ruins of Wolf House (London's dream house which mysteriously burned to the ground the night of its completion), Beauty Cottage (the cottage where London wrote much of his later work), and the House of Happy Walls (the home that Charmian London built after her husband's death). The House of Happy Walls is now an interesting museum that depicts London's life through numerous photographs, writings, and furnishings that belonged to the author. From the museum, paths lead to the other homes and the grave site. From the park return to Arnold Drive and travel south (past the Sonoma State Home) to Madrone where you turn left, crossing over to Highway 12 which takes you into Sonoma.

Sonoma is a gem of a town. By simply exploring the boundaries of its main square you will glimpse some of California's most important periods in history. (A small admission price is charged to tour Sonoma's historic buildings.) On the square's northern edge sits the **Sonoma Barracks**, a two-story, adobe building that was the Mexican provincial headquarters for the Northern Frontier under the command of General Vallejo. The adjacent wood-frame **Toscano Hotel** has been restored and on weekends guides lead interesting tours through the rooms. The nearby **Mission San Francisco Solano de Sonoma**, the last Franciscan mission built in California, was restored in the early 1900s. If you visit during the week, you may see elementary-school children, dressed as missionaries with their simple cloaks and rope ties, experiencing history "hands on" as they work with crafts and tools from the days of the missionaries. In one hall of the mission is an unusually beautiful collection of watercolor paintings of many of California's missions. The long, low adobe building across the way, the Blue Wig Inn, originally built to house soldiers assigned to the mission, enjoyed a more colorful existence as a saloon and gambling room during the Gold Rush days.

Mission San Francisco Solano de Sonoma

In addition to the historic sites on Sonoma's plaza, there are numerous shops and boutiques to investigate. There are some wonderful specialty food stores where you can purchase picnic supplies. The **Sonoma Cheese Factory** on Spain Street is interesting to visit and easy to pop into between historic sites. The front of the shop has a deli and at the back, behind a glass partition, you can observe the making of cheese. On First Street East, you can purchase delicious bread at the **Sonoma French Bread Shop** and enjoy a tasty ice cream at the ice cream parlor.

Leaving the Square, go east on Napa Boulevard for 2 miles to Old Winery Road where you turn left to the **Buena Vista Winery,** the region's oldest winery located at 18000 Old Winery Road. Nestled in a wooded glen, the old stone, ivy-covered buildings are very picturesque with arched caverns and stone walls. Picnic tables are set under the trees (it is hard to find a spot in the summer). Wine tasting is offered in the old press house and a self-guided tour directs you through the old stone barn and three tunnels. At 2 pm daily there is a tour guide who gives you a presentation of the historical founding of the winery. For further information call (707) 938-1266.

General Vallejo, the military commander and director of colonization of the Northern Frontier (until the Bear Flag Revolution established California as a free and independent republic) lived nearby with his wife and their 12 children. Vallejo's Home, "**Lachryma Montis**" (translated to mean mountain tear, an adaptation of the Indian name given to a free-flowing spring that surrounds the property), is well signposted on the outskirts of town on Spain Street. In its day this lovely Victorian-style house was considered one of the most elegant and lavishly decorated homes in the area, and is still attractively furnished.

After you leave the Sonoma Valley, one more winery awaits you as you return to San Francisco. When Highway 12 dead-ends at Highway 116, turn right onto Highway 116 (signposted Petaluma) and at the intersection of Highway 121 turn left in the direction of San Francisco. A short drive brings you to the **Gloria Ferrer Champagne Caves,** a fitting grand finale for this wine country itinerary. The Ferrer family, who brought their expertise on Spanish sparkling wines to the Sonoma Valley in 1982, hails from Catalonia, Spain and, consequently, the handsome winery with its stucco walls and tiled roof resembles a small Catalonian village. A wide road sweeps up to the winery through the vineyards. The very informative tours last half an hour and are available daily between 11 am and 4 pm. They start from the tasting room, a spacious room whose windows look out over the vineyards and valley. Most of the narrative is given in a room decorated with wine-making instruments used a half a century ago in the Ferrers' winery in Spain. The riddling of the bottles to capture the sediment is explained, and then you go to the observation room to see the process of freezing then disgorging the sediment, corking, cleaning, and labeling the bottles of sparkling wine. The tour then descends into a maze of interconnected wine storage tunnels. It is awesome to stand next to towering heights of stacked bottles. The tour concludes back in the tasting room next to their beautiful Vista Terrace overlooking the Mayacamas mountains that separate the Napa and Sonoma Valleys. A fee is charged to sample the sparkling wine. For further information call (707) 996-7256.

From the Gloria Ferrer winery it is about an hour's drive back to San Francisco by continuing along Highway 121 to Highway 37 and onto Highway 101 which takes you over the Golden Gate Bridge into the city.

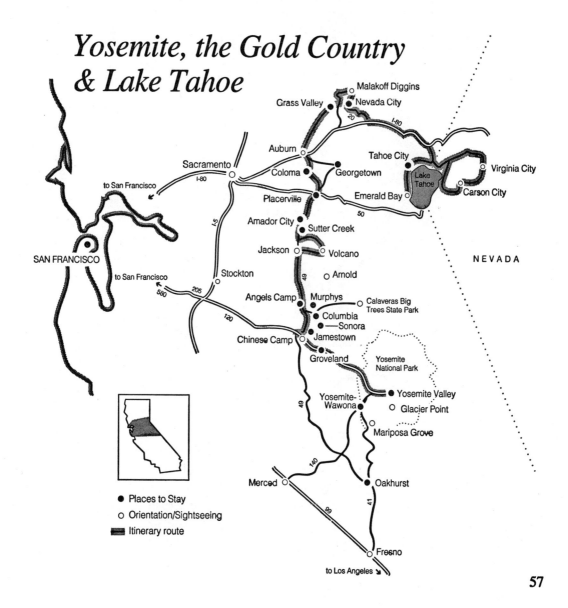

Yosemite, the Gold Country & Lake Tahoe

Malakoff Diggins
Grass Valley
Nevada City
Auburn
Sacramento
to San Francisco
Coloma
Georgetown
Tahoe City
Virginia City
Lake Tahoe
Carson City
Placerville
Emerald Bay
Amador City
Sutter Creek
SAN FRANCISCO
Jackson
Volcano
NEVADA
to San Francisco
Stockton
Arnold
Angels Camp
Murphys
Calaveras Big Trees State Park
Columbia
Sonora
Chinese Camp
Jamestown
Groveland
Yosemite National Park
Yosemite-Wawona
Yosemite Valley
Glacier Point
Mariposa Grove
Merced
Oakhurst
Fresno
to Los Angeles

● Places to Stay
○ Orientation/Sightseeing
▬ Itinerary route

Yosemite, the Gold Country & Lake Tahoe

Half Dome, Yosemite

This itinerary features two of California's most spectacular natural attractions, majestic Yosemite National Park and beautiful Lake Tahoe, and links them together by one of California's best kept secrets—the spirited, nostalgic, Gold Rush towns which string along the Sierra foothills. These colorful towns date back to 1848 when the cry went up that gold had been found at Sutter Creek, precipitating the rush to California by men eager to make their fortunes. Overnight, boom towns sprang up around every mining camp, with a cluster of similar-style saloons, restaurants, hotels, dance halls, and homes.

Gold Rush fever quickly cooled and many of the towns were left, quietly forgotten, until tourists rediscovered their charm. Today these benignly neglected towns have been spruced up and bustle with activity: antique shops, art galleries, nifty boutiques, attractive restaurants, and appealing inns are tucked into old Victorian houses lining sleepy streets. The highway that runs through the mother lode country is numbered 49 after the gold-seeking miners who were known as the Forty-Niners.

Recommended Pacing: We recommend a minimum of two nights in Yosemite and suggest that you try to stay at accommodation in the park (see page 60 and 61). Either before or after visiting Yosemite, you have a perfect opportunity to explore California's Gold Rush Country. Rather than backtracking, plan to progress through the region, spending at least one night in the south and at least one night in the north. From the northern region of the Gold Country it is a logical continuation on to Lake Tahoe. Many people enjoy Lake Tahoe as a resort, basking on its sandy beaches in the summer and skiing down the snow-covered peaks that ring its waters in the winter. If you are visiting Lake Tahoe as a tourist, we recommend a two-night visit.

Weather Wise: Heavy snow is the norm at Tahoe and Yosemite during the winter, while most of the Gold Rush towns are beneath the snow line and experience heavy winter rains. During summer months the days are hot in Yosemite and Tahoe, and several degrees warmer in the Gold Country.

As you read through this itinerary, please be aware that each of the areas featured could well be a destination in itself. Yosemite and Lake Tahoe are especially popular resorts and an entire vacation could easily be dedicated to either one. If that is your desire, just extract from the itinerary the portion that suits your interests. However, the Gold Country is not as well known and makes a super link between Yosemite and Tahoe—or, for that matter, also a great destination in its own right.

Since Yosemite makes a most convenient first-night stop from either San Francisco or Los Angeles, driving directions are given from both so that you can tailor the trip to your own needs. Much of the first day of this itinerary is spent driving to Yosemite National Park, about a four- to five-hour drive from San Francisco or a six- to seven-hour drive from the Greater Los Angeles area. A brief description of what to see and do during your stay in San Francisco is included in *San Francisco to Los Angeles via the Coast*, while the list of attractions of the much larger, more sprawling Los Angeles are included in *Leisurely Loop of Southern California.*

Leave San Francisco east over the Bay Bridge, in the direction of Oakland. Once across the bridge, stay in the middle lane and follow signs for Highway 580, heading east, signposted Stockton. Stay on Highway 580 for about 48 miles until you come to Livermore where Highway 580 meets Highway 205 which you take, continuing east, following signs for Manteca. Near Manteca, take Highway 120 east, directly to the northern gate of Yosemite National Park. Total driving distance is about 200 miles.

Leave Los Angeles heading north on Highway 5 until you come to the junction of Highway 99 which you take north (signposted Bakersfield). Continue on Highway 99 to the north edge of Fresno where you take Highway 41 north, directly to the southern gate of Yosemite National Park. Total driving distance is about 300 miles.

The main attractions of the over 1,000 square miles of **Yosemite National Park** lie within the narrow 7-mile-long **Yosemite Valley** which is where you should try to stay if at all possible. A two- or three-night stay in the park is recommended. From hotels through tented cabins, all accommodations in Yosemite are controlled by the **Yosemite Concessions Services (YCS)** for information call (209) 372-0265. It is necessary year-round to make reservations well in advance by phoning (209) 252- 4848.

From the stately and very expensive **Ahwahnee** hotel, through lodges, cabins, tented camps, and regular campsites, Yosemite has accommodations to suit every pocketbook. If your taste in hotels runs to grand, stay at The Ahwahnee. **Yosemite Lodge** provides more moderately priced accommodations in both cabins and motel/hotel-type rooms. Still less expensive are the tented camps that provide canvas tents on wooden board floors (you do not need sleeping bags since beds and linens are provided). The budget choice is regular camping. But please remember—space is very limited in every category and reservations are essential.

While the attractions of staying in the valley cannot be denied, a more relaxed, serene, country atmosphere pervades the **Wawona Hotel**, located within the park, but about a 27-mile drive south of the valley on Highway 41. With its shaded verandahs overlooking broad rolling lawns, the hotel presents a welcoming picture. Bedrooms with private bathrooms are at a premium—most rooms use communal men's and women's bathrooms (sometimes situated quite a distance from your bedroom).

Yosemite Valley, an awe-inspiring monument to the forces of nature, is bounded by magnificent scraped granite formations—**Half Dome, El Capitan, Cathedral Rock, Clouds Rest**—beckoning rock climbers from around the world. And over the rocks, cascading to the valley far below, are numerous high waterfalls with descriptive names such as Bridalveil, Ribbon, Staircase, and Silver Strand. Below the giant walls of rock the crystal-clear River Merced wends its way through woodlands and meadows of flowers. Undeniably, this is one of the most beautiful valleys anywhere in the world.

A first stop should be the information center to obtain pamphlets, books, and schedules. The park service offers a remarkable number of guided walks, slide shows, and educational programs—look over the possibilities and select the ones that most appeal to you.

Once you are in the valley, park your car and restrict yourself to travel aboard the free shuttle buses as you can do most of your sightseeing by combining pleasant walks with shuttle-bus rides. Alternative modes of transportation are on horseback on guided trips and by bike (bicycles can be rented in the park). Because the valley is flat, it has miles of paths for biking—a very unstrenuous, efficient way of getting around.

Be warned that during the summer months Yosemite Valley is jammed with cars and people—spring and fall are much more civilized times to visit.

Within the park, but beyond the valley floor, are many areas of great natural beauty. Situated just inside the park's southern perimeter is the **Mariposa Grove** of giant sequoias. It was here that John Muir, the great naturalist who fathered the idea of the national park system, persuaded President Theodore Roosevelt to add the 250-acre grove of trees to the Yosemite park system. A tram winds through the grove of sequoias as the driver tells the stories of these giant trees—some of the largest in the world.

To the south of the valley Highway 41 climbs for about 10 miles (stop at the viewing point just before the tunnel) to the Glacier Point turnoff. It is a 15-mile drive to the spectacular **Glacier Point**—a vista point over 3,000 feet above the valley floor. From Glacier Point everything in the valley below takes on Lilliputian proportions: the ribbon-like River Merced, the forest, meadows, and waterfalls all dwarfed by huge granite cliffs. Beyond the valley a giant panorama of undulating granite presents itself. The ideal photographic time to visit is early in the morning or evening. Rangers at Glacier Point offer evening interpretive programs.

Leave Yosemite by the northern gate on Highway 120 to **Groveland**, a handsome old town shaded by pines. The nearby town of Big Oak Flat is little more than a couple of houses strung along the road. As Highway 120 drops steeply down 5 miles of twisting road to Highway 49, the shady pine forests of the mountains give way to rolling, oak-studded foothills, the typical scenery of the Gold Country.

Heading north on Highway 49, detour into **Chinese Camp**, home to over 5,000 Chinese miners in the 1850s and now almost a ghost town sleeping under a profusion of delicate Chinese trees of heaven.

The main street of **Jamestown** is off Highway 49 and therefore free of traffic. With its wooden boardwalks, balconies, and storefronts, Jamestown has managed to retain much of the feel of the Gold Rush days. Inviting shops, particularly the emporium, merit a browse, the western-style saloons are full of local color, and the **The National Hotel** as well as the **Jamestown Hotel** have been restored to a beauty such as the Gold Rush days never witnessed. Just above Main Street on Fifth Avenue is the **Railtown 1897 State Historic Park** where visitors can see old freight and passenger cars, steam trains, and the roundhouse. The park is open on weekends when tours of the roundhouse are conducted.

Leaving town, continue up the main street and cross Highway 49 onto a peaceful little road that takes you through the countryside to Columbia. Follow signs for Columbia or, wherever a junction is unmarked, continue straight. A 15-minute drive brings you to Parrot Ferry Road on the outskirts of the town.

In the 1850s **Columbia** was one of the largest towns in California, with many saloons, gaming halls, and stores. Today the main street is closed to car traffic and has been restored as a state park to reflect the dusty, raucous days when Columbia was the "gem of the southern mines." The renovated buildings of Main Street are like exhibits that make learning fun. Be sure to visit the Wells Fargo office, fire station, candy store, mining museum, and concession shops

City Hotel, Columbia

where costumed citizens sell goods appropriate to the period. You can enjoy a cold sarsaparilla at the saloon, munch candy rocks at the Candy Kitchen and pan for gold at the mining shack. It is great fun to climb aboard a stagecoach for a ride through the town or take a tour to the Hidden Treasure Mine.

Both the **Fallon** and **City Hotel** have been restored (at vast expense) by the state of California to mirror the look of two of Columbia's hotels in Gold Rush days. The City Hotel on Main Street has a less ornate Victorian decor, reflecting the Columbia of the 1860s.

Parrot's Ferry Road leads north from Columbia, crosses the dam and continues through hilly countryside in the direction of Murphys. If you would like to try your hand at rappelling into the largest cavern in California, you have the opportunity at **Moaning Cavern.** (You can, of course, take the saner descent down a spiral staircase into a room capable of holding the Statue of Liberty.) The rappel is exciting, and with outfitting, instruction, and a boost of confidence, you descend through a small opening into the well-lit cavern—a most exhilarating experience.

From the caves a short drive brings you to Highway 4 where you turn east (right) for about a 20-mile drive to **Calaveras Big Trees State Park,** a 6,000-acre preserve of forest including two magnificent stands of sequoia trees. A 45-minute self-guided tour takes you through the North Grove and the nearby visitors' center provides information and history on these mammoth trees. If you have time and interest, you can visit the more distant South Grove of giant sequoias.

Leaving the park, retrace your route down Highway 4 and detour into **Murphys,** a sleepy Gold Rush town sheltered under locust and elm trees where several old buildings and an **Old Timers' Museum** reflect its Gold Rush heritage. Well signposted from the center of town is another cavern complex, **Mercer Caverns**, with rooms of stalactites, stalagmites, and other interesting limestone formations. You might also want to detour a beautiful winery, **Kautz Ironstone,** set on the hill outside Murphys. (Turn off Main Street up the road to the side of Murphy's Hotel, at the stop sign, turn right on Six Mile Road and travel 1 mile). The grounds are absolutely gorgeous in their landscaping and at the end of an extremely informative tour it is a memorable experience tasting wine while listening to the winery's magnificent organ from the old Alhambra Theater. Tours are offered daily at 11 am, 1 pm, and 3 pm, the winery is closed Christmas and Thanksgiving. Kautz Ironstone Winery, 1894 Six Mile Road, Murphys, CA 95247, tel: (209) 728-1251.

At the junction of Highways 4 and 49 sits **Angels Camp**, a pleasant town with high sidewalks and wooden-fronted buildings. Today Angels Camp's fame results not from mining, but from the frog-jumping contests held every May. There is even a monument to a frog taking the place of honor on the main street along which almost all the shops sell items carrying a frog motif.

Leave Angels Camp traveling north on Highway 49 through San Andreas where nearly all evidence of Gold Rush days has been obliterated by modern shopping centers and commercial businesses. On the outskirts of the town Highway 49 makes a sharp turn to the east (right) which is signposted Jackson. A 7-mile drive brings you to **Mukulumne Hill** which in its heyday was one of the more raucous mining towns, though now it seems to be quietly fading away. Turn off Highway 49 and loop through town past the impressive (though genteelly shabby) Hotel Leger and turn left in front of the crumbling I.O.O.F building, then through the residential area and back onto the main road.

Jackson still supports roughly the same population as it had during the Gold Rush—consequently, modern shopping centers and sprawling suburbs are the order of the day. Turn right at the first stop sign in town and almost immediately left to the main street. Set above the old town in an impressive Victorian home is the **Amador County Museum**, 225 Church Street. The various rooms have rather eclectic exhibits from the Gold Rush era: for example, the kitchen is full of 19th-century cookware while a small upstairs bedroom displays Indian baskets. Set in an adjacent building is a scale working model of the North Star Stamp Mill which crushes tiny stones.

Retrace your route to where you turned off Highway 49 and turn left on Highway 88 signposted for Lake Tahoe and Pine Grove. Just outside Pine Grove turn left (signposted for your next two destinations, Indian Grinding Rock State Park and Volcano) and follow one of the gold country's prettiest backroads to **Chaw'se Indian Grinding Rock State**

Park. A giant slab of limestone has over 1,000 grinding mortars worn into it by Indian women grinding acorn meal. A typical Miwok village has been built nearby with a ceremonial roundhouse and various tree-bark dwellings. The adjacent cultural center, built in the style of an Indian roundhouse, has interesting displays from several local Indian tribes.

Just a short drive takes you past the turnoff for Sutter Creek and into **Volcano**, one of the smallest (population 100), prettiest Gold Country towns which boasted the first lending library and theater group in the state. Now it is a tiny one-street town whose most impressive building is the three-storied, balconied **Saint George Hotel**. Several weathered building fronts give an impression of what the town looked like in more prosperous days. Three miles beyond the town lies **Daffodil Hill** where over 25,000 daffodil bulbs provide a colorful spring display.

Follow the narrow wooded ravine alongside Sutter Creek as it twists down to the town of the same name. **Sutter Creek** rivals Nevada City as the loveliest of the Gold Rush towns. Its main street is strung out along busy Highway 49 but somehow the noisy logging trucks, and commercial and car traffic do not detract from its beauty. False wooden store fronts support big balconies which hang over the high sidewalks of the town. Today many of the quaint wooden buildings are home to antique, craft, and gift shops.

Amador City and **Drytown**, the first two towns you encounter after leaving Sutter Creek as you head towards Placerville on Highway 49, have an old-world charm and are worth exploring. However, following them are a string of commercial towns that offer nothing of attraction to the tourist although the intervening countryside is still most attractive. Follow Highway 49 as it weaves through the commercial sprawl of **Placerville**, crosses Highway 50, and climbs out of town.

It is an 8-mile drive along Highway 49, through apple orchards and woodlands, to Coloma where the Gold Rush began. Or you can make it a 25-mile drive by taking a right turn east just after leaving Placerville onto Highway 193, a narrow road which twists down a thickly forested canyon to Chili Bar (a popular spot for rafters to launch) and then does a spectacular weaving climb out of the valley through Kelsey and into **Georgetown**. Stop to explore Georgetown's shaded streets and then pick up Marshall Road (turn left behind the gas station) which takes you down to Highway 49 where you turn south into Coloma.

Set on the banks of the American River, the scant remains of the boom town of **Coloma** are preserved as **Marshall Gold Discovery State Historic Park**. It all began in 1848 when James Marshall discovered gold at **Sutter's Sawmill**. The remaining historic buildings are scattered over a large area, each separated by expanses of green lawn and picnic places along the banks of the river. The residential part of town is a sleepy little cluster of attractive houses set back from the river—it is hard to believe that there was once a population of over 10,000 here. The museum shows a short film on gold discovery and provides information for a self-guided tour. A duplicate of Sutter's original sawmill, looking like a big shed, sits on the bank of the river. For a change of transportation, a number of companies offer one-day rafting trips on the American River from Coloma.

Auburn lies 20 miles farther north along Highway 49 which weaves through its suburbs, crosses Highway 80, and continues as a fast, wide road for approximately 24 miles into Grass Valley. An alternative, far more attractive, and just a few miles longer route, is to take Highway 80 north to the Colfax-Grass Valley exit and follow Highway 174 through pretty woodlands and orchards into Grass Valley. (The following sightseeing suggestion, Empire Mine State Park, is signposted on your left as you near town.)

Grass Valley has a booming economy and sprawls far beyond its historic boundary. Its old downtown buildings housing everyday stores attest to its prosperity. Save town explorations for adjacent Nevada City and concentrate on Grass Valley's **Empire Mine State Park** at the southern end of town. This hard-rock mine produced $100,000,000-worth of gold before it closed. An exhibition depicts the mining methods used by miners

Nevada City

who came here from the Cornish tin mines in England. Park personnel offer tours of the mine buildings, the most interesting of which is the opulent home of William Bourne, the mine's original owner.

The adjacent town of **Nevada City** is as handsomely quaint as Grass Valley is functional. The old mining stores and saloons have been cleverly converted into pleasant restaurants, antique stores, and the like. It is a most attractive town for wandering around. Many settlers came here from the east bringing with them the deciduous trees of their home states, so Nevada City is one of the few places in California that has the glorious fall foliage.

As a conclusion to your Gold Country explorations, take a 45-mile round trip to **Malakoff Diggins** where high-powered jets of water were blasted at a mountainside to extract gold. The method was very successful, but it clogged waterways for miles and left a lunar landscape where there had once been a forested mountainside. This is a very pleasant summer evening trip, but rather than run the risk of returning down narrow country roads in the dark, make the loop as you leave Nevada City for Lake Tahoe. The route is quite well signposted, but it gives you reassurance to have in hand the map from Nevada City Chamber of Commerce. (916) 265-2692. Leave Nevada City going north on Highway 49, following it through wooded countryside for 11 miles to the marker directing you right to Malakoff Diggins (signposted Tyler Foote Crossing Road). The narrow paved road leads you through the forest and, just as you are beginning to wonder quite where you are going, a signpost directs you right down a dirt road into **North Bloomfield**, a town of white-painted houses and buildings set behind picket fences under forest shade. (The town is being restored by the park service and the museum/ranger station is a useful informational stop.) The road through town leads to the diggins proper, a vast lunar landscape of awesome scars. If the weather is inclement, turn back at this point and return to Nevada City by way of the paved highway. Otherwise, continue along the well-maintained dirt road (forking left and downhill at junctions) which leads you down through some lovely scenery to a narrow wood-and-metal bridge spanning a rocky canyon of the South Yuba River where you pick up the paved road that brings you back to Highway 49 on the outskirts of Nevada City.

Leave Nevada City on Highway 20 east, a freeway which soon becomes a two-lane highway passing through forests and along a high ridge giving vistas of the Sierras. As Highway 20 ends, take Highway 80 towards Truckee, a fast freeway which climbs into the Sierra mountains through ever-more-dramatic rugged scenery.

The freeway climbs over **Donner Pass** and by **Donner Lake**, both named in honor of the group of settlers led by George Donner who in 1846 became snowbound while trying to cross the Sierra Nevada in late fall. Harsh conditions and lack of food took many lives and resulted in the survivors resorting to cannibalism.

Take Highway 89, the Tahoe City exit, and follow it alongside the rushing **Truckee River** to **River Ranch**, an inn where in summertime it is great sport to sit on the patio and watch the river tumbling by.

Follow the Truckee River to its source, **Lake Tahoe**. Tucked in a high valley, Lake Tahoe is a vast, blue, icy-cold lake ringed by pine forests and backed by high mountains. The lake has about 70 miles of shoreline, a maximum depth of 1,645 feet, and a summer temperature of about 65 degrees. When people from the San Francisco Bay Area say they are "going to the mountains," Tahoe is usually where they're heading. While certain enclaves have their share of hot dog stands, McDonald's restaurants, and glitzy gambling casinos, there are many unspoilt areas where you can enjoy the exquisite beauty of the lake and its surrounding stunning scenery. For bikers and joggers, a marvelous, seemingly endless trail traces a path along the lakefront and down the Truckee River.

Tahoe City combines rustic, folksy shops, restaurants, and everyday stores with two quite interesting tourist attractions: Fanny Bridge and the Gatekeeper's Cabin. **Fanny Bridge** is very close: just turn right at the supermarket, and there it is. You will see immediately the derivation of "Fanny" when you see the tourists leaning over the railing to watch the trout gobble up the food tossed to them. On the same side of the bridge where the fish feed, outlet gates are opened and shut to control the level of the lake—the entire flow of water exiting from Lake Tahoe is regulated here as the water runs into the Truckee River. The other attraction of Tahoe City, the **Gatekeeper's Cabin**, sits on the bank of the Truckee. The rustic old cabin, once home to the man who controlled the river level, is now an attractive small museum operated by the local historical society.

Hugging the shoreline, Highway 89 opens up to ever-more-lovely vistas as the road travels south. Nine miles south of Tahoe City brings you to **Sugar Pine State Park** with its many miles of hiking trails, and camping and picnic sites. In summer you can tour the nicely furnished Ehrman Mansion, once the vast lakeside summer home of a wealthy San Francisco family.

You will know by the sheer beauty of your surroundings when you are at **Emerald Bay**. The road sits hundreds of feet above a sparkling, blue-green bay and miles of Lake Tahoe stretch beyond its entrance. Center stage is a small wooded island crowned by a

Emerald Bay, Lake Tahoe

stone tea house. A 1½-mile trail winds down to the lake—it seems a lot farther walking up—and in summer you can tour **Vikingsholm**, the 38-room lakeside mansion built in 1929 and patterned after a 9th-century Norse fortress. It is the finest example of Scandinavian architecture in America and is filled with Norwegian furniture and weavings.

Just below Emerald Bay a trail leads from the parking lot up a ¼-mile steep trail to a bridge above the cascading cataract of **Eagle Falls** which offers fantastic views of Lake Tahoe. A mile farther up the trail is **Eagle Lake**, in an isolated, picture-perfect setting.

A memorable outing from Tahoe is a day trip to Nevada's silver towns, Virginia City and Carson City. Leaving Tahoe City, follow the northernmost shore of the lake across the Nevada state line and take Highway 431 from Incline Village over Mount Rose to the stop light at Highway 395. Cross the highway and go straight ahead up the winding Geiger Grade, Highway 341, to **Virginia City**. Built over a honeycomb of silver mines, in its heyday Virginia City had a population of over 30,000. Its wooden sidewalks, colorful saloons (you must visit the Bucket of Blood Saloon), and false-front buildings with their broad balconies make it a town straight out of a John Wayne movie. The stores sell everything from homemade candy to western boots and several have been reconstructed as museums. You can walk up to the old cemetery, take a steam-train ride, or tour a mine.

Leaving town, travel on through Gold Hill and Silver Hill to Highway 50 where you turn south for the 7-mile drive to **Carson City,** the state capital. The town itself has little of interest except for the **Nevada State Museum**, just across the street from the Nugget Casino on the main road. The highlight of the museum is the re-created silver mine in the basement. You walk along rail car lines in semi-darkness, past exhibits of miners at work and mine machinery—a lot safer than going down a working mine.

To return to Tahoe go south on Highway 395, the main street of town, to Highway 50 west. Turn right and when you come to Lake Tahoe turn right, following the lake to Tahoe City.

Leaving Lake Tahoe it is a fast four- to five-hour freeway drive, via Highway 80, to the San Francisco Bay area. If you are going to Los Angeles, take Highway 80 to Sacramento and Highway 5 south to Los Angeles—a fast eight- to nine-hour drive.

San Francisco to the Oregon Border

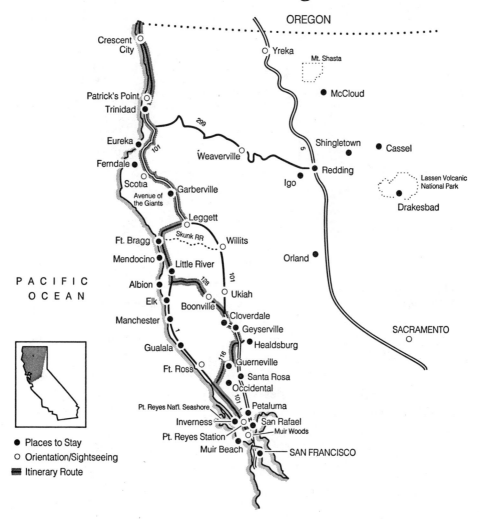

OREGON

Crescent City

Yreka

Mt. Shasta

McCloud

Patrick's Point
Trinidad

299

Weaverville

Shingletown

Cassel

Eureka

101

Redding

Ferndale

Igo

Scotia
Avenue of the Giants

Garberville

Lassen Volcanic National Park

Drakesbad

Leggett

Ft. Bragg   Skunk RR   Willits

Mendocino   Little River

Orland

Albion

128

Elk   Boonville

101

Ukiah

Manchester

Cloverdale
Geyserville

Gualala

116

Healdsburg

Ft. Ross

Guerneville
Santa Rosa
Occidental

PACIFIC OCEAN

1

SACRAMENTO

Petaluma

Pt. Reyes Nat'l. Seashore
Inverness

101

San Rafael
Muir Woods

Pt. Reyes Station

Muir Beach   SAN FRANCISCO

- ● Places to Stay
- ○ Orientation/Sightseeing
- ▓ Itinerary Route

San Francisco to the Oregon Border

Mendocino

If your heart leaps with joy at the sight of long stretches of deserted beaches, rugged cliffs embraced by wind-bent trees, sheep quietly grazing near crashing surf, and groves of redwoods towering above carpets of dainty ferns, then this itinerary will suit you to perfection. Nowhere else in California can you travel surrounded by so much natural splendor. Less than an hour after crossing the Golden Gate Bridge, civilization is left far behind you and your adventure into some of California's most beautiful scenery begins. The first part of this route includes many well-loved attractions: Muir Woods, the Russian River, Sonoma County wineries, the Mendocino Coast, and the Avenue of the Giant Redwoods. Then the route becomes less "touristy" as it reaches the Victorian jewel of Ferndale, the bustling town of Eureka, and the coastal hamlet of Trinidad, and concludes amongst the giant coastal redwoods of Redwood National Park.

Recommended Pacing: You can cover the distance between San Francisco and Mendocino in a day. It is approximately a four-hour drive if you are traveling inland on Highway 101 and then cutting west over at Cloverdale on Highway 128 back to the coast just south of Mendocino. It is approximately a six-hour journey if you follow Highway 1 as it hugs the coast all the way north. However, if time allows, follow our routing and spend a night just north of San Francisco near Point Reyes National Seashore (more if you want to take advantage of the hiking and biking trails), and a night or two in the Healdsburg/Russian River area before arriving in Mendocino. Allow two nights for the Mendocino area and two nights for the Eureka area before continuing up the coast to Oregon.

Weather Wise: The weather along California's northern coast is unpredictable: beautiful warm summer days suddenly become overcast when the fog rolls in (July and August). The prettiest months are usually June, September, and October. Rain falls during the winter and spring, while fall enjoys beautiful crisp clear days.

San Francisco, a city of unsurpassed beauty, is a favorite destination of tourists and it is no wonder: the city is dazzling in the sunlight, yet equally enchanting when wrapped in fog. The setting is spectacular: a cluster of hills on the tip of a peninsula. San Francisco is very walkable and if you tire, a cable car, bus, or taxi is always close at hand. Enough sightseeing suggestions to occupy several days begin on page 16.

Avoiding commuter hours and congestion, leave San Francisco on the **Golden Gate Bridge** following Highway 101 north. After you cross this famous bridge pull into the vista point for a panoramic view of this most lovely city. For another spectacular detour, take the very first exit after the viewing area, Alexander Avenue, turn left back under the freeway, and continue as if you are heading back onto the Golden Gate Bridge, but, instead, take a quick right to the **Marin Headlands**. Some of the city's most spectacular skylines are photographed from the vantage point of these windswept and rugged headlands looking back at the city through the span of the Golden Gate. The road continues through the park and eventually winds back to Highway 101. Information and maps are available at the visitors' center located in the old Fort Barry Chapel. Signs in the park direct you to the center which is open daily, 9:30 am–4:30 pm, tel: (415) 331-1540. Not to be missed is the **Marine Mammal Center**, where injured seals and other marine animals are nursed back to health by a multitude of volunteers. (415) 289-7325.

After returning to Highway 101, continue on to the Mill Valley exit. Circle under the freeway and follow signs for Highway 1 north. As the two-lane road leaves the town behind and winds up through the trees, watch closely for a sharp right turn to **Muir Woods**. The road takes you high above open fields and down a steep ravine to the Muir Woods entrance and car park. A park volunteer gives out a map and information and there is no charge for admission to the park. Near the park entrance a cross section of a trunk of one of the stately giant coastal redwoods gives you an appreciation of the age of these great trees. Notations relate the tree's growth rings to significant historical occurrences during the tree's lifetime: 1066—the Battle of Hastings, 1215—the Magna Carta, 1492—the discovery of America, 1776—the Declaration of Independence. But this tree was only a baby—some date back over 2,000 years. Your brochure guides you on the walk beneath the redwoods or you can take a guided tour with one of the rangers. Allow about an hour for the park, longer if you take a long walk or just sit on one of the benches to soak in the beauty.

Leaving the park, continue west to the coastal road Highway 1. Turn left and then, almost immediately, right. There is a small sign marked **Muir Beach**, but it is easy to miss. Just before you come to the beach you arrive at the **Pelican Inn**, a charming re-creation of an English pub that fortunately also offers lodging. The adjacent Muir Beach is a small half-moon beach bound at each end by large rock formations.

Return to Highway 1 and head north along a challenging, winding section of this beautiful coastal road. The road descends to the small town of **Stinson Beach** where by entering the state park you can gain access to a fabulous stretch of wide white sand, bordered on one side by the sea and on the other by grassy dunes. This is a perfect spot to stretch and enjoy a walk along the beach.

Leaving Stinson Beach, the road curves inland bordering **Bolinas Lagoon,** a paradise for birds, and then leaves the water and continues north for about 10 miles to the town of Olema. At Olema you leave Highway 1 and take the road marked to Inverness, just a short drive away.

If the weather is fine, allow time to explore **Point Reyes National Seashore,** a spectacular wilderness area stretching along the sea. If you happen to be in the area on a weekend, call ahead to the park, (415) 663-1200, to find out what special field trips (such as tidepool studies, bird watching, and sights and sounds of nature) are being offered. The Ranger Station, located in a handsome redwood building at the entrance to the park, has maps, leaflets, books, a museum, and a movie theater where a presentation

gives interesting information on the park. Be sure to stop here before your explorations to obtain a map and study what you want to see and do. A short stroll away from the ranger station is the "earthquake trail" where markers indicate changes brought about by the 1906 earthquake. Also within walking distance is the **Morgan Ranch** where Morgan horses are raised and trained for the park system. If the weather is clear, a drive out to **Point Reyes Lighthouse** is a highlight that should not be missed. As you drive for 45 minutes across windswept fields and through dairy farms to the lighthouse

Point Reyes Lighthouse

you realize how large the park really is. When you arrive, it is a ten-minute walk from the parking area to the viewing area. From there, steps lead down to the lighthouse. Be prepared: it is like walking down a 30-story building and once down, you have to come back up! In winter and spring it is a perfect place from which to watch for migrating gray whales.

After a visit to the lighthouse, look on your map for **Drakes Bay,** one of the many beaches along this rugged strip of coast, and named for the explorer seeking lands for Queen Elizabeth I of England. He is purported to have sailed into the bay on the *Golden Hinde*, and christened it Nova Albion, meaning New England. If you are hungry, there is a café at Drakes Bay where you can have a bite to eat. Another interesting stop is at the **Johnson Oyster Company** on Sir Francis Drake Boulevard—a sign directs you to it on the left on the drive toward Point Reyes Lighthouse. Stop to see the demonstration of how oysters are cultivated in the bay for 18 months before being harvested

If you choose to continue on to the northernmost point of the peninsula, travel Pierce Point Road which ends at the Tule Elk Range. Before 1860 thousands of tule elk roamed here but were hunted to extinction, then in 1978 two bulls and eight cows were successfully reintroduced and now the herd numbers about 250. Trails lead through this wilderness and research area to the Tomales Point Bluff or a shorter distance down to McClures Beach and Elephant Rock.

Retrace your route through the park to **Point Reyes Station** where the **Station House Café,** a delightful restaurant with delicious, imaginative food, beckons you into its dining room or tranquil, brick-paved, cottage-garden patio. Continue north on Highway 1 as the road winds through fields of pastureland and creameries and then loops back and follows for a while the northern rim of **Tomales Bay,** providing lovely vistas across the water to the wooded hills and the town of Inverness. About a 20-minute drive brings you to the village of Marshall, and soon after, the road heads inland through rolling ranch land bound by picket fences, passing the towns of **Tomales** (the **Tomales Bakery,** located in the old barbershop and open Thursday through Monday, is worth visiting—rivaling anything you would sample in France) and Valley Ford before turning west to Bodega Bay and the small town of Jenner. From here it is about a 15-minute drive to **Fort Ross**. "Ross" means "Russian" and this is the site where the Russians, in the early part of the 19th century, built a fort to protect their fishing and fur interests in California. After browsing through the museum, follow the footpath through the woods and enter the courtyard bounded by the weathered wooden buildings where the settlers lived and worked. Be sure not to miss the pretty Russian Orthodox chapel in the southeast corner of the compound. When you have finished roaming through the encampment, take the dramatic walk along the bluffs above the ocean (707) 847-3286.

Leaving the fort, retrace your path to Jenner and follow Highway 116 inland along the banks of the **Russian River**. This is a tranquil stretch of road, passing through dense forests that open up conveniently to offer views of the very green water of the Russian River. (In winter after heavy rains the river can become a rushing torrent—no longer green and tranquil.) On weekends this road is very congested, but midweek and off season this is a very pretty drive. The largest resort along the river is **Guerneville** and just a few miles beyond the town you come to the **Korbel Winery**, a picturesque large building banked with flowers. The last guided tour usually leaves at 3 pm—to be safe, call to double check the schedule: (707) 887-2294. Korbel is famous for sparkling wines and the tour and video presentations are especially interesting. Three Korbel brothers came to this area from Bohemia to harvest the redwoods and ended up harvesting grapes. There is also a tour of the pretty rose garden nestled on the slope to the left of the winery.

Sampling champagne at Korbel will whet your appetite for additional wines from Sonoma County. Leaving the winery, continue for a short distance along River Road, watching for a left-hand turn for Westside Road (if you go over the bridge, you have gone too far). Westside Road winds its way to Healdsburg, past vineyards, meadows with cows grazing, pretty apple orchards, and several wineries, including **Hop Kiln**

Winery and the nearby **Rochioli Winery** which are open for tasting until 5 pm. The architecture at Hop Kiln is very interesting, with whimsical chimneys jutting into the sky. As the name implies, the winery was originally used for drying beer hops. For more information call Hop Kiln Winery, telephone (707) 433-6491 or for the Rochioli Winery, telephone (707) 433-2305.

Nearby **Healdsburg** has an attractive main square lined with quaint shops and restaurants.

Leaving Healdsburg, follow Highway 101 north for the half-hour drive to Cloverdale where you take Highway 128 heading northwest toward the coast. At first the road twists slowly up and over a rather steep pass. After the summit, the way becomes more gentle as you head down into the beautiful **Anderson Valley**, well-known for its delicious wines. Whenever the hills spread away from the road, the gentle meadows are filled with vineyards. If time permits, stop at the **Navarro Winery**, housed in an attractive contemporary building where wine tasting is offered. For further information call (707) 895-3686. As the road leaves the sunny open fields of grapes, the sun almost disappears as you enter a majestic redwood forest, so dense that only slanting rays of light filter through the trees. Upon leaving the forest, Highway 128 soon merges with the coastal Highway 1 (about a 60-mile drive from where you left Highway 101). Here you join Highway 1 going north through Albion and Little River, and then on to Mendocino.

Mendocino is an absolute jewel: a New-England-style town built upon headlands that jut out to the ocean. It is not surprising that the town looks as if it were transported from the East Coast because its heritage goes back to adventurous fishermen who settled here from New England, and, upon arrival, built houses like those they had left behind. (In fact, the "New England" setting, seen in the popular television series *Murder She Wrote,* was filmed here.) Tucked into the many colorful wood-frame buildings are a wealth of art galleries, gift shops, and restaurants. Do not let your explorations stop at the quaint town, but venture out onto the barren, windswept headlands—a visit to Mendocino would not be complete without a walk along the bluffs. In winter or spring there is an added bonus: spouts of water off the shoreline are an indication that a gray whale is present.

Mendocino makes a most convenient base for exploring the coast. However, if breathtaking views are more important to you than quaint shops and restaurants, then overnight instead 16 miles south of Mendocino in **Elk**, a tiny old lumber town hugging the bluffs along one of the most spectacularly beautiful stretches of the sensational Mendocino coastline. Elk has several places to stay that are described in detail in the inn section of this guide—each has its own personality, each has a magnificent ocean view. Note: If you choose to overnight in Elk instead of the town of Mendocino, when Highway 128 merges with Highway 1, go south to Elk instead of north to Mendocino.

Staying in this area, you could most successfully be entertained by doing absolutely nothing other than soaking in the natural rugged beauty of the coast. However, there are some sightseeing possibilities. Just north of the town of Mendocino you come to **Fort Bragg**. This is a sprawling town that, when compared to the quaintness of Mendocino, has little to offer architecturally except for an extremely colorful fishing harbor. At 18220 N. Highway One you find the 47 acres of the **Mendocino Coast Botanical Gardens**. The mild rainy winters and cool summers provide ideal growing conditions for the collections in the gardens which are sheltered by a native pine forest. The gardens include a fern-covered canyon, coastal bluffs, a rocky inter-tidal habitat, and wheelchair-accessible trails that connect everything together. There are lots of places to picnic including the sheltered Cliff House with its spectacular views of the ocean. Two electric carts are available for those with special needs. (707) 964-4352.

The most popular attraction in Fort Bragg is the **Skunk Railroad** which runs between Fort Bragg and Willits. During the summer months you can either take the all-day trip which makes the complete round trip to **Willits,** or choose a half-day trip leaving in the morning or the afternoon. The train follows the old logging route through the redwood

forests. Frankly, you will have already seen lovelier glens of redwood trees than those you will view on the ride, but the outing is fun, especially if you are traveling with children. The train station is in the center of town just after you pass over the rail tracks. Call ahead for reservations: (707) 964-6371.

Leaving the Mendocino area, continue to follow the coast north and enjoy a treasury of memorable views: sometimes the bluffs drop into the sea, other times sand dunes almost hide the ocean and at one point the beach sweeps right up to the road. At Rockport Highway 1 turns inland and twists and turns its way through forests and over the coastal range on 20 miles of narrow winding road. Arriving at **Leggett** (just before the junction with Highway 101), look for a sign to your right indicating a small privately owned redwood park where you can drive through a hole in a redwood tree.

From Leggett continue north along Highway 101 signposted for Eureka. However, rather than rushing all the way up Highway 101, follow the old highway, called **The Avenue Of The Giants**, that weaves through the **Humboldt Redwoods State Park**. This is a 33-mile-long drive, but we suggest you select the most beautiful section by skipping the first part and joining the Avenue of the Giants at Myers Flat. As you exit at Myers Flat, the two-lane road passes a few stores and then glides into a spectacular glen of redwoods. A lovely section of the forest is at **Williams**

Grove. Stop at the nearby park headquarters and obtain a map which directs you off the Avenue of the Giants to **Rockefeller Forest,** the oldest glen of redwoods left in the world—some date back over 2,000 years. The trees are labeled and a well-marked footpath guides you through the forest to the Big Tree, an astounding giant measuring 17 feet in diameter and soaring endlessly into the sky, and to the Flat Iron Tree (another biggie with a somewhat flattened-out trunk) located nearby in an especially serene grove of trees.

About ten minutes after rejoining Highway 101, exit to **Scotia.** Established in 1869, the entire town—homes, shops, school, hotel—is owned by the largest lumber company in the world. The picturesque little redwood homes are dominated by the **Pacific Lumber Company.** You will find the small shopping center worth visiting just for the sake of seeing the redwood building constructed from pillars made from whole tree trunks. Drive to the museum—an all-redwood building resembling a Grecian temple with redwood-tree (bark and all) pillars instead of marble. The museum displays photos, artifacts, and machinery used in the logging camps. It is here you obtain your redwood shingle giving directions for the self-guided mill tour. Pass in hand, you follow the "yellow brick road," a well-marked trail, highlighted with yellow arrows, which guides you throughout the factory. Your first stop is at the hydraulic de-barker where you watch through windows the bark stripped from the logs by high-pressure water which sweeps back and forth over each log like a broom. Bits of bark and sprays of water cover the windows while the entire building rumbles as the giant logs are stripped naked. The next stop is the saw mill where logs are pulled back and forth beneath a giant-sized rotary saw which slices them into large boards. Walking along the overhead ramp, you watch the entire process from the first touch of the saw until the various-sized boards are neatly wrapped and bound tightly with straps. The Pacific Lumber Company mill is closed on weekends and holidays. Passes are given out for tours Monday through Friday, 7:30 am–2:00 pm. It is best to check times in advance of your arrival by calling (707) 764-2222.

Ferndale

Returning to Highway 101, about a 10-mile drive brings you to the Ferndale exit. Founded in 1852, **Ferndale** is the westernmost town (more of a village than a town) in the continental United States. Its downtown with its gaily painted Victorian buildings has changed very little since the 1890s. **Main Street** is a gem, lined with delightful little galleries and stores—a favorite being the irresistible candy shop where you view, through the window, hand-dipping of delectable chocolates. Many visitors enjoy the **Repertory Theater** on Main Street where some excellent plays are produced. (707) 725-2378. Epitomizing the colorful character of the town is **The Gingerbread Mansion** and the historic bed and breakfast, **The Shaw House**. Stop at Ferndale's **museum** to learn more about her past as you tour Victorian rooms and see displays of old dairy and smithying equipment. Open Wednesday through Sunday 11–4 pm, Shaw and 3rd Street, (707) 786-4466.

Centerville Beach is 5 miles west of Ferndale on Centerville Road (turn right on Ocean Avenue at the end of Ferndale). Here you have 9 miles of beaches backed by dairy farms to the north and steep cliffs to the south. Watch for harbor seals in the breakers and tundra swans which congregate in the Eel River bottoms north of Centerville Road from mid-November to February.

Leaving Ferndale, retrace your way to Highway 101 and continue north for the 10-mile drive to **Eureka**. The area surrounding the 101 is full of fast-food chains, gas stations, and commercial establishments, but a small portion of this large town, the **Old Town**, is worth a visit (G and D between 1st and 3rd). On the northwestern edge of this restored project lies the ornate **Carson Mansion** (2nd and M), the most photographed ornate Victorian mansion in northern California. Just a short stroll from the Carson Mansion lie the **Carter House Victorians**, a complex of three Victorian buildings offering accommodation and dining.

About 20 miles beyond Eureka exit the 101 for the coastal hamlet of **Trinidad**. Although the houses are now mostly of modern architecture, Trinidad Bay has an interesting history. It was discovered by the Portuguese in 1595, claimed by the Spaniards in 1775, flourished in the 1850s Gold Rush as a supply port for the miners, and was later kept on the map by logging. Now Trinidad is a sleepy little cluster of homes nestled on the bluffs overlooking a sheltered cove where an untouristy wharf stretches out into the bay. Next to the wharf is the **Seascape Restaurant** where you can dine on fish straight from the little fishing boats. Stroll the mile-long path along the headlands enjoying the views and in winter the crashing rollers.

Return almost to the 101 and turn left on Patrick's Point Drive as it winds through conifers often just out of view of the rocky coastline to **Patrick's Point State Park**. (707) 677-3570. The price of admission affords you the opportunity to stroll beside the crashing waves at Agate Beach (you may well find an agate) or enjoy the rocky vistas from the coastal trail which brings you to Wedding Rock and Patrick's Point. Also within the park is a re-created Yurok village which recalls the days when the Yurok Indians camped in this area.

From here, Highway 101 leaves the coast where the waves pound the shore and ventures inland past quiet lagoons (Big Lagoon, Stone Lagoon, and Freshwater Lagoon). At the end of Freshwater Lagoon you enter **Redwood National Park** and turn left for the **Redwood Information Center** set at the edge of the beach (1 mile south of Orick). Enjoy the exhibits, equip yourself with maps, and set off into the park which contains some of the world's tallest trees.

Passing through **Orick,** it seems that there are more small stores advertising every imaginable item made from redwood than there are houses. So if you've always craved taking an 8-foot redwood Indian home to Aunt Tilda, this is a perfect opportunity to stop and buy one.

Turn right onto Bald Hill Road and climb steeply into the trees to **Lady Bird Johnson Grove** where you follow a 1-mile walk which loops through the stillness of a coastal redwood forest with the trees towering high above you and the forest floor carpeted with ferns.

Return to the 101 north and continue for 1½ miles, turning left on Davison Road where a large herd of elk roam the pastures that lead to **Gold Bluffs Beach** (4 miles) where traces of gold were found during the Gold Rush and on to **Fern Canyon** (8 miles from 101) where you proceed along a steep narrow canyon walled with ferns and follow a short looping trail which criss crosses the creek.

Returning to the 101 as it continues north, cross the Klamath River and pass through the fishing resort of Klamath to reach the coastside town of **Crescent City**. Much of the town's waterfront was destroyed by a tidal wave resulting from an earthquake in Alaska in 1964. While this itinerary concludes at the Oregon border, a convenient, very lovely place to make your base in southern Oregon is the **Tu Tu Tun Lodge** in Gold Beach, telephone (541) 247-6664.

Leisurely Loop of Southern California

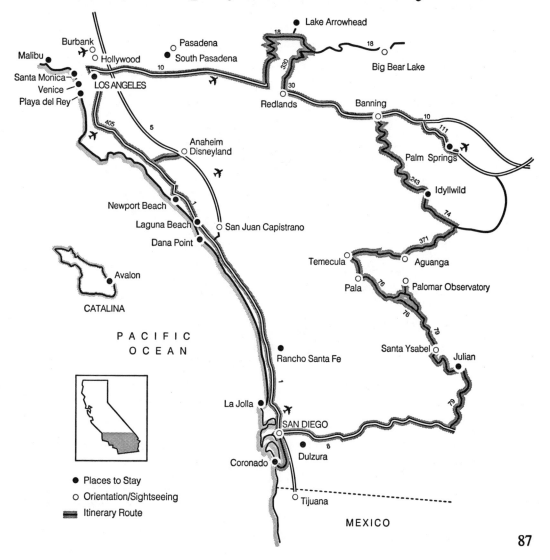

Malibu

Burbank ✈
○ Hollywood

Santa Monica
Venice
Playa del Rey
LOS ANGELES

Pasadena
○ South Pasadena

10

Lake Arrowhead

18
330

18
○
Big Bear Lake

30
Redlands ○

Banning ○

10
111 ✈
Palm Springs

405

5

Anaheim
○ Disneyland

243
Idyllwild ○

74

Newport Beach

Laguna Beach

Dana Point

○ San Juan Capistrano

371
Aguanga ○

Temecula ○
Pala ○

76
Palomar Observatory ○

76

Avalon ●

CATALINA

79

Santa Ysabel ○
Julian ●

PACIFIC
OCEAN

Rancho Santa Fe ●

79

La Jolla ●

✈
SAN DIEGO

Coronado ●

Dulzura ●

8

○ Tijuana

MEXICO

● Places to Stay
○ Orientation/Sightseeing
▬ Itinerary Route

87

Leisurely Loop of Southern California

Disneyland

Los Angeles and San Diego are popular destinations, attracting travelers from around the world to a wealth of sightseeing treats. But in addition to visiting these justifiably famous cities, we hope to entice you to venture out into the countryside to explore lesser-known sightseeing gems: quaint Balboa Island with its handsome yachts, charming La Jolla with its idyllic beaches, picturesque Julian exuding its Gold Rush heritage, secluded Idyllwild nestled in the mountains, glamorous Palm Springs where movie stars still steal away, beautiful Arrowhead with its crystal-clear lake. Perhaps nowhere else can you discover within only a few short miles such a rich tapestry of places to visit—all so different, all so appealing. White sand beaches, forests with towering pines, deserts rimmed with snow-peaked mountains, bountiful orchards, historical mining towns, and shimmering blue lakes all await your discovery.

Recommended Pacing: Greater Los Angeles is an enormous metropolis of cities and suburbs connected by an overwhelming maze of very busy freeways—during the commuter rush hours it can take hours to get from one side of the city to the other. Choose a hotel or motel close to the principal attraction you are visiting in Los Angeles and use it as a base for your other sightseeing. If you are just visiting Disneyland, stay in the area for two nights—the more attractions you want to include, the longer the recommended stay: if you include San Diego or La Jolla, add two nights; if you visit Palm Springs, add another and possibly include one additional night for Lake Arrowhead.

Weather Wise: The weather along the coast is warm year round and there is very little winter rain. Julian has a more temperate climate—though sometimes in the summer it has the odd very hot day and in the winter the occasional snowfall. Palm Springs can be boiling hot, but with a dry heat, during the summer, and is ideal in the winter, with warm days and cool mountain-desert nights. Lake Arrowhead is a mountain resort with warm summer weather and snow in winter.

If you are going to be staying for an extended period of time in **Los Angeles**, supplement this guide with a book totally dedicated to what to see and do. There is also a wealth of free information available from the Los Angeles Visitors' Bureau: (213) 624-7300—they will send you a very useful packet of information. We are not going to attempt to detail all of Los Angeles' sightseeing possibilities, but just briefly mention a few highlights.

Disneyland: The wonderland created by Walt Disney needs no introduction. What child from two to ninety-two has not heard of this Magic Kingdom, home to such lovable characters as Mickey Mouse, Donald Duck, Pluto, and Snow White? The park is a fantasy land of fun, divided into various theme areas. You enter into Main Street USA and from there it is on to Tomorrowland, Fantasyland, Frontierland, and Adventureland, each with its own rides, entertainment, and restaurants. Disneyland is open every day of the year. The park is located at 1313 Harbor Boulevard in Anaheim. For further information call (714) 999-4565.

Huntington Library, Art Gallery, and Botanical Gardens: The home and 207-acre estate of the late Henry Huntington are open to the public and should not be missed by any visitor to the Los Angeles area. Huntington's enormous home is now a museum featuring the work of French and English 18th-century artists. What makes the museum especially attractive is that the paintings are displayed in a homelike setting surrounded by appropriately dramatic furnishings. Nearby, in another beautiful building, is the Huntington Library—a real gem containing, among other rare books, a 15th-century copy of the Gutenberg bible, Benjamin Franklin's handwritten autobiography, and marvelous Audubon bird prints. The gardens of the estate merit a tour in themselves and include various sections such as a rose garden, a Japanese garden, a camellia garden, a cactus garden, an English garden, and a bonsai garden. Located at 1151 Oxford Road in San Marino, the estate is open Tuesday through Friday noon—4:30 pm, and Saturday and Sunday 10:30 am—4:30 pm. For information on special events and shows call (818) 405-2281.

J. Paul Getty Museum: Even non-art enthusiasts enjoy the J. Paul Getty Museum, a replica of an ancient Roman villa from Herculaneum, dramatically set in 10 acres of garden. The reflecting pool, bronze statues, and marble columns add to the grandeur of this very special museum that features many Greek and Roman sculptures and an excellent collection of 18th-century European art. Either a taxi must drop you off at the front gate or you must call ahead to make a parking reservation—you cannot just walk or drive up to the museum. The museum is located at 17985 Pacific Coast Highway, Malibu, open Tuesday through Sunday 10 am–5 pm. For information call (310) 458-2003.

NBC Television Studios: Los Angeles is the television capital of the world. To get an idea of what goes on behind the screen, visit the NBC Television Studios and take their one-hour tour that gives you a look at where the stars rehearse, how costumes are designed, how stage props are made, and what goes into the special effects. The tour also visits some of the show sets. The studios are located at 3000 West Alameda Avenue in Burbank. For further information call (818) 840-3537.

The Norton Simon Museum of Art: The Norton Simon Museum of Art is without doubt one of the finest private art museums in the world, set in a beautiful Moorish-style building accented by a reflecting pool and manicured gardens. Norton Simon and his actress wife, Jennifer Jones, share their incredible collection of art including paintings by such masters as Rubens, Rembrandt, Raphael, Picasso, and Matisse. The museum, open Thursday through Sunday noon–6 pm, is located at 411 West Colorado Boulevard in Pasadena. For further information call (818) 449-6840.

Pueblo de Los Angeles: With all the tinsel of modern-day Los Angeles, it is easy to forget that this city grew up around a Spanish mission. You catch a glimpse of the town's history in Pueblo de Los Angeles, a little bit of Mexico where Hispanic people sell colorful Mexican souvenirs and operate attractive restaurants. The 42-acre complex of old buildings (some dating back to the 1780s) has been restored and is now a state park. Pueblo de Los Angeles is located at 130 Apse de la Plaza, Los Angeles. For further information call (213) 628-1274.

The *Queen Mary*: If you take Highway 710 west to Long Beach, the freeway ends at the waterfront with the *Queen Mary* docked alongside: you can go aboard and wander through the biggest ocean liner ever built. A portion of the ship is a hotel, the rest a museum, re-creating the days of splendor when the *Queen Mary* was queen of the seas.

Universal Studios: Visiting Universal Studios, the biggest, busiest movie studio in the world, is like going to a vast amusement park and there is so much to see and do that you must spend a whole day here. Included in the admission price is a two-hour tram journey which takes you around the 420-acre lot, out of the real world and into make-believe: along the way you encounter the howling fury of King Kong and tremble in a terrifying 8.3 earthquake. Water World, a live sea war spectacular, Back to the Future, a time-travel ride from the age of the dinosaurs to 2015, and Backdraft's raging 10,000 degrees firestorm thrill you with their excitement, while the animal actors' stage show and the re-creation of the zany Lucille Ball sitcoms give you comic relief from adrenaline rushes. The studios are just off the Hollywood Freeway at the Universal Center Drive exit in Universal City. For further information call (818) 508-9600.

It takes only a couple of hours to whip down the freeway between Los Angeles and San Diego, but, instead, follow our sightseeing suggestions and dawdle along the way to enjoy some of southern California's coastal attractions en route.

Drive south from Los Angeles on Highway 405, the San Diego Freeway, until you come to Highway 73, the Corona del Mar Freeway, which branches to the south toward the coast. Take this, then in just minutes you come to Highway 55, Newport Boulevard. Exit here and stay on the same road all the way to **Newport Beach**. Soon after crossing the bridge, watch for the sign to your right for Newport Pier. (In case you get off track, the pier is at the foot of 20th Street.) Try to arrive mid-morning so that you can capture a glimpse of yesteryear when the **Dory Fleet** comes in to beach, just to the right of the pier. The dory fleet, made up of colorfully painted, open wooden fishing boats, has been putting out to sea for almost a hundred years. It is never certain exactly what time the fleet will come in (it depends upon the fishing conditions), but if you arrive mid-morning, the chances are you will see the fishermen preparing and selling their catch-of-the-day from the back of their small boats. If seeing all the fresh fish puts you in the mood for lunch, walk across the street to the **Oyster Bar & Grill**—the food is excellent and the clam chowder truly outstanding. If you want to overnight in Newport Beach, **Doryman's Inn**, just steps from the pier, is highly recommended.

From Newport Beach, continue south along the long, thin peninsula: the next community you come to is **Balboa**. In the center of town there is a clearly signposted public parking area next to Balboa Pier: leave your car here and explore the area. The beach is beautiful, stretching the entire length of the peninsula, all the way from the southern tip to beyond Newport Pier. Stroll along the beach and then walk across the peninsula (about a two-block span) to the Balboa Pavilion, a colorful Victorian gingerbread creation smack in the center of the wharf. Next to the pavilion are several booths where tickets are sold for cruises into the harbor. One of the best of these excursions is on the *Pavilion Queen* that makes a 45-minute loop of the bay. Buy your ticket and, if you have time to spare until the boat leaves, wander around the nostalgic, honky-tonk boardwalk with its cotton candy, Ferris wheel, saltwater taffy shops, and penny arcade. But be back in time to board your boat because the Balboa harbor cruise should not be missed. The trip is a boat fancier's dream: over 9,000 yachts are moored in the harbor. Also of interest are the opulent homes whose lawns stretch out to the docks where their million-dollar cruisers are moored.

A block from the Balboa Pavilion is the ferry landing—you cannot miss it. After your cruise, retrieve your car and follow signs to the Balboa Ferry. You might have to wait in line a bit because the little old-fashioned ferry only takes three cars at a time. When your turn comes, it is just minutes over to **Balboa Island**, a delightful, very wealthy community. Park your car on the main street and poke about in the pretty shops, then walk a few blocks in each direction. The homes look quaint and many seem quite small and simple, but looks are deceiving—the price tags are very high.

From Balboa Island there is a bridge across the harbor to the mainland. Almost as soon as you cross the bridge, turn right, heading south on Highway 1 through the ritzy community of **Corona del Mar**. Although there is still a quaintness to the area, exclusive boutiques, expensive art galleries, palatial homes, and trendy shops hint at the fact that this is not the sleepy little town it might appear to be.

From Corona del Mar, Highway 1 parallels the sea which washes up against a long stretch of beach bound by high bluffs. The area seems relatively undeveloped except for its beach parks. About 11 miles south of Corona del Mar the road passes through **Laguna Beach**, famous for its many art galleries, pretty boutiques, and miles of lovely sand. In summer, from mid-July through August, Laguna Beach is usually packed with tourists coming to see the Pageant of the Masters, a tableau in which town residents dress up and re-create paintings. Two dozen living paintings are staged each evening and viewed by spectators in an outdoor amphitheater.

Continue south along the Coastal Highway. Soon after passing Dana Point, take the turnoff to the east on Highway 5 to **San Juan Capistrano.** Watch for signs directing you off the highway to **Mission San Juan Capistrano** (just two blocks from the freeway). This mission, founded by Father Junipero Serra in 1776, has been carefully restored to give you a glimpse of what life was like in the early days of California. Although located in the center of town, the mission creates its own environment since it is insulated by lovely gardens and a complex of Spanish adobe buildings. Another point of special interest at San Juan Capistrano is that the swallows have chosen it as "home," arriving every March 19th (Saint Joseph's Day) and leaving October 23rd. Visit the mission and then retrace your route to Highway 1 and continue south about an hour to **San Diego.**

The San Diego Visitors' Bureau—(619) 232-3101—will send you a packet of valuable information for touring its many attractions. A recently completed train line makes it easier and more fun than ever to get around San Diego and its environs. You can actually board the train in Old Town and journey to the Mexican border. San Diego offers a wealth of attractions and amusements—we featuresome of our favorites.

Balboa Park: Balboa Park is without a doubt one of the highlights of San Diego. One of the most famous attractions within the park is the **San Diego Zoo,** one of the finest in the world. A good orientation of the zoo is to take either the 40-minute bus tour or else the aerial tramway. Most of the more than 3,000 animals live within natural-style enclosures with very few cages. The Children's Zoo is especially fun, with a nursery for newborn animals and a petting zoo. But Balboa Park offers much more than its splendid zoo. There are fascinating museums and exhibits within the 1,400-acre park: the Museum of Man, the Aerospace Museum, the San Diego Museum of Art, the Timken Art Gallery, the Natural History Museum, the Reuben H. Fleet Space Theater and Science Center, the Hall of Champions, the Museum of Photographic Arts, the Lily Pond, and the Botanical Building. Most of the museums are housed in picturesque Spanish-style buildings. For information call (619) 239-0512.

Coronado: While in San Diego take the bridge or the ferry over to Coronado, an island-like bulb of land tipping a thin isthmus that stretches south almost to the Mexican border. Here you find not only a long stretch of beautiful beach, but also the Del Coronado Hotel, a Victorian fantasy of gingerbread turrets and gables. The Del Coronado, locally referred to as "The Del," is a sightseeing attraction in its own right and makes an excellent choice for a luncheon stop.

The Embarcadero: The Embarcadero is the downtown port area located along Harbor Drive. From here you can take a harbor cruise or visit one of the floating museums tied up to the quay, such as the *Star of India*, built in 1863, a dramatic tall-masted ship that carried passengers and cargo around the world and the *Medea*, a turn-of-the-century luxury yacht. For information call (619) 234-9153.

Heritage Park: Just adjacent to **Old Town** is Heritage Park, where some of San Diego's Victorian heritage is preserved. Next to the spacious village green, a street lined with fabulous Victorian houses slopes gently uphill. The houses were moved here from other areas of San Diego to save them from the bulldozers and now these intricate creations house small shops and offices (do not miss the doll shop with a wonderful collection of doll houses and antique toys).

La Jolla: Be sure to visit La Jolla, "The Jewel," a sophisticated town just north of San Diego. Classy shops line the streets and spectacular homes, secluded behind high walls, overlook the ocean. La Jolla is home to a branch of the University of California and within its Scripps Institution of Oceanography is an excellent aquarium and museum featuring marine life from California and Mexico. However, what really makes La Jolla so special are her beautiful white sand beaches sheltered in intimate little coves. You may prefer to stay here rather than in San Diego.

Mexico: Mexico lies just south of San Diego. Do not judge the many wonders of Mexico by its border town of **Tijuana,** but if you would like to have a taste of Mexico, take one of the "shopping and sightseeing" tours that leave from downtown for the short drive to the border. You can drive across the border, but the packaged bus tour takes all the hassle from the trip. United States citizens need only carry identification such as a driver's license if they are staying in Mexico for less than 72 hours. For further information call Gray Line Tours at (619) 491-0011.

Mission San Diego de Alcala

Mission San Diego de Alcala: The oldest of the chain of missions that stretches up the coast is Mission San Diego de Alcala. The mission was originally closer to San Diego but was moved to its present site (10818 San Diego Mission

Road) in 1774. To reach the mission, head east on Highway 8; it is signposted to the north of the highway beyond the intersection of Highway 15. For information call: (619) 281-8449.

Old Town: Old Town is where San Diego originated. Just southeast of the intersection of Highways 5 and 8 you see signposts for the oldest sections of San Diego. The area has been designated as a city park and several square blocks are accessible to pedestrians. Make the Historical Museum your first stop and orient yourself by viewing a scale model of San Diego in its early days. Although small in area, Old Town is most interesting to visit as many of the buildings are open as small museums, such as the Machado-Steward Adobe, the Old School House, and the Seeley Stables (an 1860s stage depot with a good display of horse-drawn carriages). If you are in Old Town at mealtime, you can choose from many attractive restaurants. For further information call (619) 291-4903.

Seaport Village: Just a little way south of the Embarcadero is Seaport Village, a very popular tourist attraction and fun for adults and children alike. Situated right on the waterfront, it has little paths that meander through 23 acres of a village of shops and restaurants built in a colorful variety of styles from Early Spanish to Victorian. Street artists display their talents to laughing audiences. An old-time merry-go-round (an import from Coney Island) jingles its gay melody, irresistibly beckoning the child in all of us to climb aboard.

Sea World: San Diego's marine display is in Mission Bay Park. Set in a 150-acre park which includes a 1-acre children's playland, Sea World features one of California's famous personalities, Shamu, the performing killer whale who delights children of all ages with her wit and aquatic abilities. Penguin Encounter is a particularly fun exhibit where you watch comical penguins waddling about in their polar environment, while Shark Encounter presents one of the largest displays of sharks in the world and provides the terrifying thrill of being surrounded by these efficient killing machines as you walk through an acrylic tube. For further information call (619) 226-3901.

Wild Animal Park: This is a branch of the San Diego Zoo 30 miles north of the city near Escondido—truly a zoo on a grand scale. The animals roam freely in terrain designed to match their natural habitat. You feel as if you are on a safari in Africa as you watch for lions and other animals while you tour the park on the Wgasa Bushline Monorail tour. There are also several open theaters where animal shows are presented. For further information call (619) 234-6541.

Leaving San Diego, Highway 8 takes you east and winds through shrub-filled canyons dotted with ever-expanding housing suburbs. About 30 minutes after the highway leaves the city, watch for the sign for Highway 79 where you turn north toward Julian. The road weaves through an Indian reservation and the scenery becomes prettier by the minute as you climb into the mountains and enter the **Cuyamaca Rancho State Park**. There are not many opportunities to sightsee en route, but if you want to break your journey, you can pause at the park headquarters and visit the Indian museum or the museum at the **Old Stonewall Mine.** Leaving the park, the road winds down into Julian.

Julian is a small town that can easily be explored in just a short time. What is especially nice is that, although it is a tourist attraction, the town is not "tacky touristy." Rather, you get the feeling you are in the last century as you wander through the streets and stop to browse at some of the antique shops, visit the small historical museum in the old brewery, and enjoy refreshment at the soda fountain in the 1880s drug store. If you want to delve deeper into mining, just a short drive (or long walk) away on the outskirts of town is the **Eagle Mine,** founded by pioneers from Georgia, many of them soldiers who came here after the Civil War. Tours are taken deep into the mine and a narration gives not only the history of the mine, but the history of Julian.

If you are in Julian in the fall, you can enjoy another of Julian's offerings—apples. Although you can sample Julian's wonderful apples throughout the year (every restaurant has its own special apple pie on the menu), the apple becomes king during the fall at harvest time. Beginning in October and continuing on into November, special craft shows and events are held in the Julian Town Hall, and, of course, apples are featured at every meal in every restaurant. You might also want to visit one of the packing plants on the edge of town where you can buy not only apples, but every conceivable item that has apples as a theme.

It is only a short drive north from Julian on Highway 79 to **Santa Ysabel** where you turn right at the main intersection. At this junction you see **Dudley's Bakery**, a rather nondescript looking building that houses a great bakery: loyal customers drive all the way from San Diego just to buy one of their 21 varieties of tasty bread. As you leave Santa Ysabel you come to **Mission Santa Ysabel**, a reconstructed mission that still serves the Indians. This is one of the less interesting missions, but you may want to see the murals painted by the local Indians.

About 7 miles after leaving the mission, Highway 79 breaks off to the east and you continue north on Highway 76. In five minutes you come to Lake Henshaw. Just beyond the lake turn northeast (right) on East Grade Road which winds its way up the mountain to the **Palomar Observatory**. Just near the parking area is a museum where you learn about the observatory through photos and short films. It is a pleasant stroll up to the impressive white-domed observatory that houses the Hale telescope—the largest in the United States. A flight of steps takes you to a glass-walled area where you see the giant telescope whose lens is 200 inches in diameter, 2 feet thick, and took 11 years to polish. You cannot see the telescope in operation because it is used only at night, but it is fun to imagine scientists scanning the heavens.

After viewing the observatory, loop back down the twisting road to the main highway and when it intersects with Highway 76 turn northwest (right), driving through hills covered with groves of avocado and orange trees. In about 12 miles you come to **Pala** and the **Mission San Antonio de Pala**, established in 1810, one of the few remaining active "asistancias" (missions built in outlying areas to serve the Indians). The mission is small, but the chapel holds great beauty in its rugged simplicity enhanced by thick adobe walls, rustic beamed ceiling, and Indian paintings. A bell tower stands alone to the right of the chapel, a picturesque sight; to the left are a simple museum and souvenir shop.

From Pala it is about a ten-minute drive north on S16 to Temecula. Just before you enter town the road intersects with Highway 79 and you head east for 18 miles to Aguanga where Highway 371 takes you northeast for 21 miles to Highway 74. As you head north on 74 the mountain air becomes sweeter and the scenery increasingly prettier as you enter the forest. In about 12 miles you see signs for **Idyllwild** to the northeast. Turn here on Highway 243 and very soon you come to the small resort tucked into the mountains high above Palm Springs. Homey little restaurants, antique stores, and fascinating gift shops make up the town. If you are interested in handmade items, stop at **Maggie's Attic**. Originally the store featured handmade items from 15 local artisans—now Maggie has 750 suppliers, not only from every state, but from around the world. There is a Christmas section with a marvelous selection of Santa Claus ornaments. The shop is located in an old six-room house at 54380 North Circle Drive.

Leaving Idyllwild, continue north on Highway 342 to Banning where you turn east (right) on Highway 10. In about 12 miles you come to Highway 111 where you turn right and follow signs to Palm Springs (about a ten-minute drive). **Palm Springs** was first discovered by the Indians who came to this oasis to bathe in the hot springs which they considered to have healing qualities. The same tribe still owns much of Palm Springs and rents their valuable real estate to homeowners and commercial enterprises. The hot springs are still in use today.

During the winter season the town is congested with traffic and the sidewalks are crammed with an assortment of people of every age, size, and shape dressed in colorful sporty clothes. Palm Springs used to be deserted in summer when the days are very hot. However, more and more tourists are coming in June, July, and August, attracted by the lower hotel rates. Although the temperature in the summer months is frequently well above 110 degrees, it is a dry heat and not unbearable in the mornings and balmy

Aerial Tramway, Palm Springs

evenings. In fact, due to the altitude, evenings often require a sweater. So if your visit is in summer, plan your sight-seeing for early and late in the day and spend midday in the comfort of your air-conditioned inn.

In addition to the pleasures of basking in the sun or playing on one of the many golf courses in the area, Palm Springs offers a variety of sightseeing. The most impressive excursion is to take the **Aerial Tramway** (located just north of town off Highway 111) from the desert floor up 2½ miles into the San Jacinto Mountains. In summer you go from sizzling heat to cool mountain forests, while in winter you go from desert to snow. The weather atop the mountain is often more than 40 degrees cooler than in Palm Springs, so remember to take the appropriate clothing. At the top are observation decks with telescopes, a restaurant, and miles of hiking trails.

If you enjoy deserts, be sure not to miss the **Living Desert Outdoor Museum** (closed in summer) where 6 miles of trails wind through different types of desert found in the United States. Tour booklets are available at the entrance to assist you along the trails. If you are interested in the rich and famous, join a bus tour that takes you by the outside of their magnificent homes—many movie stars have second homes in Palm Springs.

Palm Springs is a convenient place to end this itinerary because it is a quick, easy freeway-drive back to Los Angeles. But, if time permits, squeeze in one more contrasting destination, the exclusive Alpine resort of Lake Arrowhead.

Leave Palm Springs and head north on Highway 111 for about 10 miles to Highway 10 and turn west for Banning. Approximately 20 miles past Banning at Redlands, exit from the freeway on Highway 30 and drive north for a few minutes until Highway 38 travels into the hills. As the road begins to climb up from the valley the scenery becomes prettier with every curve—the dry desert brush is gradually left behind, replaced by evergreen trees. At the town of Running Springs turn west on Highway 18. This is called the "**Rim of the World Highway**," a road where sweeping vistas of the valley floor can be glimpsed through the clouds. Be aware that fog often hovers around this drive and then, instead of admiring beautiful views, you creep along in thick gray mist.

Lake Arrowhead village is a newly built cluster of restaurants and shops along the lakefront. The lake is bordered by magnificent estates of the wealthy from southern California. The magnet of Lake Arrowhead is not any specific sightseeing, but rather the out-of-doors experience: although lakefront and beach access is restricted and private, you can take leisurely walks through the forest, picnic in secluded parks, explore the lake by paddle boats, or rent bicycles for a bit of fresh-air adventure. You also must take the hour-long ride on the nostalgic steamer that circles the lake.

When it is time to complete your itinerary, retrace your path back to the valley and follow Highway 10 back into Los Angeles. Unless you encounter unexpected traffic, the trip should take about two hours.

Places to Stay

The location of the Albion River Inn is splendid, right on the bluff overlooking the handsome bay formed by the mouth of the River Albion as it flows into the ocean. Although this is a newly built hotel, the architecture creates the ambiance of a New England village: softly hued clusters of cottages perch on the cliffs surrounded by a meadow where long grass waves in the wind. Gardens filled with brightly colored flowers line the walkways along the bluff and the quiet is broken only by the deep-throated call of the foghorn. Each of the bedrooms offers a sweeping view of the inlet where the fishing boats bob about in the ever-changing tides. All of the rooms are spacious, romantic, and very private and all have wood-burning fireplaces. The decor is most attractive and although not antique, reflects the hand of a professional decorator. There is an excellent restaurant adjacent to the inn with picture windows overlooking the sea—it is a good idea to request dinner reservations in advance. A hearty breakfast is offered each morning including fresh juices, seasonal fruits, made-to-order eggs, toast, home-fried potatoes, omelets, etc. Coffee makers are set up in each room so that guests can enjoy hot drinks whenever they want. *Directions*: From San Francisco drive north on Highway 101 to Cloverdale, west on Highway 128 to Highway 1, and north 3 miles to Albion. The Albion River Inn is on the northwest side of the Albion bridge.

ALBION RIVER INN
Innkeepers: Flurry Healy & Peter Wells
3790 N. Highway One, P.O. Box 100
Albion, CA 95410
Tel: (707) 937-1919 Fax: (707) 937-2604
20 bedrooms with private bathrooms
Double: $160–$250
Open all year
Credit cards: MC, VS
Children accepted

Amador City with its quaint old-west style houses was a bustle of activity during the Gold Rush days. Now it's a peaceful place (except for the logging trucks which rumble through town periodically), with its old wooden stores full of antique and craft shops and the Imperial Hotel, looking as though it belongs in a cowboy movie. There is immediate charm as soon as you walk into this renovated western hotel where you wouldn't be surprised to see prospectors leaning at the bar. Beyond the bar lies a spacious, high-ceilinged dining room, its red-brick walls hung with fanciful Victorian art. Dining is casual and the menu is short: usually three appetizers, seven entrees, five or six desserts. Upstairs, the six bedrooms are a delight—nothing fancy or frilly, but each well thought-out and accompanied by a small, sparkling bathroom with tub or shower and heated towel bar. Room 6, decorated warmly in tans and navy, is a real winner with an elaborate art-deco bed. The whimsical hand-painted headboard in room 5 is echoed in the paintings of clothes on the closet in room 3. Rooms 1 and 2 share the large balcony at the front of the hotel. There are two sets of adjoining rooms. Guests help themselves to early-morning coffee and tea before going in for breakfast. *Directions:* Amador City straddles Highway 49, 6 miles north of Jackson. The Imperial Hotel is on your right at the bend in the main street.

IMPERIAL HOTEL
Innkeepers: Bruce Sherrill & Dale Martin
14202 Highway 49, P.O. Box 195
Amador City, CA 95601
Tel: (209) 267-9172 Fax: (209) 267-9249
6 bedrooms with private bathrooms
Double: $80–$95
Open all year
Credit cards: all major
Children accepted

A guest at our own inn recommended Cooper House with raves as a perfect retreat in the Gold Rush country. Built in 1911, Cooper House was home to Dr. George P. Cooper, accommodating both his family and patients of the gold-mining community. Set above the heart of town, shaded by trees, and enjoying lush green lawns and terraced gardens, Cooper House was and is still today considered one of the finest homes in town. Enter off the porch to the living room warmed by a large open fireplace. Just off the living room, the Cabernet room enjoys a little sitting area (a queen sleeper) an en-suite bedroom, and a bathroom tucked around the corner. It is a nice setup for those traveling with children. Across the hall from Cabernet, the Chardonnay suite is a cozy room with access to a private deck. Climb the stairs to the Zinfandel Suite which used to serve as Dr. Cooper's office and examining room. With its private entrance from the street, this suite also enjoys a private deck off the French doors and lots of sunshine. Innkeepers Kathy and Tom are very welcoming. Refreshments are offered in the afternoon and a Continental breakfast is served each morning. For recreation, the public swimming pool is close by and Kathy can also direct you to the "Fireman's Hole"—a natural pool with a rope swing—perfect for swimming or gold panning on a hot Gold-Country afternoon. *Directions*: Take Raspberry Street off Main, then turn left on Church Street.

COOPER HOUSE
Innkeeper: Kathy Reese
1184 Church Street, P.O. Box 1388
Angels Camp, CA 95222
Tel: (209) 736-2145
Fax: (Visitors' Center) (209) 736-9124
3 bedrooms with private bathrooms
Double: $90
Open all year
Credit cards: all major
Children accepted

It was wonderful to find that the grand Bayview Hotel, built in 1878, has been attractively refurbished and once again offers comfortable and reasonable accommodation in the seaside village of Aptos. This handsome white Victorian's first floor is now leased and accommodates an attractive restaurant which can offer guests the convenience of dining or the luxury of room service. A lovely wood-banistered stairway winds up to the second and third floors and the 11 guestrooms of the hotel. The rooms are all attractive in their individual decor and vary in size which is reflected in the price: the Cascade room with its full-size bed tucked into a cubby of sunny yellow and rose colors, small yet inviting, is priced at $90; the Loma Prieta room, with both a full-size and a queen-size bed under high ceilings, dressed in colonial blue-and-white stripes, is very appealing and costs $115; rooms on the third floor such as the Seacliff with its king-size bed, large Roman tub, gas fireplace, and side windows are priced at $150. All the guestrooms have private baths and direct-dial phones, and television sets are available upon request in many of the rooms. Gwen Burkard's attention to detail and special touches such as fresh flowers, books, robes, and spotless housekeeping are ever-present and ensure a comfortable stay. *Directions:* Located 10 miles south of Santa Cruz. Take the Seacliff Beach exit off Highway 1 east into town.

BAYVIEW HOTEL
Owners: Pat & Tom O'Brien
Innkeeper: Gwen Burkard
8041 Soquel Drive
Aptos, CA 95003
Tel: (408) 688-8654 Fax: (408) 688-5128
11 bedrooms with private bathrooms
Double: $90–$150
Open all year
Credit cards: all major
Children accepted

Aptos, just two hours south of San Francisco, is best known as a beach resort. Most tourists never realize that tucked into the coastal hills are beautiful redwood glens and adjacent to a 10,000-acre forest of redwoods, creeks, and trails is Mangels House, an elegant, large, redwood home, built in the 1880s, painted white and wrapped in a two-tiered verandah. Once the holiday home of the wealthy Mangels family, whose fortune was in sugar beets, Mangels House now belongs to Jacqueline and Ron Fisher. You enter into a large living room dominated by a tall stone fireplace surrounded by two comfortable floral-patterned sofas and an easy chair. To the left is a formal dining room where a full breakfast is served each morning. The five delightful bedrooms at the top of a lovely staircase vary considerably in size, and each is individual in decor and pretty and fresh in its furnishings. One of the nicest aspects of Mangels House is that it is nestled in the woodlands, yet is only a five-minute drive to the beach. *Directions:* From Santa Cruz, drive 6 miles south on Highway 1, taking the Seacliff Beach-Aptos exit over the freeway (away from the bay). Turn right at the traffic light to Soquel Drive. Just before the Aptos Station Shopping Center turn left onto Aptos Creek Road (also the entrance to the state park). The house is a half mile farther on your right.

MANGELS HOUSE
Innkeeper: Jacqueline Fisher
570 Aptos Creek Road
Aptos, CA 95003
Mail: P.O. Box 302, Aptos, CA 95001
Tel: (408) 688-7982 Fax: none
5 bedrooms with private bathrooms
Double: $105–$150
Closed Christmas
Credit cards: all major
Children accepted over 12

The lovely Ballard Inn is located in the Santa Ynez Valley, a lush region of rolling hills planted with vineyards or sectioned off with white picket fences. Set just off the road, the Ballard was built as an inn, but carries the appearance of a gracious sprawling residence. White picket fences enclose its narrow front garden and a wide porch winds round it. The dining room, serving bountiful breakfasts (with an offering of two or three hot selections) and gourmet dinners (Wednesday through Sunday evenings), is located just off the entry to the right. To the left, another cozy room invites you to linger over a buffet of afternoon hors d'oeuvres, or venture on into the sitting room where large deep sofas steal you away for lazy conversations in front of an open fireplace. Guestrooms are located upstairs or in a neighboring wing just off the graveled driveway. Rooms are comfortable and attractively decorated, each with a small, functional private bathroom. Although, at first, rooms overlooking the front garden seem preferable to those overlooking the parking, select a room at the back for quiet as locals do head off to work and early-morning traffic breaks the silence of the country morning. A final note: If you like horses, ask about the neighboring miniature horse farm. We visited in spring when every mother was matched with a miniature foal—adorable. *Directions:* Take Route 246 off Highway 101 in the direction of Solvang. Travel north on Alamo Pintado Road and then east on Baseline Road. The Ballard Inn is on the right.

THE BALLARD INN
Owners: Steve Hyslop & Larry Stone
Innkeeper: Kelly Robinson
2436 Baseline Avenue, Ballard, CA 93463
Tel: (805) 688-7770 Fax: (805) 688-9560
15 bedrooms with private bathrooms
Double: $150–$220
Closed Christmas
Credit cards: all major
Children accepted

Deetjen's Big Sur Inn, established in the 1930s by "Grandpa" Deetjen from Norway, is a complex of weathered, wood-sided buildings, trimmed in white and topped by green roofs, tucked just off Highway 1 on a narrow road winding back beside a mountain stream into a redwood grove. Deetjen's is very rustic in decor and comfort; however, it exemplifies all that is Big Sur—the attitude, the lifestyle, a desire to enjoy a setting of beauty and nature, uncluttered by possessions. The first building in the complex houses the four intimate rooms that comprise the restaurant. Each candlelit room is set under low-beamed ceilings, warmed by a seemingly ever-burning fireplace and decorated with a wonderful collection of old chairs, benches, and tables dressed with linens. Accommodation is offered in buildings with individual names and characters. Old hand-hewn doors (without locks or keys) open to a medley of varying room configurations, all warmed by fireplaces, wood-burning stoves, or electric heaters. The doorway of Edy's Room, like a tree house with vaulted ceilings and a private deck, is framed by a tree limb and accessed by climbing a rambling stairway. Downstairs in the same building the Franklin Room is cozy with dark-paneled walls and a fire-stove. If you have accommodation in a complex of four attached buildings, you will be lulled to sleep by the sound of the rushing stream below. *Directions*: Located on Highway 1 to the south side of Big Sur.

DEETJEN'S BIG SUR INN
Innkeeper: Laura Moran-Etheridge
Highway 1
Big Sur, CA 93920
Tel: (408) 667-2377 Fax: none
20 rooms, 15 with private bathrooms
Double: $75–$155
Open all year
Credit cards: MC, VS
Children welcome with certain restrictions

The Post Ranch Inn is a stunning resort (two swimming pools, health spa, hiking trails, ocean-view restaurant and bar, library) built on 98 acres overlooking the Big Sur coast. Great care has been taken to preserve the natural beauty and tranquillity of the pristine site (homesteaded in the mid-1800s by William Post and his Indian wife, Anselma Onesimo). The reception building is just off Highway 1 and guards the private drive that winds up to the cliff, the restaurant, and accommodations. Cars are left discreetly near the reception area and guests are transported to their rooms by van. You can select from Ocean Houses snuggled into the hillside high above the ocean with roofs of sod and wildflowers or the circular Coast Houses, all with panoramic water views. Across the way Tree Houses up on stilts, the circular Mountain House, and the six-unit Butterfly House all have forest and mountain views. Each room is named for one of Big Sur's early settlers and is appropriately designed with wood siding inside and out, handsome slate in the bathrooms, and accents of deep-sea-blue fabrics. All of the rooms have fireplaces, Jacuzzi tubs, and mini-bars. Although extremely expensive, there are few places in California where one can enjoy accommodation perched above the ocean. *Directions:* Located 30 miles south of Carmel, on the west side of the Highway 1.

POST RANCH INN
Owner: Michael Freed
Director: Larry Callahan
Highway 1, P.O. Box 219
Big Sur, CA 93920
Tel: (408) 667-2200 or (800) 527-2200
Fax: (408) 667-2824
30 bedrooms with private bathrooms
Double: $285–$545
Open all year
Credit cards: all major
Inappropriate for children

Ventana, surrounded by 240 acres of meadows and forests, is nestled in Big Sur, a gorgeous stretch of coast where the hills plunge down to meet the crashing sea. In contrast to the coastline, there is nothing rugged about Ventana. It pretends to be somewhat rustic, but in reality, behind the weathered wooden façade of the cottages lies a most sophisticated, deluxe resort where guests are pampered and provided with every luxury. The Ventana has grown in stages, so each cluster of natural-wood buildings has its own patina of age. The exteriors are not outstanding, but, inside, each guestroom is spacious and decorator-perfect. The decor varies (depending upon which section you are in) but each guestroom has the same country ambiance with natural-wood paneling, luxurious fabrics, and wicker chairs. Most rooms have a large terrace with a latticed wood screen—some have private hot tubs. All have a pretty view either of the hills and forest or to the sea on the far horizon. There are three lounges: one where wine and cheese are served in the afternoon and two where breakfast (a scrumptious buffet of home-baked pastries and fruit) is set out each morning. Guests can either take a tray to their room, or eat on one of the tables in the lounge or outside on the terrace. There are two 75-foot swimming pools with adjacent hot tubs (some areas are designated as clothing optional), a fitness center, and a gourmet restaurant. *Directions:* Thirty miles south of Carmel on the east side of Highway 1.

VENTANA
Director: Randy Smith
Highway 1, Big Sur, CA 93920
Tel: (408) 667-2331 or (800) 628-6500
Fax: (408) 667-2419
60 bedrooms with private bathrooms
Double: $215–$575
Open all year
Credit cards: all major
Inappropriate for children

Within strolling distance from the sweet, old-fashioned town of Calistoga with its quaint shops and cute restaurants is the prettily elegant Christopher's Inn which displays the remarkable talents of Christopher Layton, a San Francisco architect and landscape designer. Three nondescript small homes have been transformed into one exceptionally charming inn. Christopher's "magic touch" has come into play again with the recent acquisition of two homes adjacent to the property that now house three extremely spacious rooms. The guestrooms, which vary from pocket size to comfortable, in the original inn are decorated in a cozy English-country style with Laura Ashley linens, window and wall coverings; while the three suites in the newly opened rooms have more of a French-country feel. Each room has either a porch or private garden patio area, and five offer the romance of a fireplace. One of the favorite rooms of returning guests has a fireplace, antiques, and a sleigh bed. Each morning a basket is delivered to your room with a bounty of delicious treats: fresh coffee, juice, croissants or Danish, fresh fruit with yogurt, or warm baked cobbler. Details such as the carefully tended landscape, fresh flowers, and antiques make this an appealing place to stay. *Directions*: Coming north on Highway 29, the inn is 500 yards past the John Deer tractor sales barn, on the right side of the road, before the blinking light at the intersection of Foothill Boulevard and Lincoln.

CHRISTOPHER'S INN
Innkeepers: Adele & Christopher Layton
1010 Foothill Boulevard
Calistoga, CA 94515
Tel: (707) 942-5755 Fax: none
13 bedroom with private bathrooms
Double: $125–$250
Open all year
Credit cards: all major
Children accepted

With the Hanns Kornell Winery as its neighbor, the Larkmead Country Inn is tucked a short distance off the Saint Helena Highway on Larkmead Lane. Set behind a fieldstone fence and gates, this lovely two-story, white clapboard home was built by one of the first wine-producing families in the Napa Valley. Its broad porches shaded by magnificent sycamores, magnolias, and cypress trees provide a lovely place to settle after a day of wine tasting. The entrance to the inn is at back and up a flight of stairs to the second floor. Owned and managed by Joan and Gene Garbarino, the inn is beautifully furnished with antiques, lovely paintings, prints, and Persian carpets. Guests are encouraged to enjoy the warm ambiance of the central living room with a large fireplace, bay window, and upstairs porch. The four guestrooms are named after wines of the Napa Valley and appropriately look out over the surrounding vineyards. Chardonnay and Chablis are twin-bedded rooms while Chenin Blanc and Beaujolais are furnished with queen beds. Each room is attractively furnished, is air conditioned, and has a private bath or shower. Chablis and Beaujolais enjoy the privacy of an enclosed porch. *Directions*: Located 4½ miles north of Saint Helena off Highway 29 on Larkmead Lane. Look for the home on the right just before the Hanns Kornell Winery—there is no sign advertising the inn.

LARKMEAD COUNTRY INN
Innkeepers: Joan & Gene Garbarino
1103 Larkmead Lane
Calistoga, CA 94515
Tel: (707) 942-5360 Fax: none
4 bedrooms with private bathrooms
Double: $100–$125
Closed December & January
Credit cards: none accepted
Children accepted over 14

Although located on the Silverado Trail, one of the two main arteries through the Napa Valley, Scarlett's Country Inn, tucked in a pocket canyon, is blissfully hidden from the road. The inn consists of two buildings: the original turn-of-the century farmhouse with two suites, and behind it, a newer ranch house with dining room, kitchen, and one guestroom. Ask to stay in the original farmhouse which is charming, like a doll house with just two suites, each with its private entrance. The Gamay Suite has a bathroom on the first floor and upstairs a small parlor plus a bedroom tucked under the eaves. The Camellia Suite on the first floor is a real prize, with a living room with sofa bed, wood-burning fireplace, and a wet bar, plus a separate bedroom. In front of the house the lawn is shaded by a large tree from which hangs a wonderfully nostalgic, old-fashioned rope swing. In the rear garden, is a beautiful swimming pool, tranquilly set amongst the trees. In addition there is an aviary with colorful finches and two plump hens (Blondie and Blackie). Although small, Scarlett's Country Inn offers many niceties often lacking in much fanciers hotels: daily fresh flowers in each of the rooms, turn-down service at night, and complimentary wine upon check-in. *Directions:* Located about mid-way between Calistoga and Saint Helena on the Silverado Trail. Watch carefully for the address number (3918) indicating a small lane leading east from the main road to the inn.

SCARLETT'S COUNTRY INN
Innkeeper: Scarlett Dwyer
3918 Silverado Trail, North
Calistoga, CA 94515
Tel: (707) 942-6669 Fax: (916) 992-1336
E-mail: scarletts@aol.com
3 bedrooms with private bathrooms
Double: $95–$150
Open all year
Credit cards: none accepted
Children accepted

The Silver Rose Inn enjoys a lovely setting on acreage just off the Silverado Trail and offers accommodations in two separate buildings. The Inn On The Knoll is set on an oak-studded knoll terraced above a magnificently landscaped pool carved out of the natural rock hillside, and looks out over vineyards, open fields, and surrounding hillsides. Flagstone steps lead up to the front door of this relatively new two-story building of wood and shingle. From the entrance you look down into the large Gathering Room with its huge stone fireplace and vaulted ceilings and up to the railed walkway that leads to the nine guestrooms whose names denote their individual themes from the Oriental Suite with its large private balcony and Jacuzzi tub to Peach Delight which is frilly and cute. A second recently completed building, Inn The Vineyard, provides for an additional eleven theme rooms, from the most elegant, the two-room Vineyard Suite, to a nostalgic decor of Greta Garbo in Hello Hollywood. The inn is also fortunate to have a natural hot spring on the property which flows from their wells at 150 degrees and enables the inn to offer a full-service spa for the exclusive use of guests. *Directions:* From downtown Calistoga travel east on Lincoln Avenue and take the Brannon Street cutoff to the Silverado Trail. Take a short jog south on the Silverado Trail and then the first, almost immediate, left on Rosedale Road. The entrance to the Silver Rose Inn is just on the right.

SILVER ROSE INN
Innkeepers: Sally & J. Paul Dumont
351 Rosedale Road
Calistoga, CA 94515
Tel: (707) 942-9581 Fax: (707) 942-0841
20 bedrooms with private bathrooms
Double: $175–$255
Open all year
Credit cards: all major
Inappropriate for children

For a homey, bed-and-breakfast atmosphere, Zinfandel House is just the place. From the moment you're greeted cheerily over the front deck railing of this brown, wood-sided, contemporary home by innkeeper Bette Starke, a sense of warm hospitality pervades your stay. A wonderful view overlooking vineyards and mountains awaits from atop the deck, as the inn is perched high on the west side of the valley. Two of the bedrooms are cozily decorated and share a bath, though one of these is available with private bath on request. The largest room, with its own bath, shares the view with a reading room and comfortable living room. All three have goose-down pillows, comforters, and handmade quilts. The Starkes, long-time residents of the Napa Valley, offer their knowledge on food, wine, and the area, and will gladly make dinner reservations at the many very good restaurants nearby. Their guest book is a delightful collection of comments and memories—Bette takes Polaroid photos of everyone who stays with them and they become part of her extended family. *Directions:* Four miles north of Saint Helena on Highway 29, watch for Larkmead Lane on the right. About 200 yards past Larkmead Lane, slow down and look for a group of mailboxes: opposite these, you turn left up Summit Road, bear left around some old farm buildings, and go slowly up three tenths of a mile from the highway to the inn's marked driveway on your left.

ZINFANDEL HOUSE
Innkeepers: Bette & George Starke
1253 Summit Drive
Calistoga, CA 94515
Tel: (707) 942-0733 Fax: (707) 942-4618
E-mail: zinhouse@aol.com
3 bedrooms, 2 with private bathrooms
Double: $75–$100
Open all year
Credit cards: MC, VS
Inappropriate for children

As an alternative to the cute and frilly bed and breakfasts near Cambria's shops and galleries, the Blue Whale offers guests more privacy and the opportunity to stroll for miles along Moonstone Beach. The front room and parlor enjoy views across the road to the beach and expansive ocean through six large picture windows. It is here that guests are served a delicious breakfast, and wine, cheese, and cookies are set out in the afternoon. Stretching out behind the main building are the newly constructed guestrooms, each opening at an angle onto a border of front garden that buffers the rooms from the parallel parking. Country in their decor, the rooms are attractive in their light-pine furnishings, chintz and floral fabrics, and canopy beds. Each of the spacious bedrooms has television, telephone, a refrigerator, and a tiled modern bathroom. The innkeepers extend a warm welcome and offer gracious service. Motels and hotels line the beach frontage and without a doubt The Blue Whale is the best of the bunch. *Directions:* Turn west off Highway 1 north at the exit sign for Moonstone Beach. Follow Moonstone Beach Drive past the hotels which line this coastal frontage to the Blue Whale.

THE BLUE WHALE
Owner: Fred Ushijima
Innkeepers: Kathleen & Bob Hathcock
6736 Moonstone Beach Drive
Cambria, CA 93428
Tel & fax: (805) 927-4647
6 bedrooms with private bathrooms
Double: $160–$205
Open all year
Credit cards: MC, VS
Inappropriate for young children

The J. Patrick House benefits from the enthusiasm and care of its relatively new owners, Barbara and Mel Schwimmer. Built as an authentic log cabin, the J. Patrick House, lovingly named for the previous owner's father, is a newly constructed inn where great care has successfully established an old-world ambiance. The living room is especially inviting with its country knickknacks and open log fire surrounded by comfy sofa and chairs. In the evenings appetizers such as gingered eggplant or vegetable paté are offered with a selection of three wines. Breakfast, a vegetarian repast of fruit, muffins, bread, homemade granola, hot beverages, and freshly squeezed orange juice, is served in a cheerful nook off the cozy living room which overlooks a small but lovely garden. One bedroom is upstairs in the main house while the remainder are in an annex across the back garden. Named for counties in Ireland, each room has a wood-burning fireplace or stove and window seat. Each room has its own personality and all have a private bath and shower except one which has only a shower. The back bedrooms enjoy a lovely little sitting room where guests are treated in the evening to milk and "killer" chocolate chip cookies. *Directions*: Exit off Highway 1 east on Burton Drive and travel half a mile. The house is on the right.

J. PATRICK HOUSE
Innkeepers: Barbara & Mel Schwimmer
2990 Burton Drive
Cambria, CA 93428
Tel: (805) 927-3812 or (800) 341-5258
Fax: (805) 927-6759
8 bedrooms with private bathrooms
Double: $110–$160
Open all year
Credit cards: all major
Children accepted over 15

This pretty little Victorian, freshly painted in a warm butter-cream and dressed with green trim, sits at the heart of the original downtown area of Cambria. A gate in the picket fence opens to a brick walkway leading through the garden to the small porch and entry of this lovely inn. Inside, the decor is refreshing, clean, light, and attractive, with whitewashed walls and the warm patina of natural pine floors. Named for the couple who inhabited the home for much of its century-plus history, the inn has photos and memorabilia of their lives proudly displayed throughout its rooms. The house has five simple and extremely tasteful guestrooms, all intimate in size, with modern and functional bathrooms. Downstairs at the back of the inn overlooking a wooded garden, the Garden Room, formerly the kitchen, enjoys its own private entrance and porch. At the front of the inn, the Parlor Room, once used as a school classroom, is now a pretty bedroom with a bay window and bird's-eye-maple furnishings. Upstairs, the Village Room, the Gothic Room, and Louise's Room are all attractive and enjoy the character added by the pitches and angles of the roof-line. *Directions:* From Highway 1 turn east on Burton Drive; at the stop sign turn left (still Burton) and wind down the hill, cross the bridge, and the house is on the left.

THE SQUIBB HOUSE
Owner: Bruce Black
Innkeeper: Martha Gibson
4063 Burton Drive
Cambria, CA 93428
Tel: (805) 927-9600 Fax: (805) 927-9606
5 bedrooms with private bathrooms
Double: $95–$125
Open all year
Credit cards: MC, VS
Inappropriate for children

The Inn at Depot Hill, just two blocks up the hill from the beach and picturesque village of Capitola-by-the-Sea, dates back to 1901 when it was built as a Southern Pacific railroad station. Limited in terms of the size of the property, the grounds are minimal. Inside, the inn's imaginative decor reflects the theme of first-class train travel at the turn of-the century: the bedrooms are handsomely decorated and named after different parts of the world—as if a guest were taking a railway journey and stopping at different destinations. Suzie Lankes (whose grandfather was an architect for the Southern Pacific Railroad) has added many of her own caring touches such as real linen sheets, lacy pillowcases, and sumptuous feather beds. There is a wealth of other amenities: writing desks, tasteful cupboarded televisions and VCRs, fireplaces, bathrobes, hairdryers, luxurious marble bathrooms, some Jacuzzi tubs on private outdoor patios, and even mini-televisions in all of the bathrooms. An elegant breakfast is served each morning either in the dining room, or in the romantic walled garden, or is brought to your room. Complimentary early-evening wine and hors d'oeuvres, and late-evening desserts and port are served from the dining-room buffet. Suzie and Dan are not present as innkeepers, but oversee a managed staff. *Directions:* South on Highway 1 from Santa Cruz. Take the Park Avenue exit, turn right and go 1 mile. Turn left onto Monterey, then immediately left into the inn's driveway.

THE INN AT DEPOT HILL
Owners: Suzie Lankes & Dan Floyd
250 Monterey Avenue, Capitola, CA 95010
Tel: (408) 462-3376 Fax: (408) 462-3697
E-mail: lodging@innatdepothill.com
12 bedrooms with private bathrooms
Double: $165–$250
Open all year
Credit cards: all major
Children accepted

The Cobblestone Inn is a remarkable conversion of a rather ordinary motel into a country inn with great appeal: the central parking courtyard has been paved and enhanced with trees, flowers, and creepers, a brick patio has been set with tables and chairs, and the inn has been attractively decorated and furnished in an appealing English-country style. The Cobblestone Inn is one of a group of small hotels that pride themselves on having perfected the art of personalized innkeeping. This one is certainly no exception. The staff are young, enthusiastic, and attentive, and you feel thoroughly spoiled by all the little extras: flowers, fruit, balloons announcing special occasions, a handwritten note welcoming you by name, your bed turned down at night, and a newspaper at your door in the morning. Guestrooms all open onto an outdoor stairwell. Besides their delightful decor, bedrooms have every amenity: good reading lights, refrigerator, phone, television, and fireplace. Beverages and snacks are always available. Hearty hors d'oeuvres arrive in the evening. A full buffet breakfast is served and you can take it outside to the patio to enjoy the sunshine of a Carmel morning. With all this comfort and attention, it is not surprising that reservations need to be made well in advance. *Directions:* From Highway 1 take the Ocean Avenue exit, then turn left on Junipero. The Cobblestone is on your right on the corner of 8th Street.

COBBLESTONE INN
Innkeeper: Suzi Russo
Corner of Junipero & 8th Street
P.O. Box 3185
Carmel, CA 93921
Tel: (408) 625-5222 Fax: (408) 625-0478
24 bedrooms with private bathrooms
Double: $95–$175
Open all year
Credit cards: all major
Children accepted

The Mission Ranch, which in days long past was a working farm, was bought and renovated with great sensitively to its heritage by Clint Eastwood. The inn is located on 22 acres, just a pleasant walk from the center of Carmel, yet a world away in tranquillity (in fact, sheep still graze in the meadow that stretches out to the sea in front of the hotel). The ranch offers a wide range of accommodations in terms of setting, views, and price. The least expensive guestrooms are found in the old barn, while more deluxe rooms are located in small meadow-front cottages. The latter have fireplaces and private porches with old-fashioned rocking chairs that beckon you to watch the sun set over the sea. There are also six bedrooms in the charming old farmhouse which has an ornate Victorian-style living room with heavy oak furniture and grand piano. Whichever room you choose, you cannot help being captivated by the peaceful beauty of the property and its well maintained gardens. For exercise, there are six tennis courts and a workout room, plus, of course, a lovely beach within a 15-minute walk. A Continental buffet breakfast including fruits, cereals, juices, and pastries is served in the clubhouse next to the tennis courts. The restaurant, open for dinner, has an attractive terrace where guests can dine outside on warm evenings. *Directions:* From Highway 1 turn west onto Rio Road, then left at the Mission (Lausuen Road), and wind round the Mission to the ranch.

MISSION RANCH
Owner: Clint Eastwood
Innkeeper: John Purcell
26270 Dolores, Carmel, CA 93923
Tel: (408) 624-6436 Fax: (408) 626-4163
31 bedrooms with private bathrooms
Double: $85–$225
Open all year
Credit cards: all major
Children accepted

Just a block or two off Ocean Avenue, the principal shopping district of Carmel, and just a block or two up from the beautiful blue waters and white sand of its glorious beach is the charming San Antonio House. Set back from the road, San Antonio House is nestled amongst its own little garden areas with ivy-covered walls and a lush front lawn shaded by trees—walk under a lovely trellis to another, almost secret garden at the back. The San Antonio House has the feel of a cottage set in the Cotswolds. Each of the four guestrooms enjoys its own private entrance and wood-burning fireplace. Although not spacious, the rooms are cozy and intimate, a delightful retreat on a foggy coastside day. The Patio room opens onto the front garden with its own private stone patio secluded behind a border of colorful flowers; The Dollhouse is reached by a little stairway, is decorated with lace, tapestry, cuddly bears, and a dollhouse and has a cozy little day-bed tucked under the eaves in a separate alcove; Treetops, the most spacious room, located above the carriage house, is secluded and overlooks the gardens; and the delightful Garden Room is country-cozy—its sitting area in front of its fireplace is an inviting spot to linger away an afternoon. A bountiful Continental breakfast is served on a tray to be enjoyed in the privacy of your room or in the garden. *Directions:* Take Ocean Avenue west off Highway 1, then turn south on San Antonio. San Antonio House is in the first block on the east side.

SAN ANTONIO HOUSE
Owners: Dianna & Larry Wells
Innkeeper: Sarah Anne Lee
San Antonio between Ocean & 7th
P.O. Box 3683, Carmel, CA 93921
Tel: (408) 624-4334 Fax: none
4 bedrooms with private bathrooms
Double: $130–$175
Open all year
Credit cards: MC, VS
Children accepted over 12

With the ocean three blocks away, Sea View Inn is within easy walking distance of the much-photographed Carmel beach and it may just be possible to catch the tiniest glimpse of the ocean through the trees from the third floor of the inn. This large Victorian house looks as though it were once a large home, when in fact it has always been an inn. Cream-colored board-and-batten wainscoting accented by a plate rail displaying antiques and interesting bric-a-brac sets the welcoming mood for the living room and adjacent parlor—both rooms are warmed by cozy fireplaces. Games, books, and magazines add a comfortable, lived-in feel. The largest bedrooms are found on the second floor. Room 6 has a new, elegant decor with an Oriental rug, Ralph Lauren prints, and white shutters at the window. The adjacent room 7 has stark white walls and window blinds with a dramatic Oriental-style four-poster bed draped with blue-and-white Chinese-motif fabric. The four tiny bedrooms tucked under the steeply slanting attic ceilings on the third floor provide the snuggest of accommodation. Each is lavishly decorated in a mellow English-floral print gathered into canopies and covering huge bed pillows. *Directions:* Take the Ocean Avenue exit from Highway 1 to Camino Real where you turn left—Sea View Inn is just after 11th Street on the left-hand side.

SEA VIEW INN
Owners: Diane & Marshall Hydorn
Innkeeper: Margo Thomas
Camino Real between 11th & 12th Streets
P.O. Box 4138
Carmel, CA 93921
Tel: (408) 624-8778 Fax: (408) 625-5901
8 bedrooms, 6 with private bathrooms
Double: $80–$130
Open all year
Credit cards: MC, VS
Children accepted over 12

Sunset House, a beige stucco building colored by a handsome green door and flowers at the windowboxes, is set in a residential district of Carmel just a few blocks from the heart of downtown. Although each of the guestrooms is its own comfortable hideaway, the inviting salon is a welcome spot to settle, meet other guests, and on weekends enjoy a selection of wines from the Fike's personal cellar. Two guestrooms are found upstairs in the house. The North Room, dressed in colors of forest green, antique gold and rose, offers a cozy sitting area in front of a handsome brick hearth and ocean views over neighboring rooftops. The South Room, enjoying the other side of the same brick fireplace, has a decor of greens and peach and a day-bed that can accommodate a third person. Off the front drive, the West Room, set under beamed cathedral ceilings, is very cottagey in its decor and intimate with its corner fireplace. The Patio Room, tucked off the back garden and elegantly colored in soft beiges, is luxurious with a whirlpool tub and canopy bed set again before a wood-burning fireplace. In the Fike's home across from the inn is also a lovely, secluded studio with a kitchenette, deck and wonderful ocean views. Breakfast is delivered to the privacy of the guestrooms. *Directions:* Take Highway 1, turn west on Ocean Avenue, then south on Camino Real.

SUNSET HOUSE
Innkeepers: Camille & Dennis Fike
S.E. Camino Real, P.O. Box 1925
Carmel, CA 93921
Tel & fax: (408) 624-4884
E-mail: sunsetbb@redshift.com
4 rooms & 1 studio, with private bathrooms
Double: $165–$195
Open all year
Credit cards: all major
Children welcome

Carmel's quaint gingerbread architecture, profusion of colorful flowers, and tall, shady trees are all happily combined at the Vagabond's House Inn. Set around a flagstone courtyard shaded by a giant oak tree and surrounded by fuchsias, azaleas, camellias, and rhododendrons, the inn is made up of a group of attached story-book English cottages, brick and half-timbered, topped by a thick shake roof, making this one of Carmel's most appealing-looking inns. Most of the guestrooms open directly onto the courtyard with its fountain and profusion of flowers including colorful fuchsias cascading from hanging boxes set in the oak tree. Many of the bedrooms have been refurbished and are very inviting, with pretty coordinating fabrics on the comforters, cushions, and window coverings. There are at least two antique clocks in every bedroom, and many have their own fireplace (be sure to request a room with a wood-burning as opposed to gas fireplace) and cozy sitting nook. In the morning you phone reception to let them know when you would like a breakfast tray brought to your room. When you check in, be sure not to miss the antique toy collection in the lounge. *Directions:* Take the Ocean Avenue exit from Highway 1, turn right on Dolores Street, and go a few blocks to 4th Street. The Vagabond's House Inn is on the corner of 4th Street and Dolores.

VAGABOND'S HOUSE INN
Owner: Dennis Le Vett
Innkeeper: Honey Spence
Dolores & 4th Street, P.O. Box 2747
Carmel, CA 93921
Tel: (408) 624-7738 or (800) 262-1262
Fax: (408) 626-1243 Fax: none
11 bedrooms with private bathrooms
Double: $85–$165
Open all year
Credit cards: all major
Children accepted over 12

We tend not to recommend hotels versus inns, and yet every once in a while we happen on one, be it large or small, where the service is exceptional and welcoming and we find we want to share it with our readers. The Tickle Pink Inn is a lovely, romantic retreat and the fact that it is family-owned and -operated is evident in the quality and caring of the service. Set high on the hillside above the well-known Highlands Inn, the Tickle Pink is a two-story pink motel-like building which hugs the hillside and looks out through the greenery of cypress trees to the distant rugged ocean. Rooms are attractively decorated with light-pine furnishings in warm colors of beiges, creams, and pinks. Most guestrooms have their own private deck and handsome stone fireplace; all enjoy a TV with VCR (movies are available for rent), terry robes, and coffee service. Included in the room rate is a lovely afternoon buffet of wine and an assortment of cheeses and fruit, and an appealing Continental breakfast served either in your room or on the patio off the lounge. Ocean views vary depending on the location within the inn, but the staff is extremely helpful in describing the differences in accommodation and patient in assisting you with a selection over the phone. *Directions:* The Tickle Pink is located 4 miles south of Rio Road in Carmel just off Highway 1. Highland Drive is marked by a sign for both the Highlands Inn and the Tickle Pink.

TICKLE PINK INN
Owners: The Gurries Family
Innkeeper: Mark Watson
155 Highland Drive
Carmel Highlands, CA 93923
Tel: (408) 624-1244 Fax: (408) 626-9516
34 bedrooms with private bathrooms
Double: $149–$289
Open all year
Credit cards: all major
Children accepted

Sitting just off the Carmel Valley Road, in the warmth of the Carmel Valley sun, is a lovely inn, charming in its simple accommodation and rich in its history. Originally a working ranch of some 7,000 acres, Rancho Los Laureles was acquired in later years by the Pacific Improvement Company then, in the early 1930s, by Muriel Vanderbilt Phelps who built stables for her racehorses and the large pool that exists today. A complex of white clapboard, single-story buildings sprawling along the expanse of green lawn provides accommodations which are best described as country-simple, with clean, functional, and attractively priced rooms. My favorite rooms, converted from the former stables, with attractive knotty-pine-paneled walls and traditional furnishings, were some of the most reasonably priced. Above the lodge, the Hill House offers the most luxurious accommodation, with three bedrooms, two baths, a living room with fireplace, full kitchen, and its own stables. The master suite is complete with a Jacuzzi and deck overlooking the valley and mountains. In Muriel Vanderbilt's former home you find the Vanderbilt Restaurant, a lovely informal dining room overlooking the pool, the intimate Library which can be reserved for private dinner parties or functions, and the popular Los Laureles Saloon, a handsome mahogany-paneled room warmed by a stone fireplace. Los Laureles guests have access to the equestrian facilities and restaurant of the very exclusive neighboring resort, Stonepine, which is under the same management. *Directions:* Travel the G16 10½ miles east of Highway 1 from Carmel.

LOS LAURELES
Director: Daniel Barduzzi
313 W. Carmel Valley Road, P.O. Box 2310
Carmel Valley, CA 93924
Tel: (408) 659-2233 Fax: (408) 659-0481
30 bedrooms with private bathrooms
Double: $98–$450
Open all year
Credit cards: MC, VS
Children accepted

Threading into the hills east of Carmel is the beautiful Carmel Valley where, unlike Carmel, which tends to be foggy, almost every day is blessed with sunshine. Here, tucked into its own 330-acre oasis, is Stonepine, built by the Crockers, an early-California dynasty of great wealth. Anticipation of the very special treat awaiting builds as impressive, wrought-iron gates open magically, allowing you to enter. The road crosses a small bridge then winds through the trees, ending in the courtyard of a beautiful home, Italian in feel with a muted-pink façade accented with red-tile roof, shuttered windows, and fancy grille-work. Inside, a quiet elegance emanates from every niche and corner. No expense is spared in the splendid furnishings which give no hint that this is a commercial operation. You definitely feel like a guest in a private mansion as you roam from library to sitting room to dining room, each decorated to perfection. The dining room, handsomely lined in mellow antique paneling, is set exquisitely for dinner each night with fine crystal and china. Upstairs are eight beautiful guestrooms, plus there are four bedrooms in the paddock house and two in the Briar Rose Cottage. Although there is a swimming pool and a tennis court, Stonepine was built as a ranch, and horses are the main attraction. Stonepine is very expensive and exclusive. *Directions:* Signposted on the right after leaving Carmel Valley Village going east on G16.

STONEPINE
Owner: Gordon Hentschel
Director: Daniel Barduzzi
150 E. Carmel Valley Road
Carmel Valley, CA 93924
Tel: (408) 659-2245 Fax: (408) 659-5160
14 bedrooms with private bathrooms
Double: $225–$375
Open all year
Credit cards: all major
Children accepted over 12

Cassel is a town of a few houses, an old-fashioned general store and an inn (Clearwater House) set upon the banks of Hat Creek, California's famous trout water, and catering specifically to fly-fishermen. You enter through the front porch/tackle room—full of waders, boots, rods, and vests—into the living room with fish prints hung on the wall, an old fishing basket decorating a side table, and a library of books about fly fishing. Comfy sofas are drawn around the fire, Oriental rugs cover the wood floor, and guests dine together at the long polished cherry-wood table. The bedrooms, with flowery spreads and country curtains, are quite small and very plainly decorated. Each has a small basic bathroom. Created by Dick Galland, a former wilderness guide, the inn is run on a day-to-day basis by Lynn Bedell who offers a sincerely warm welcome and ensures that guests are well fed—cookies and drinks are always available. Fishing guides and two- to five-day schools are available for beginning, intermediate, or advanced fly fishers. Enjoy a game of tennis and views towards the distant hills from the top-notch tennis court. There are driving tours and hiking in nearby Lassen National Park and spectacular waterfalls around Burney. *Directions:* From Redding take Highway 299 east through Burney, continue 2 miles beyond the intersection of the 299 and 89, turn right for the 4-mile drive to Cassel. Cross the creek and the inn is on your right.

CLEARWATER HOUSE
Innkeepers: Lynn Bedell & Dick Galland
21568 Cassel Road, P.O. Box 90
Cassel, CA 96016
Tel & fax: (916) 335-5500
E-mail: d1trout@aol.com
7 bedrooms with private bathrooms
Double: $240–$300, includes all meals
Open last Saturday in April to November 15th
Credit cards: MC, VS
Children accepted

Staying at the Inn on Mt. Ada is like stepping into a fairy tale—suddenly you are "king of the mountain." This is not too far from reality, since the inn is the beautiful Wrigley family mansion (chewing gum, you know), their vacation "cottage" built high on the hill overlooking Avalon harbor. If you arrive by ferry at Catalina Island, you cannot miss the house: the mansion appears like a white wedding cake to your left above the harbor. The inn is expensive, but money seems almost immaterial, because, once through the door, you have bought a dream. You are truly like a pampered guest in a millionaire's home, with hardly a hint of commercialism (until you pay the bill) to put a damper on the illusion. The lounges and dining room have been redecorated with soft, pretty colors and traditional furniture and fabrics appropriate to the era when the house was built. Upstairs are six individually decorated bedrooms, the grandest having a fireplace, sitting area, and a terrace with breathtaking views of the harbor. Rates include all the extras such as complimentary use of your own golf cart, a full scrumptious breakfast, a deli-style lunch, and traditional country-inn dinner. Coffee, tea, soft drinks, fruit juice, and freshly baked cookies are always available in the den and sun porch. *Directions*: Boats from Long Beach, San Pedro, and Newport Beach. Helicopters from Long Beach and San Pedro.

INN ON MT. ADA
Innkeepers: Marlene McAdam & Susie Griffin
P.O. Box 2560, 398 Wrigley Road
Avalon, Catalina, CA 90704
Tel: (310) 510-2030 Fax: (310) 510-2237
6 bedrooms with private bathrooms
Double: $273–$676*
*Includes all meals
Closed Christmas
Credit cards: MC, VS
Children accepted over 14

The Shelford House, a stately white Victorian farmhouse dating back to the 1880s, is located just to the east of Cloverdale, perched on a small knoll overlooking fields of grapes. A large porch, complete with an old-fashioned swing, wraps around the front of the home. Downstairs, the parlor is very formal, decorated with fussy Victorian furniture. Upstairs, there are two fresh and pretty bedrooms with their individual bathrooms. A downstairs bedroom has a private bathroom. On most of the beds there are beautiful quilts, every one of them lovingly made by hand. Behind the main home is an annex where three more guestrooms are built above the carriage house. These rooms each have a private bathroom and share a parlor. The bedroom in front has a real country view out over the pool to the horse corral and fields of grapes. The Brennocks offer, for an extra charge, a tour of many local wineries in their 1929 Model A Ford. You may also enjoy lunch in their wine-barrel gazebo. After your wine tour, the pool is most inviting on a hot day. Note: As the book goes to press I have just been advised of new ownership. I have yet to meet the Bennocks, and would greatly appreciate feedback from readers. *Directions:* Take the main street through the town of Cloverdale, Highway 101, and turn east on First Street to River Road. After the bridge, you see the inn on your right.

THE SHELFORD HOUSE
Innkeepers: Lou Ann & Bill Brennock
29955 River Road
Cloverdale, CA 95425
Tel: (707) 894-5956 or (800) 833-6479
Fax: none
6 bedrooms with private bathrooms
Double: $90–$125
Open all year
Credit cards: all major
Children accepted

The Coloma Country Inn, a handsome early-American farmhouse, was built in 1852, four years after gold was discovered at Sutter's Mill which is located just down the street. Today Coloma is a sleepy little village where the scant remains of the heady Gold Rush days are separated by wide green lawns sloping up from the American River which give it the air of being a well-kept park. The Coloma Country Inn sits in the middle of the park, its wrap-around porch inviting guests to relax and sip a glass of wine while soaking in the beauty of the surrounding tranquil countryside. Inside, the decor is perfectly lovely, simple, very appealing American country style, though some rooms do have some Victorian pieces. Each bed is accented by a lovely antique quilt from Cindi's large collection. Some rooms feature a balcony or brick patio with a rose garden. An 1898 carriage house features two new suites, each with its own flowering courtyard and kitchenette. Behind the inn is an attractive pond with a little boat moored at the dock. The surrounding Gold Country is a great attraction to visitors to these parts, but, if you are looking for alternative means of transportation, Alan, a commercial hot-air-balloon pilot, can arrange to take you aloft. If you are game for more excitement, he can arrange one-or two-day raft trips on the nearby river. *Directions:* Take Highway 50 from Sacramento to Placerville, then exit on Highway 49 heading north for the 8-mile drive to Coloma.

COLOMA COUNTRY INN
Innkeepers: Cindi & Alan Ehrgott
345 High Street, P.O. Box 502
Coloma, CA 95613
Tel: (916) 622-6919 Fax: none
7 bedrooms, 5 with private bathrooms
Double: $89–$175
Open all year
Credit cards: none accepted
Children accepted

Columbia is a state-preserved town whose shops and stores have been re-created to show life in the heyday of the California Gold Rush. On Main Street is the exquisitely restored City Hotel. Prior to 1874 the building was a gold assay office, the state company headquarters, an opera house, and a newspaper office. Now it is owned by the state of California and partially staffed by students from Columbia College's hotel management program (consequently the staff, dressed in their period costumes, are exceedingly young and wonderfully friendly). The excellent restaurant and the conviviality of the adjacent What Cheer bar provide an especially pleasant way to spend an evening. The high-ceilinged bedrooms have Victorian or early-American furniture. The very nicest rooms open directly onto the parlor, rooms 1 and 2 having the added attraction of balconies overlooking Main Street. All the bedrooms have private en-suite toilets and washbasins. It is not a problem to have showers down the hallway when slippers, robes, and little wicker baskets to carry soap, shampoo, and towels are provided. A bountiful Continental breakfast is served on the buffet in the dining room. *Directions:* From Sonora take Highway 49 north for the 4-mile drive to Columbia.

CITY HOTEL
Owner: California State Parks System
Manager: Tom Bender
Main Street
Columbia State Historic Park, CA 95310
Tel: (209) 532-1479 or (800) 532-1479
Fax: (209) 532-7027 E-mail: info@cityhotel.com
10 bedrooms with half baths
Showers down the hall
Double: $75–$95
Closed one week in January
Credit cards: all major
Children accepted

The Fallon Hotel is owned and operated in the same way as the nearby City Hotel in this gem of a Gold-Rush town. The hotel opened in 1986 after receiving a $4,000,000 refurbishment from the state of California. The bedrooms are perfect reflections of the opulent 1880s, with patterned ceilings, colorful, ornate wallpaper, and grand antique furniture. Front rooms have shaded balconies. All have en-suite pull-chain toilets and ornate washbasins. Like the nearby City Hotel, showers are down the hall and slippers, bathrobes, and baskets of toiletries are handily provided. One downstairs room has wider doors for wheelchair access. A simple buffet-style Continental breakfast is served in the adjoining ice-cream parlor. In the Fallon Hotel building is the Fallon Theater, offering a year-round schedule of contemporary dramas, musicals, and melodramas. When making reservations at either the City or Fallon hotels, ask about their excellent value-for-money theater and dinner packages. *Directions:* From the San Francisco area take Highway 580 for 60 miles, then Highway 120 east to Sonora and Highway 49 north from Sonora for the 4-mile drive to Columbia which is off the main highway.

FALLON HOTEL
Owner: California State Parks System
Manager: Tom Bender
Washington Street
Columbia State Historic Park, CA 95310
Tel: (209) 532-1470 or (800) 532-1479
Fax: (209) 532-7027
E-mail: info@cityhotel.com
13 bedrooms with half baths
Showers down the hall
Double: $55–$95
Open all year
Credit cards: all major
Children accepted

Barbara Gage's lovely old two-story home with its weathered brick exterior, a restored former stage stop, sits just a garden's distance from the Middle Fork of the Feather River. You enter into the coolness of the house into the front room with a lovely old trestle table banked by two wonderful old benches set before a large open fireplace. Stools are drawn up to a counter in front of the open country kitchen. The two guestrooms on the first floor are off the large (what was once the front) porch of the home, set with wicker furniture, and both have private bathrooms. The Parlor Room is for the romantic—a warm paneled library room with a fireplace and double Victorian brass bed, while the larger Trading Post Room has a western theme and one single and two double beds. Cross the bridge and follow a forested footpath to the charming white one-bedroom cottage with its inviting porch, dear little kitchen, lovely small central sitting area with wood-burning pot-bellied stove, and small back bedroom with private bath. The inn is set on 250 acres and Barbara proudly claims her 1-mile (2-mile if you count both sides of the river!) frontage on the Feather River which she also makes available to non-resident fishing enthusiasts. *Directions*: From Cromberg on Highway 89 take the Old Cromberg Road and follow it as it winds down past the wonderful old cemetery to the bottom of the hill and Twenty Mile House.

TWENTY MILE HOUSE   ***New***
Innkeeper: Barbara Gage
Old Cromberg Road
P.O. Box 30001
Cromberg, CA 96103
Tel: (916) 836-0375 Fax: (916) 836-2128
2 bedrooms, 1 cottage, with private bathrooms
Double: $110
Open all year
Credit cards: none
Children accepted by prior arrangement

The Blue Lantern Inn, perched on a bluff offering unparalleled views of the fascinating harbor of Dana Point and the blue Pacific, is an outstanding inn on southern California's Riviera. The new construction is designed in a Cape Code style—a most appealing building whose many gables, towers, and jutting roof lines create a whimsical look. The façade is painted a soft gray made even prettier by its crisp white trim. Inside, the color scheme reflects the sea with the use of hues of periwinkle blue, soft lavender, and sea-foam green. Each of the 29 guestrooms is individually decorated—some with light-pine, some with wicker, others with dark-mahogany furniture. The traditional-style furnishings are mostly reproductions and are of excellent quality. Each room has a gas log fireplace and spacious bathroom with Jacuzzi tub. Many of the rooms capture magnificent views of the sea. Breakfast is served each morning in the lounge, a cheerful room where sunlight streams through the wall of windows. Off the reception area is the library where tea is served in the afternoon. Other amenities include a conference room and a well equipped exercise room. The Blue Lantern is more of a sophisticated small hotel than a cozy bed and breakfast, but the management is superb and the warmth of welcome cannot be surpassed. *Directions:* From the Pacific Coast Highway 1, turn west on Street of the Blue Lantern and go one block.

BLUE LANTERN INN
Innkeeper: Lin McMahon
34343 Street of the Blue Lantern
Dana Point, CA 92629
Tel: (714) 661-1304 Fax: (714) 496-1483
29 bedrooms with private bathrooms
Double: $135–$350
Open all year
Credit cards: all major
Children accepted

The Ritz-Carlton Laguna Niguel is truly a gem—without a doubt, one of the finest beach resorts in California. As such (even though it is larger than most hotels in this guide) we want to share its merits with our readers. There is a magic to the management of the Ritz-Carlton group: they instill the warmth and charm of a small inn into a large hotel. All the help—from the bell hop to the maid who turns down your bed—seem to take genuine pride in making your stay very special. In addition to the fabulous service, the hotel is a showplace of refined elegance. A wide entrance hall leads to a nautical-style bar where wood paneling and bookshelves create a cozy niche to settle for afternoon tea or a refreshing drink. The lounge which stretches out to the left of the bar features a continuous row of arched windows, accented by thick louvered shutters, which frame a panorama of the ocean. The color scheme throughout repeats the colors of the sea: pastel peaches, creamy whites, beiges, and light turquoise. Accents of fine antiques, outstanding oil paintings, enormous displays of fresh flowers, and large potted palms add to the feeling of utter luxury. In addition to the two miles of beach stretching below the hotel, there are two swimming pools, four tennis courts, and an adjacent eighteen-hole golf course. *Directions*: From highway 5, take the Crown Valley parkway exit west to the Pacific Coast Highway, go south 1 mile, and turn right on Ritz-Carlton Drive.

THE RITZ-CARLTON LAGUNA NIGUEL
Manager: John Dravinski
One Ritz-Carlton Drive
Dana Point, CA 92629
Tel: (714) 240-2000 Fax: (714) 240-0829
393 bedrooms with private bathrooms
Double: $235–$2,750 (breakfast not included)
Open all year
Credit cards: all major
Children accepted

Deep within Lassen National Park lies Drakesbad Guest Ranch, set in an idyllic high mountain valley. A broad sweep of grassy meadow cut by a tumbling river gives way to towering pines rising to rocky peaks. There's no electricity at Drakesbad—the warm glow of a kerosene lamp lights your cozy paneled bedroom. Furnishings are simple: polished pine-log chairs and beds topped by quilts, simple country curtains, and a pine dresser and bedside table. Our favorite rooms are in the little cabins that nestle at the very edge of the meadow with their smart modern bathrooms and sliding doors which open to a tiny deck where you can sit and watch the deer grazing at twilight. Other cabins nestle in the pines. Rooms upstairs in the main lodge have half baths. Evenings are for books, games, and conviviality by the fireplace in the lodge, conversation around the campfire, or star-gazing from the soothing warmth of the swimming pool which is fed by the natural warmth of a hot spring. Days are for walks, horseback riding, and swimming. A bell is rung to announce meals which are served in the rustic pine dining room whose tables are topped with flowery mats and napkins. It's a family place full of people who came as children returning year after year with children and grandchildren—some who remember when guests slept in tents on the meadow. *Directions:* Turn left at the fire station in Chester and follow Warner Valley Road to the ranch. The last 4 miles are dirt road.

DRAKESBAD GUEST RANCH
Innkeepers: Billie & Ed Fiebiger
End of Warner Valley Road
Lassen National Park, Chester, CA 96020
Winter tel: (916) 529-1512 Fax: (916) 529-4511
Summer tel: ask operator—Drakesbad 2 via 916 Susanville
19 bedrooms with private bathrooms
Double: $170–$185 (includes all meals)
Open second Fri. in June to second Sun. in October
Credit cards: MC, VS
Children very welcome

Tucked seemingly miles away deep in the countryside, Brookside Farm is actually only a 35-minute drive from the outskirts of San Diego. Sally and Edd Guishard have done a remarkable job of converting an ordinary complex of farm buildings into an inviting inn. The location and mood set the theme of many of the rooms: the Bird's Nest tucked under the eaves has lovely bird stenciling on the walls, while Captain Small's room has a red-and-blue quilt and blue-checked chairs. Four rooms, Peter Rabbit's House, Room with a View, Jennie's Room, and La Casita, are housed within the walls of the old the barn. The original well house is now the Hunter's Cabin and has a rustic decor, wood-burning stove, and planked floors and overlooks the creek through a wall of paned windows and screened porch. Edd is responsible for the inn's stained glass windows as well as being a wonderful chef. On weekends he prepares an inviting four-course dinner, inviting guests to share in the preparation (he owned several restaurants in the San Diego area before moving here). On weekday nights, a complimentary supper is served to guests. The setting of the inn is lovely: play badminton on the lawn, laze away the hours on the patio, or relax in the spa under the grape arbor. *Directions*: From San Diego take Highway 94 east to Dulzura, go 1½ miles past the café, then right on Marron Valley Road.

BROOKSIDE FARM B & B INN
Innkeepers: Sally & Edd Guishard
1373 Marron Valley Road
Dulzura, CA 91917
Tel: (619) 468-3043 Fax: none
11 bedrooms with private bathrooms
Double: $80–$115
Open all year
Credit cards: all major
Inappropriate for children

The Elk Cove Inn, on the south edge of town as the road winds down the hill, is one of the town's grandest homes and enjoys a million-dollar view of cove and towering rock weathered by the crashing sea. Its new owner, Elaine Bryant, a charming hostess, takes great pride in extending a warm welcome and lavishing southern hospitality and attention on her guests. In the main house, the gathering room is set with breakfast tables in front of two walls of windows looking out on the spectacular coastline—a wonderful, memorable spot for a morning repast. The bedrooms' decor is feminine and a bit fussy, with silk- and fresh-flower arrangements, patterned comforters, throw pillows, lace, and floral wallpapers. In the main house, three rooms are found on the first floor. The smallest, off the back hallway, has a bed dressed in blue gingham and a small bathroom. Upstairs there are three rooms, all with private bath (although the bath for one room is down the hall), and an intimate sitting area with television, VCR, microwave, and stocked refrigerator. The four bedrooms in the two separate cottages enjoy full ocean views through large picture windows. Three new suites under construction (completion spring 1997) will each enjoy a large living room with a spectacular view and deck, a large bath equipped with Jacuzzi, and a spacious bedroom. *Directions*: Elk is 15 miles south of Mendocino, or 6½ miles south of the junction of Highway 128 on Highway 1.

ELK COVE INN   **New**
Innkeeper: Elaine Bryant
6300 South Highway 1, P.O. Box 367
Elk, CA 95432
Tel: (707) 877-3321 or (800) 275-2967
Fax: (707) 877-1808
13 bedrooms with private bathrooms
Double: $98–$298
Open all year
Credit cards: all major
Inappropriate for children

The Griffin House, a pretty little clapboard house painted gray with white trim and with a white picket fence, dates back to the late 1800s when it served as the local doctor's office and pharmacy. Later, five cottages were added behind the office to house some of the lumber men coming to the growing town of Elk. The present owner, Leslie Lawson, has opened an Irish pub in the main house and renovated the cottages for guests. The pub offers evening meals and good cheer (winter opening hours vary). The garden cottages are pleasant, but truly outstanding are the three doll-house-like cottages on the edge of the bluff. In fact, these three separate little houses offer the most sensational views anywhere on the California coast. Each of these cottages, named after one of the early settlers of Elk, has a wood-burning stove, a sitting area, a wall of window overlooking the coast, and a private redwood deck with chairs and table. These tiny cottages are simple in decor, nothing contrived or quaintly cute, just providing old-fashioned comfort. But, I promise you, these cottages offer a vista so breathtaking that you will be back again and again. Leslie, the very gracious, warm-hearted owner, is a natural at innkeeping—which she finds a breeze by comparison to her previous job as Dean of Students at the University of California at Santa Barbara where she "mothered" 18,000 students. *Directions:* Off the west side of the Highway 1, at the center of Elk.

GRIFFIN HOUSE
Innkeeper: Leslie Griffin-Lawson
5910 South Highway 1, P.O. Box 172
Elk, CA 95432
Tel: (707) 877-3422 Fax: none
E-mail: elklgl@aol.com
4 rooms & 3 cottages, with private bathrooms
Double: $85–$150
Open all year
Credit cards: all major
Pub open seasonally, children accepted

The Harbor House has a fantastic location—on one of the prettiest bluffs along the Mendocino coast. There is even a little path, with benches along the way, winding down the cliff to a secluded private beach. The home was built in 1916 as a guest house for the Goodyear Redwood Lumber Company, so it is no wonder that everything inside and outside is built of redwood. The inn is appealing, reflecting the ambiance of a beautiful, elegant country lodge. You enter into a charming redwood-paneled living room dominated by a large fireplace, also made of redwood. An Oriental carpet, comfortable sofas, beamed ceiling, soft lighting, and a piano tucked in the corner add to the inviting warmth. Doors lead from the lounge to the verandah-like dining room, stretching the length of the building, with picture windows looking out to the sea. A broad wooden staircase leads upstairs to comfortably furnished, homey bedrooms. Other guestrooms are in adjacent cottages. Most of the bedrooms have sea views, and all but one have wood-burning fireplaces. Included in the room rate are both a fixed-menu dinner and breakfast—and the food is good with home-baked breads, freshly ground coffee, garden vegetables, and, of course, wonderful seafood. *Directions:* Take Highway 101 north from San Francisco to Cloverdale, then Highway 128 west to the ocean and Highway 1 south for 5 miles to Elk.

HARBOR HOUSE
Innkeepers: Helen & Dean Turner
5600 South Highway 1, P.O. Box 369
Elk, CA 95432
Tel: (707) 877-3203 Fax: none
10 bedrooms with private bathrooms
Double: $140–$270*
*Includes breakfast & dinner
Open all year
Credit cards: none accepted
Children accepted over 12

The Sandpiper House Inn is superbly positioned on a bluff overlooking the most beautiful section of the Mendocino coast. The front of the gray-shingled house, enclosed with a white picket fence, is most inviting. But just wait: it is not until you come inside and look out the windows to the ocean that you realize what a prize you have discovered. Behind the house, a beautifully tended green lawn embraced by an English garden stretches out to the edge of the bluff below which the waves crash against awesome rock formations. Benches are strategically placed to capture the glory. A path leads down the steep incline with a half-way resting point before continuing on down to the private beach. Because of the setting the house would be a winner if it were just a shell within, but, happily, the interior does justice to the setting. The decor is unpretentiously lovely with an elegant homelike ambiance and excellent taste. Four of the bedrooms capture the sensational view and as I saw each one it became my favorite. Choose Evergreen for complete privacy, a luxurious bathroom, and fireplace; Headland for its garden patio and view capturing sitting area; Clifton for its bay window with chairs placed to capture the view; and Weston for its breathtaking panoramic view of rocky headland and vast expanse of seascape through windows at the foot of the bed. To add perfection, the owners are as warm and gracious as their home they share with guests. *Directions:* Located on Highway 1 at the north end of the village.

SANDPIPER HOUSE INN
Innkeepers: Claire & Richard Melrose
5520 South Highway 1, P.O. Box 149
Elk, CA 95432
Tel: (707) 877-3587 Fax: none
5 bedrooms with private bathrooms
Double: $120–$215
Open all year
Credit cards: all major
Children accepted over 12

Carter House Victorians are a group of three buildings: the majestic Carter House, the adorable Bell Cottage next-door, and the adjacent Hotel Carter. The inns are the dream of Mark Carter who grew up in Eureka and, after restoring several Victorian homes, chose to build his own (the Carter House), using the original plans for a Victorian house designed by the architect who built the Carson Mansion, a Victorian showplace in Eureka. All of their bedrooms are generously appointed with antique furniture, original artwork, and cozy flannel robes to make guests really feel "at home." While the Carter House offers the most delightful antique-filled rooms, if you are in the mood for something more sensuous, opt for a suite. The suites at the Hotel Carter offer large whirlpool tubs with marina views (in the bedroom), fireplaces, king beds, large showers with two heads, entertainment centers, and well-stocked refrigerators (not complimentary). The Hotel Carter's lobby and dining room are the center for socializing—guests enjoy hors d'oeuvres and wine in the early evening, a nightcap of homemade cookies and tea before bed, outstanding dinners, and bountiful breakfasts. The ebullient Mark Carter sets the friendly welcoming tone for this delightful inn. *Directions:* Take Highway 101 north to Eureka. The highway turns into 5th Street. From 5th Street, turn left on L Street and go two blocks.

CARTER HOUSE VICTORIANS
Innkeepers: Christi & Mark Carter
301 L Street
Eureka, CA 95501
Tel: (707) 445-1390 Fax: (707) 444-8067
E-mail: carter52@carterhouse.com
32 bedrooms with private bathrooms
Double: $95–$350
Open all year
Credit cards: all major
Children accepted over 12

Brothers Cornelius and John Daly came from Ireland to Eureka and in 1895 founded a successful chain of northern California clothing shops. When their business flourished the brothers returned to Ireland in search of wives, married sisters Annie and Eileen, and returned to Eureka to build them impressive homes next door to each another. Now Annie and Con's home is a delightful bed and breakfast run with warm enthusiasm by Sue and Gene Clinesmith who fell in love with their house while visiting their son at Humboldt State University. Sue and Gene have lavished time and attention on their lovely home and the result is that it is an extremely comfortable place for guests to stay. Enjoy wine and cheese in the parlor, watch a movie in the den, or relax in the wicker parlor or on the back patio overlooking the garden. Upstairs, I particularly enjoyed the Garden View and Victorian Rose suites with their spacious bedrooms, sitting rooms (in what were once sleeping porches), and modern bathrooms. A short walk takes you through Eureka's more commercial district to its attractive historic old town (between D and G and 1st and 3rd streets) with its attractive shops and restaurants occupying restored buildings. *Directions*: From San Francisco take Highway 101 275 miles north to Eureka. The highway turns into 5th Street. From 5th Street turn right into H Street: The Daly Inn is on your left.

THE DALY INN
Innkeepers: Sue & Gene Clinesmith
1125 H Street,Eureka, CA 95501
Tel: (707) 445-3638 or (800) 321-9656
Fax: (707) 444-3636
E-mail: dalyinn@humboldt.com
5 rooms, 3 with private bathrooms
Double: $80–$140
Open all year
Credit cards: all major
Children accepted

Ferndale is a jewel—a wonderfully preserved Victorian town 5 miles from the northern California coast. Happily, the town's most beautiful Victorian, a fantasy of ornate turrets and gables, is an inn, The Gingerbread Mansion. Walking through the parlors and breakfast room is like taking a step back into Victorian times. While the bedrooms continue the Victorian theme, I feel certain that the prude Victorians would be quite aghast at several of Ken Torbert's more sensuous rooms. If money is no object, request the Empire Suite, an open-plan bedroom and bathroom combination where you can soak in a claw-foot tub in front of one of the fireplaces (there are two), relish the complexity of operating a shower with eight heads, and sleep in a king-size bed where towering Ionic columns (pillars) soar to the rafters. Alternatively, request your room by whether you want a tub in the room (Lilac), his-and-her tubs in the room (Gingerbread), fireplaces (five rooms), or a sleeping loft for a child (Hideaway). I particularly enjoyed the Garden Room with its fireplace, old-style bathroom, and French windows opening onto a private balcony overlooking the clipped hedges and colorful flowerbeds of the garden. Guests often combine their stay with a play performed by the Ferndale Repertory Company. *Directions:* Ferndale is approximately 250 miles north of San Francisco. From Highway 101 traveling north, take the Fernbridge/Ferndale exit, following signs to Ferndale. When you reach Main Street, turn left at the Bank of America and go one block.

THE GINGERBREAD MANSION
Innkeeper: Ken Torbert
400 Berding Street, Ferndale, CA 95536
Tel: (707) 786-4000 Fax: (707) 786-438
E-mail: kenn@humboldt1.com
9 bedrooms with private bathrooms
Double: $140–$350
Open all year
Credit cards: MC, VS
Children accepted over 10

The quaint Victorian town of Ferndale lies almost midway between San Francisco and Ashland, making it an ideal stop for those traveling between these two lovely spots. Situated on Main Street on a 1-acre parcel which isolates it from the road, the Shaw House was built in 1854 by Seth Shaw, one of the founders of Ferndale. Now it is the home of Norma and Ken Bessingpas who do an excellent job of welcoming guests to their bed and breakfast and making certain that they have all the necessary information to enjoy this lovely area. A memento of the house's historic importance is the gilded overmantle in the parlor to which Norma has added a garland festooned with fairylights and next to it placed a tailor's dummy wearing a Victorian bridal gown. The adjacent library is a restful place to relax. Up the main staircase you find four guestrooms ranging from a snug bedroom with a bathroom down the hall to the spacious Honeymoon room with its domed ceiling and large bathroom with claw-foot tub and shower. I also very much enjoyed the privacy offered by the three ground-floor rooms which have their own entrances and patios. Main Street has changed very little since the 1890s and offers galleries, antique shops, restaurants (guests usually dine at Curleys Grill), and an excellent bookstore. *Directions*: Coming from San Francisco on Highway 101, take the Fernbridge/Ferndale exit and follow signs to Ferndale. The Shaw House is on the right on Main Street.

THE SHAW HOUSE
Innkeepers: Norma & Ken Bessingpas
703 Main Street, P.O. Box 1125
Ferndale, CA 95536-1125
Tel & fax: (707) 786-9958
E-mail: shawhse@humboldt1.com
7 rooms with private bathrooms
Double: $75–$135
Open all year
Credit cards: all major
Children accepted

The Lodge at Noyo River has a superb location on the hillside overlooking Fort Bragg's harbor, definitely one of the most colorful fishing harbors along the coast of California. Rooms are available in three sections of the hotel—either in the newly built annex featuring seven spacious suites, each with a private balcony and offering all the latest modern amenities, two in separate outside cottages, or in the more appealing, original old family home which now has two gorgeous suites, each with private sunroom and fireplace, and five lovely upstairs bedrooms. These bedrooms in the main house just ooze with character. Although not decorator-perfect, they are refreshingly "real" in their decor: old-fashioned, comfortable rooms which make you feel you are really stepping back to the last century. Ask for room 1. This is just a gem, a spacious corner room with a king-sized bed and an enormous bathroom tucked under the eaves sporting a wonderful claw-footed tub. But the best feature of room 1 is the view: from the windows you look down through the trees to the picturesque River Noyo where the colorful boats dock, protected from the sea. Breakfast is served either in the dining room or, when weather permits, outside on the deck overlooking the harbor. *Directions:* From Highway 1, just north of the bridge spanning the Noyo River, take North Harbor Drive which loops down to the fishing harbor. Before reaching the harbor, jog left when you see the sign.

THE LODGE AT NOYO RIVER
Manager: Charles Reinhart
500 Casa del Noyo Drive
Fort Bragg, CA 95437
Tel: (707) 964-8045 Fax: (707) 964-5354
16 bedrooms with private bathrooms
Double: $99–$149
Open all year
Credit cards: all major
Children accepted

You would think you were in England instead of northern California when you first see the large Tudor-style Benbow Inn. The English theme continues as you step inside the lounge with its large antique fireplace flanked by comfortable sofas, antique chests, paintings, needlepoint, cherry-wood wainscoting, two grandfather clocks, potted green plants, and a splendid Oriental carpet. At tea time complimentary English tea and scones are served along with mulled wine when the days are nippy. The dining room, too, is very English: a beautiful, sunny room with beamed ceiling and dark-oak Windsor chairs. Both the reception hall and the dining room open out to a pretty courtyard overlooking the river. The traditionally decorated bedrooms vary in size—all the way up from small bedrooms located both in the main hotel and in an annex which also opens onto the courtyard. The one disadvantage of the Benbow Inn is its proximity to the freeway, but loyal guests do not seem to mind. A wonderful feature here is the very special Christmas celebration—events including Christmas movies, caroling, and dancing are planned each day, and there is a very festive English Christmas dinner. *Directions:* Drive north on Highway 101. Just south of Garberville, take the Benbow exit. The hotel is on west side of the freeway.

BENBOW INN
Owners: Teresa & John Porter
Innkeeper: Patsy Watts
445 Lake Benbow Drive
Garberville, CA 95440
Tel: (707) 923-2124 Fax: (707) 923-2122
E-mail: benbowinc@hol.com
55 bedrooms with private bathrooms
Double: $115–$295
Closed January 2 to mid-April
Credit cards: MC, VS
Children accepted

Georgetown's unusually wide, tree-lined streets faced by wood-frame buildings give character and charm to this town perched high on a hill 9 miles above the South Fork of the American River. The American River Inn was once a boarding house for gold miners who came to make their fortune, but they certainly did not have today's luxuries of a spa and swimming pool. The main house is a picture-perfect Victorian whose interior beautifully complements the lovely exterior. Inside, the individually decorated bedrooms are furnished with antiques appropriate to the period and the bathrooms have claw-foot tubs and pull-chain toilets. A nifty-gifty shop occupies a small front room. A full breakfast is served in the dining room or on the patio and guests have the use of a comfortable parlor. Across the lawn and past the swimming pool and spa is the Queen Ann House which is perfect for seminars, retreats, or wedding parties. A more recent addition to the complex are the Woodside Mine Suites, very basic non descript rooms with little charm. Guests with children are usually offered the suites—it is disappointing not to be able to enjoy the character of the old home. The inn is happy to make arrangements for white-water rafting, kayaking, bicycling, or hot-air ballooning. *Directions:* From Sacramento take Highway 50 or 80 to Auburn or Placerville, then Highway 49 to 193 which brings you into Georgetown. The American River Inn is on Main Street at Orleans.

AMERICAN RIVER INN
Innkeepers: Maria & Will Collin
Main at Orleans Street, P.O. Box 43
Georgetown, CA 95634
Tel: (916) 333-4499 or (800) 245-6566
Fax: (916) 333-9253
17 bedrooms, 8 suites, 18 with private bathrooms
Double: $85–$118
Open all year
Credit cards: all major
Children accepted over 8

Mary Jane and Jerry Campbell have perfected innkeeping in the decade and a half that they have opened their home to overnight guests. Time has served not to weather but rather enrich their enthusiasm and warmth of welcome. The Campbell Ranch Inn, in the heart of the Sonoma county wine country, is a contemporary home whose appeal lies in its hosts and its absolutely spectacular location. Set on the 35-acre hillside with a backdrop of fir and pine trees, views from the inn stretch out across its lovely garden and swimming pool to the miles and miles of vineyards that carpet the surrounding countryside and rolling hills. It is a beautiful setting, very quiet and very soothing—the perfect escape. If you could survive on a bountiful breakfast and the wonderful homemade pie offered each evening as dessert, you might never choose to venture back down the Campbells' drive. The idyllic setting encourages you to relax, read by the pool, or perhaps muster up energy for a game of tennis. With the exception of one cottage, the guestrooms (all with king-sized beds) are actual bedrooms in the Campbell home. They are furnished as they were for their family and are nondescript in their decor. The cottage affords more privacy and has a sitting room with a fireplace and vine-covered deck with million-dollar views in addition to a bedroom and bathroom. The cottage is just adjacent to the spot where Jerry keeps his model trains. *Directions:* On Highway 101, 80 miles north of San Francisco, take the Canyon Road exit at Geyserville and travel west 1-6/10 miles.

CAMPBELL RANCH INN
Innkeepers: Mary Jane & Jerry Campbell
1475 Canyon Road
Geyserville, CA 95441
Tel: (707) 857-3476 or (800) 959-3878 Fax: none
5 bedrooms with private bathrooms
Double: $100–$165
Open all year
Credit cards: all major
Inappropriate for children

It is hard not to notice Beltane Ranch, a pale-yellow board-and-batten house encircled on both stories by broad verandahs, set on the hillside off the Valley of the Moon Road. Rosemary, the owner, will probably be in the cozy country kitchen when you arrive, but if she is away from home, she will write you a welcoming note on the chalkboard hung by the back door. The house has no internal staircase, so each room has a private entrance off the verandah—which was probably a very handy thing when this was the weekend retreat of a San Francisco madam. Incidentally, this also explains the rather southern architecture of the house as "madam" hailed from Louisiana. The bedrooms, decorated in family antiques, have a very comfortable ambiance. Chairs and hammocks are placed on the verandah outside each room and offer a wonderful spot to settle and enjoy peaceful countryside views beyond Rosemary's well tended garden. Beltane has been in the family for 60 years and produces a well-known Chardonnay as well as other varieties of wines. For the energetic, there are a tennis court and walking trails. Beltane Ranch remains a personal favorite. *Directions:* From Sonoma take Highway 12 towards Santa Rosa: Beltane Ranch is on your right shortly after passing the turnoff to Glen Ellen.

BELTANE RANCH
Innkeeper: Rosemary Wood
11775 Highway 12 (Sonoma Highway)
P.O. Box 395
Glen Ellen, CA 95442
Tel: (707) 996-6501 Fax: none
4 bedrooms with private bathrooms
Double: $110–$160
Open all year
Credit cards: none accepted
Children accepted over 4

Gaige House Inn is located on the main road that weaves through Glen Ellen. New owners, Greg and Ken, are slowly making their own statement as to decor with contemporary, Indonesian, and Japanese details and have ambitious plans for major upgrades and the addition of two rooms. Many bed and breakfasts take pride in bountiful breakfasts, but how many actually have a gourmet chef in the kitchen? The Gaige House does. Another of the staff does nothing but starch and iron all the linens, which are (of course) of elegant quality. Everything is fresh and pretty, airy and light. Each of the nine bedrooms has its own personality, but all exude a similar ambiance with a predominant use of Ralph Lauren fabrics. The most outstanding room, the Gaige Suite, is a spacious, sunny room with large windows on three sides and a wrap-around deck overlooking the garden. Dominating the room is a four-poster bed with a lace-canopy trim and a bathroom (with Jacuzzi tub) as large as bedrooms in some hotels. An added bonus—a large pool is set in the lawn in the rear garden. Note: I learned of the change of ownership just a few weeks before this book went to press. I have not had an opportunity to visit or meet the new owners and would greatly appreciate feedback. *Directions:* Driving north on 12 from Sonoma, turn left on Arnold Drive which is signposted to Glen Ellen. The Gaige House Inn is on the right, just before you arrive in town.

GAIGE HOUSE INN
Owners: Greg Nemrow & Ken Burnet
13540 Arnold Drive
Glen Ellen, CA 95442
Tel: (707) 935-0237 Fax: (707) 935-6411
9 bedrooms with private bathrooms
Double: $125–$245
Open all year
Credit cards: all major
Children accepted over 14

Grass Valley has continued to prosper since the heady Gold Rush days when Cornish miners arrived from England seeking their fortunes in gold. Although the town cannot compete for charm with nearby Nevada City, it certainly has a first-class hostelry in Murphy's Inn—this small inn, its broad verandah decorated with topiary ivy baskets, was once the mansion of North Star Mine owner Edward Colman. It has been lovingly restored and refurbished. Bedrooms in the main house range from Theodosia's Suite with its king-size brass bed draped in lace sitting before the fireplace, to a cozy, small upstairs bedroom. One room just off the kitchen has a delightful pot-belly stove and sunny skylights. The entire inn is furnished in Victorian finery. The Donation Day House, just across the street, has two suites, one with a full kitchen, which could accommodate guests with children. Ted and Nancy encourage guests to make themselves at home and stock the refrigerators with juices, sodas, and goodies and supply the "best chocolate chip cookies west of the Mississippi." *Directions:* From the San Francisco area take Highway 80 to 49 north to Grass Valley, exit on Colfax, then go left on South Auburn and left on Neal.

MURPHY'S INN
Owners: Nancy & Ted Daus
Innkeeper: Linda Jones
318 Neal Street
Grass Valley, CA 95945
Tel & fax: (916) 273-6873
or Tel: (800) 895-2488
8 bedrooms with private bathrooms
Double: $100–$150
Open all year
Credit cards: all major
Children accepted

Groveland is a quaint Gold Rush town just half an hour from the west entrance to Yosemite. Highway 120 becomes Groveland's one main street as it transects the charming town. It is a great place to break the drive and stop for either breakfast or lunch at the corner PJ's Café and for those who choose to overnight and just take a day trip into the park, the Groveland Hotel offers very comfortable and attractive accommodation. Fronting Main Street, the Groveland Hotel is actually two buildings dating from 1849 and 1914 joined by a wrap-around verandah. One building dates from the Gold Rush and the other was built as a boarding house to accommodate the executives from San Francisco here to oversee the building of the massive Hetch Hetchy water project. No two rooms are alike and yet each is pleasing in its decor, decorated with a blend of antiques and attractive fabrics. Although opening onto the street, some of the main floor and front upstairs rooms enjoy lovely bay windows and there are two rooms, one with a queen the other twin beds, which each have only one window and therefore no views, but they are a great value for their price. A Continental breakfast is included in the room rate, and the restaurant also offers dinner. *Directions:* Groveland is a two hours from Sacramento along the historic stretch of Highway 120.

THE GROVELAND HOTEL
Innkeepers: Peggy & Grover Mosley
18767 Main Street, P.O. Box 481
Groveland, CA 95321
Tel: (209) 962-4000 or (800) 273-3314
Fax: (209) 962-6674 E-mail: peggy@groveland.com
17 bedrooms with private bathrooms
Double: $95–$175
Open all year
Credit cards: all major
Children accepted

With a backdrop of towering redwood and pine trees, the weathered, wood-sided cottages of the North Coast Country Inn step up the hillside just off the eastside of Highway 1. Although it does not have ocean views, the inn's wooded setting is lovely and the accommodation is some of the best in the area. Nancy and Loren Flanagan use the original old farmhouse, once part of a local sheep ranch, as their private residence and patterned the neighboring cottages after its rustic and appealing design. Each spacious guestroom cottage is attractive in its individual and country decor, enjoys its own private entrance off a porch or surrounding deck, and is equipped with dining and kitchenette areas, a wood-burning fireplace, and private bathroom. Although it was hard to select a favorite, I loved the space of the Aquitaine Room with its handsome four-poster bed, beamed ceiling, and large windows. A maze of brick walkways weaves through an immaculately-cared-for garden of green lawn and fruit trees, while a wooded path winds up the hillside to a secluded hot tub set into a two-level redwood deck, magical at night under the beauty of dramatic stars whose intensity is not diminished by city lights. Price includes a wonderful full breakfast delivered to the privacy of your cottage. In the summer of 1997 there will be two additional rooms on the hillside above the garage. *Directions:* Located at Highway 1 and Fish Rock Road, 4 miles north of Gualala and ¼ mile north of Anchor Bay.

NORTH COAST COUNTRY INN
Innkeepers: Nancy & Loren Flanagan
34591 South Highway, Gualala, CA 95445
Tel: (707) 884-4537 or (800) 959-4537 Fax: none
4 bedrooms with private bathrooms
Double: $135 (New rooms will be $165)
Open all year
Credit cards: all major
Inappropriate for children

The Old Milano Hotel has been welcoming guests since the first day the doors opened in 1905. Although built upon a bluff overlooking the ocean in what appears to be quite an isolated location, at the turn of the century the hotel was a center of activity, serving overnight stagecoach guests, lumber barons, and travelers on their way up the coast by train. Today, the old hotel has been restored to reflect its original Victorian elegance and two lovely new cottages are currently being built on the beautiful acreage. In the original hotel, none of the six guestrooms upstairs has a private bath, but all are decorated with Victorian antiques and although pocket-sized and a bit worn, most enjoy some spectacular ocean views. Just off the living room on the first floor is the largest guestroom in the old hotel, another room is tucked into a cottage in the rear garden and still another is housed in an old-fashioned train caboose set amongst the trees. The new cottages will each have two guestrooms with ocean views, private baths, and gas fireplaces. In the main house, the large dining room and wine parlor, with a massive stone fireplace, are especially attractive. Gourmet dinners are offered Wednesday through Sunday. Although it has many attributes, the hotel's most outstanding feature is its perfect location on a lawn which sweeps down to a bluff overlooking the ocean. *Directions*: The Old Milano Hotel is on the Coastal Highway just north of Gualala.

OLD MILANO HOTEL
Innkeeper: Leslie Linscheid
38300 Highway 1
Gualala, CA 95445
Tel: (707) 884-3256 Fax: none
E-mail: lll@mcn.org
13 bedrooms, 3 with private bathrooms
Double: $80–$170
Open all year
Credit cards: MC, VS
Inappropriate for children

Until it was converted to a small inn, Applewood was a private residence. The present owners, Jim Caron and Darryl Notter, have transformed it into a well tended, European-style inn—not trendy, just quietly elegant. The atmosphere is that of a country lodge, with a large stone fireplace opening on two sides, warming both the living room and a cheerful glassed-in dining room. Just off the living room is another dining room with an enormous crystal chandelier hanging above a central table surrounded by individual small tables. In addition to breakfast, with a reservation, Applewood offers their guests dinner featuring fresh Sonoma County produce, much of it grown in the hotel's own gardens. Dining-room windows look over a wooded area and a lovely swimming pool on the terrace. Guestrooms are found in the main house or in Piccola Casa, a new building that fronts the inn's lovely new courtyard entry. The immaculate bedrooms are all individual in their decor, although each has a TV, direct-dial phone, and comfortable queen bed decked with down comforter and pillows. Prices reflect the room's size and location, and whether or not it has a fireplace. The furnishings are elegant, slightly formal, but still showing the homey touch of the owners. *Directions:* On Highway 116, half a mile south of the bridge as you leave Guerneville.

APPLEWOOD
Innkeepers: Jim Caron & Darryl Notter
13555 Highway 116
(Pocket Canyon) Guerneville, CA 95446
Tel: (707) 869-9093 or (800) 555-8509
Fax: (707) 869-9170
E-mail: stay@applewoodinn.com
16 bedrooms with private bathrooms
Double: $125–$250
Open all year
Credit cards: all major
Inappropriate for children

The Zaballa House, built in the mid-1800s, has the honor of being Half Moon Bay's oldest building. Its original owner, Estanislao Zaballa, was quite the man about town. He owned much property including the general merchandise store, several stables, and a saloon on Main Street. His home on Main Street where he lived with his wife and five children is the only building remaining. Today it has been beautifully restored into one of Half Moon Bay's cutest-looking bed and breakfasts: a soft-gray-blue clapboard house with white trim and white picket fence. Downstairs, there is a small parlor as you enter and a guest dining area off the central hallway. Some of the guestrooms are located on the first floor, others are up the staircase on the second level. All are individually decorated with their own personality. My favorite bedroom is a bright and cheerful corner room on the first floor, overlooking the garden. This room is in the oldest section of the house and has white wainscoting halfway up the walls, prettily accented above by dark-blue floral wallpaper. Just behind and to the side of the inn, an addition was completed in late 1996 to accommodate a wing with additional guestrooms and shops. A bountiful breakfast is served each morning and for other meals, there are many restaurants as well as tempting shops just steps away on Main Street. *Directions:* Take Highway 1 south from San Francisco to Highway 92 in Half Moon Bay (30 miles). Turn east on 92 and then south at the first stop light onto Main Street. As you drive into town, the Zaballa House is just past the bridge on the right.

ZABALLA HOUSE BED & BREAKFAST
Innkeeper: Simon Lowings
324 Main Street, Half Moon Bay, CA 94019
Tel: (415) 726-9123 Fax: (415) 726-3921
12 bedrooms with private bathrooms
Double: $85–$170
Open all year
Credit cards: all major
Children accepted over 6

For those who love to be lulled to sleep by the rhythmic sound of crashing waves, the Cypress Inn might be just your cup of tea. It is positioned directly across the road from the 5-mile-long sandy stretch of Miramar Beach. The Cypress Inn is a contemporary building with a weathered-wood façade with turquoise trim. Giving credence to the inn's name, a windswept cypress tree towers by the entrance. Inside, a Mexican-Indian folk-art theme prevails. As you enter, there is a snug sitting area to your left with wicker chairs and sofa grouped around a fireplace. Small rather than spacious, all of the guestrooms have terra-cotta floors and are very similar in decor except that each has its own color scheme (most of the walls are painted in very bright colors). Each of the rooms has a gas-log fireplace, built-in bed with reading lamps, cactus plants, wicker chairs, a writing desk, and louvered doors opening onto private balconies—each overlooking the ocean. The adjacent Beach House offers four more quietly decorated king-bedded rooms, three of which have filtered ocean views. We particularly enjoyed Dunes Beach, decorated in soft-pink shell motif on the fabric, with its bed facing ocean-view windows. Owners Suzie and Dan are not on-site innkeepers, but oversee a managed staff. *Directions:* Take Highway 1 south from San Francisco. Turn right on Medio Avenue (1½ miles beyond the stop light at Pillar Point harbor). Cypress Inn is at the end of the street.

CYPRESS INN
Owners: Suzie Lankes & Dan Floyd
407 Mirada Road, Miramar Beach
Half Moon Bay, CA 94019
Tel: (415) 726-6002 Fax: (415) 712-0380
E-mail: lodging@cypressinn.com
12 bedrooms with private bathrooms
Double: $150–$275
Open all year
Credit cards: all major
Children accepted

The Belle de Jour Inn, a complex of farm cottages built in 1873, has a wonderful country, hillside setting. It is approached by a long drive shaded by pine trees and bordered by lush lawn. The impeccably maintained complex has five cottages with guestrooms plus a single-story farmhouse which is the home of Brenda and Tom. They run their small inn with a professional eye to detail and a genuine warmth of welcome that keeps guests coming back year after year. Once the grain and tack room, the Caretaker's Suite has a pine four-poster, king-size canopy bed topped with Battenberg lace and French doors opening onto a trellised deck. The Terrace Room is charming, with a fireplace and a whirlpool tub for two, overlooking terrace and valley. The Morning Hill Room is cozy with a wood stove and a shuttered window seat. The Atelier, with sitting room, is large and lovely. The hundred-year-old barn accommodates a magnificent deluxe, second-floor country suite with vaulted ceilings, plank wood floors, old-world antique pine furniture, fireplace, and a whirlpool tub for two in its own stained-glass alcove–very romantic. A full country breakfast is served in the owners' kitchen or on the garden deck. For a memorable wine-tasting experience, Tom will take you in his 1925 vintage auto along the backroads of the wine country. *Directions:* Traveling north on Highway 101, exit at Dry Creek Road, go east to Healdsburg Avenue. Turn left at the lights and go north for 1 mile. The entrance is directly across from the Simi Winery.

BELLE DE JOUR INN
Innkeepers: Brenda & Tom Hearn
16276 Healdsburg Avenue
Healdsburg, CA 95448
Tel: (707) 431-9777 Fax: (707) 431-7412
5 bedrooms with private bathrooms
Double: $135–$225
Open all year
Credit cards: all major
Inappropriate for children

Healdsburg's main square is a green park bordered by shops and restaurants. If you want to stay in this charming town, the Inn on the Plaza overlooking the main square is a great choice. Entrance to the Inn is through double doors into a freshly painted, high-ceilinged reception area that doubles as an art gallery and gift shop. A dramatic, long flight of stairs winds up to a central lounge where a jigsaw puzzle is left for each successive guest to work on a bit. Off the lounge are ten bedrooms decorated in a very Victorian style, a few of which overlook the old plaza through bay windows. Most have fireplaces and some have tubs for two. An enclosed rooftop room has white marble tables and chairs and lots of greenery. There are two breakfast servings: cereal, toast, jam, and hot beverages are available for early risers and later, around 9 am, a hot egg dish plus fresh fruit platter, hot muffins, and juice are served. Complimentary wine and fresh buttered popcorn are set out at 5:30 pm—on weekends, party trays are added. When you return from dinner, a delicious orange liqueur and dark chocolates await you. On Saturdays and Sundays there is a spectacular morning brunch with champagne, choice of hot entrees, salads, and dessert. The Inn on the Plaza is a very friendly, welcoming hotel and Genny or her competent staff are always there to greet you. *Directions*: The inn is on the south side of Healdsburg's main square.

INN ON THE PLAZA
Innkeeper: Genny Jenkins
110 Matheson
Healdsburg, CA 95448
Tel: (707) 433-6991 or (800) 431-8663
Fax: none
10 bedrooms with private bathrooms
Double: $115–$225
Open all year
Credit cards: MC, VS
Children by special arrangement

We greatly appreciate the letters we often receive from readers sharing a particular favorite inn along with the unwritten implication that they are astounded that we could have missed such a gem. In the case of The Cedar Street Inn, I received a letter from the owner herself! My only defense is that I simply missed the inn, tucked just off North Circle Drive on a small quiet street of the same name. Within walking distance of the cute shops and restaurants at the heart of Idyllwild, The Cedar Street Inn offers quiet accommodation in cottagey rooms which open onto a central patio. The guestrooms, some of which are housed in private cabins, are individual in decor and offer their own special appointments and appeal. To name just a few of the rooms: the Victorian Suite enjoys a large Roman tub and fireplace; the Attic is accessed by its own private spiral staircase to an outside deck and boasts a bathroom which overlooks the treetops; the Captain's Quarters is decorated in a nautical decor and is warmed by a river-rock fireplace; the Carriage House is a tri-level suite with fireplace and a bathroom equipped with both tub and shower. Patty and Gary Tompkins are your gracious innkeepers, intent on making your stay at The Cedar Street Inn a special and memorable one. *Directions*: Turn off Route 243, turn east on North Circle Drive, and then turn right on Cedar Street.

THE CEDAR STREET INN
Innkeepers: Patty & Gary Tompkins
25880 Cedar Street, P.O. Box 627
Idyllwild, CA 92549
Tel: (909) 659-4789 Fax: (909) 659-3540
8 bedrooms & 3 cabins, with private bathrooms
Double: $69–$125
Open all year
Credit cards: all major
Children welcome in cabin accommodation

Idyllwild is a mile-high village of some 3,000 residents, and with its magnificent hiking trails affords a wonderful weekend getaway from the metropolitan areas of southern California. The Fern Valley Inn is a rustic country inn of 11 log cabins nestled in the pines. On a recent visit to the inn I was fortunate to be able to get to know the owners who are enthusiastic about their role as innkeepers and have ambitious plans to refurbish and redecorate. In transition, Colleen was experimenting with new quilts and knickknacks for the various rooms at the time of my visit, but she stated that she still plans to maintain a theme for each room to be reflected in the decor. Themes vary from a southwestern motif to The School Room with its old school prints, a drawing slate, and printed rules for teachers. Rooms are supplied with coffee, teas, fruit and bread as breakfast fare. Each cottage is equipped with a refrigerator, television, and fireplace or log stove. Colleen and Mike McCann personally tend to the inn and care for their guests. The grounds are immaculately kept—swept pathways wind amongst the cottages, leading to the heated pool, rose garden, and parlor. The parlor with its porch is a welcoming place for guests to congregate and enjoy a glass of sherry or a challenging game of chess. *Directions:* Take Highway 10 west from Los Angeles to Banning and Highway 243 to Idyllwild. Turn left on North Circle, right on South Circle, left on Fern Valley Road.

FERN VALLEY INN
Innkeepers: Colleen & Mike McCann
25240 Fern Valley Road, P.O. Box 116
Idyllwild, CA 92549
Tel: (909) 659-2205 Fax: (909) 659-2630
11 bedrooms with private bathrooms
Double: $65–$105
Open all year
Credit cards: MC, VS
Inappropriate for children

The Strawberry Creek Inn, a lovely dark-shingled building with etched-glass windows, sits back off the main road on the final approach to town. It is owner-managed, with Diana Dugan and Jim Goff the lovely hosts: Jim's domain is the expansive gardens, while Diana's personal warmth is reflected in the decor—she is responsible for every nook and inviting touch. In the shingled main house the parlor is set with a large comfy sofa, tables, and chairs before the fireplace and its bookshelves are brimming with novels and games. Diana has selected coordinating wallpapers, borders, and trims in colors of rose and greens. Off the parlor in a cheerful enclosed sun porch, long trestle tables accommodate guests with a bountiful feast: French toast with bratwurst, fruit, juice, and coffee or tea is just one example of breakfast. The bedrooms are located both in the main house and in a back wing which wraps around a sunny courtyard. Each room is decked with country handmade quilts or crocheted spreads. Rooms in the main house, four upstairs and one down, are charming, and give the feeling of being "back home." The courtyard rooms were built with private fireplaces, baths, and skylights and are equipped with a small refrigerator and queen beds. A cottage on the creek offers a king bed, whirlpool tub, two baths, fireplace, kitchen, glassed-in porch and roomy back deck. A second cottage with two bedrooms and one bathroom enjoys a secluded forest setting. *Directions:* From the south, the inn is on the right on Highway 243 past South Circle Drive.

STRAWBERRY CREEK INN
Innkeepers: Diana Dugan & Jim Goff
26370 Highway 243, P.O. Box 1818
Idyllwild, CA 92349
Tel: (714) 659-3202 Fax: (909) 659-4707
9 bedrooms with private bathrooms
Double: $85–$135
Closed Thanksgiving & Christmas
Credit cards: MC, VS
Children accepted

Brigadoon Castle is spectacular. Tucked away on a private oasis of 86 acres and bounded by national forest, it is a magnificent property and a wonderfully romantic hideaway. The turreted entrance to the castle is through a handsome arched wooden door framed by ivy and wisteria. Inside, although impressive with its vaulted archways, dramatic stair, lofty ceilings, wide passageways, and regal decor, the ambiance is also welcoming and intimate. The two-tiered living room is magnificent with sofas set before its brick fireplace which rises to the loft library, a lovely room looking out through towering windows to the surrounding greenery. Outside the living room a brick terrace stretches to the edge of the woods and a path beckons on up to the hot tub. Five bedchambers are found in the main castle, each more beautiful than the next, from feminine Korysa's Garden Room with its hand-painted whitewashed sleigh bed and armoire and delicate decor to the two-level Tyler's Tree Top Room in the turret with its mural-covered walls and ceiling. The gatekeeper's house, The Cottage, has its own living room, fireplace, full kitchen, loft bedroom, deck with hot tub, and a gorgeous setting next to the rushing creek. This is hostess Geri MacCallum's adventure of a lifetime and she invites you to come to Brigadoon and let the magic stir your heart! *Directions*: A bit complicated! For a general orientation, Igo is located 15 miles south west of Redding. Call for directions.

BRIGADOON CASTLE   **New**
Innkeeper: Geri E. MacCallum
9036 Zogg Mine Road, P.O. Box 324
Igo, CA 96047
Tel: (916) 396-2785 or (888) 343-2836
Fax: (916) 396-2784
6 bedrooms, 4 with private bathrooms
Double: $125–$275
Open all year
Credit cards: all major
Children accepted by prior arrangement

The Blackthorne Inn is the whimsical creation of Susan and Bill Wigert. They have built a Hansel and Gretel house tucked among the treetops, loaded with peaked roofs, dormer windows, funny little turrets, bay windows, and an octagonal tower. You wind up through the trees to the main entry level which is wrapped by an enormous wooden deck, emphasizing the tree-house look. The living room is dominated by a floor-to-ceiling stone fireplace. Skylights, a stained-glass window, a Chinese carpet, wood-paneled walls, baskets of flowers, and walls of windows looking out into the trees make the room most appealing. The guestrooms, located on various levels, are not decorated in any particular period or style, and because of the wooded setting vary in outlook and available sunlight. The favorite choice of many is the Eagle's Nest, located in the octagonal tower, where walls of glass give the impression one is sleeping under the stars—camping at its best. (Note: It is a bit rustic as the bathroom is outside, in the dressing room opposite the hot tub.) Each of the other guestrooms has its own personality, whether it be with stained-glass windows, a private entrance, a separate sitting room, or a bay window looking out into the trees. *Directions:* Take Sir Francis Drake Boulevard off Highway 1 to Olema. Turn right, go 2 miles, then left toward Inverness, go 1 mile, then left on Vallejo Avenue (at the Knave of Hearts Bakery).

BLACKTHORNE INN
Innkeepers: Susan & Bill Wigert
266 Vallejo Avenue, P.O. Box 712
Inverness, CA 94937
Tel: (415) 663-8621 Fax: (415) 663-8635
E-mail: susan@blackthorneinn.com
5 bedrooms, 3 with private bathrooms
Double: $105–$205
Open all year
Credit cards: MC, VS
Children accepted over 14

Built as a hunting lodge by the Empire Club in 1917, this dark-shingled building highlighted with a white trim porch hung with greenery is a wonderful escape in the woods just up from the bay. Previously a restaurant only, under the artistically brilliant direction of its owner, Manka's now offers intimate accommodation and a restaurant (open Thursday through Monday) whose menu is in keeping with the theme of a hunting lodge—much of the food is grilled over an open fire. Four guestrooms are found up a narrow flight of stairs above the restaurant. They occupy the four corners of the lodge and open onto a hallway hung with antlers and old paintings which creaks round the stairwell. Two of the rooms enjoy an expanse of deck looking out through the trees to the bay. Four rooms are located in a rambling annex at the back of the wooded property. Two cabins just below the lodge and two a short drive away, both nestled on the edge of the water enjoying its own acreage and private beach, offer the guest even more privacy and rustic seclusion. We love the wonderful four-poster beds made from rough-hewn Oregon fir, enhanced by warm flannel checks and plaids, and draped with heavy throw blankets. Manka's charm is its appealing, comfortable, rustic ambiance—a homey hideaway inviting you to nestle in with a good book and romantic company. Note: Breakfast is offered from a tempting menu at tables set in the lobby in front of the fire and is additional to the cost of the room. *Directions:* Manka's is at Argyle and Callendar Street.

MANKA'S INVERNESS LODGE
Innkeeper: Margaret Grade
30 Callendar Way, P.O. Box 1110
Inverness, CA 94937
Tel: (415) 669-1034 Fax: (415) 669-1598
8 bedrooms, 1 suite, 3 cabins, with private bathrooms
Double: $115–$325 (breakfast not included)
Open all year
Credit cards: MC, VS
Children accepted

Sandy Cove Inn offers guests a spectacular setting of wilderness, beauty, and quiet. Its grounds boast a riding arena and stable, an expanse of well tended garden, and, unbelievably, its own private stretch of white sand beach on Tomales Bay. Without ever venturing beyond the fenced compound one can picnic, swim, beachcomb, tidepool, canoe, or birdwatch. In addition to a parklike setting, the inn offers very private guest accommodation in cottages of weathered wood smartly trimmed in white, each with its own entrance. One feels ultimately pampered with every need anticipated: you are provided not only with the expected amenities, but with imaginative extras such as binoculars, first-aid kits, flashlights, backpacks, hats, walking sticks, insect repellent, beach maps, and slippers at the front door—an attention to detail I have seen nowhere else. A bountiful breakfast including a hot entree is delivered to your room. The handsome guestrooms are individual in decor and offerings. The North Suite has its own fire stove, a pine bed, a decor of rich cranberry with a nautical theme, and a deck overlooking the dressage ring and stables; the South Suite, dressed with a subtle equestrian theme, enjoys a wood stove and a small sitting area overlooking the arena; and the West Suite has its own porch, a gas fireplace, and a decor of rich blues and burgundies. *Directions:* Travel Sir Francis Drake Boulevard north through Inverness. Just before the road veers inland towards Point Reyes beaches, watch for the gated entry to Sandy Cove Inn on the right.

SANDY COVE INN
Innkeepers: Kathy & Gerry Coles
12990 Sir Francis Drake Blvd., P.O. Box 869
Inverness, CA 94937
Tel: (415) 669-2683 Fax: (415) 669-7511
E-mail: sandycov@nbm.com
3 bedrooms with private bathrooms
Double: $110–$195
Open all year
Credit cards: all major
Inappropriate for children

Ten Inverness Way is a most attractive-looking inn—a cozy, redwood-shingled building fronted by a carefree, cheerful English garden. Originally built in 1904 as a family home, it was bought in 1980 by Mary Davies who converted it into an inn. A flagstone path leads from the road up a slope, through the flowerbeds to the front door. Inside, a staircase takes you to the second level and opens to the living room which has an informal ambiance with a large stone fireplace, redwood walls, Oriental carpets, comfortable furnishings, and a few antique accents. The room is not elegant nor decorator perfect, but is very inviting. This is where Mary says guests relax and make themselves at home—playing games or snuggling up on the sofa with a good book. As the tensions of city life recede, guests strike up conversations with fellow visitors. The four small bedrooms are simply decorated, but fresh and immaculately clean, with handmade quilts on the beds adding a special touch. A suite has been added, complete with French doors leading to its own garden, and kitchen. In the morning Mary or assistant innkeeper Barbara Searles serves a delicious full breakfast in the sunny breakfast room, opening through French doors off the living room. After breakfast, Point Reyes National Seashore is just waiting to be explored. *Directions*: Drive into Inverness on the main road, Sir Francis Drake Boulevard, and watch for the sign pointing to your left to Ten Inverness Way.

TEN INVERNESS WAY
Innkeepers: Mary Davies & Barbara Searles
Ten Inverness Way, P.O. Box 63
Inverness, CA 94937
Tel & fax: (415) 669-1648
5 bedrooms with private bathrooms
Double: $125–$165
Open all year
Credit cards: MC, VS
Children accepted

Jamestown, with its high wooden sidewalks and wooden storefronts with broad balconies hanging to the street, wears an air of yesteryear—you expect to see old-time cowboys emerging from the saloon and a stagecoach rumbling down its Main Street. It seems that every Gold Rush town had a hotel similar to this one, but today few can boast of a city hotel that has received the careful restoration that the Jamestown Hotel has. The outside looks much as it did in its heyday, a simple brick false-front building whose second-story balcony forms a roof above the sidewalk. The lobby, cocktail lounge (where drinks are available in a cozy fireside setting in the evening and breakfast is served in the morning), and dining room occupy the ground floor. The restaurant abounds with the same old-world ambiance as the rest of the hotel and prides itself on serving excellent food. On summer days meals are served on the patio. The bedrooms are quaintly Victorian, neat as new pins. Some are two smaller rooms made into a sitting room and bedroom combination. All have attractive, spotless bathrooms and are named for famous western personalities, being decorated with that person in mind, for example, Lola Montez, Lotta Crabtree, Jenny Lind, and Buffalo Bill. *Directions:* From the San Francisco area take Highway 580 for 60 miles, then Highway 120 east to Jamestown which is just before Sonora.

JAMESTOWN HOTEL
Innkeepers: Janet & Lee Hammond
18153 Main Street, P.O. Box 539
Jamestown, CA 95327
Tel: (209) 984-3902 or (800) 205-4901
Fax: (209) 984-4149
8 bedrooms with private bathrooms
Double: $75–$105
Open all year
Credit cards: all major
Children accepted

Built in 1859 and proudly claiming to be one of California's ten oldest hotels, the National Hotel is located on the main street of Jamestown, considered the gateway to the Gold Country. The first floor accommodates a wonderful upscale restaurant where a breakfast buffet of freshly baked muffins, fruit, hard-boiled eggs, assorted cereals, juices, coffee, and tea is set out for resident guests and where lunch, dinner, and a Sunday champagne brunch is available to residents and non-residents. You can also opt to enjoy lunch or dinner at tables set on a side terrace under the shade of a vine-covered trellis. The handsome old redwood bar in the Gold Rush Saloon offers refreshment, possible entertainment, and local gossip. A steep stairway just off the entry leads to the 11 guestrooms on the second floor. Wonderful old brass and iron beds decked with handmade patchwork quilts, handsome trunks, lovely old armoires, antique washbasins, and lace curtains at the windows dominate the decor which is pleasing and reminiscent of the Gold Rush era—but with modern comforts. Five guestrooms enjoy private bathrooms while six of the rooms sharing two hall bathrooms are furnished with in-room washbasins. The guestrooms are comfortable, air conditioned, and are all accessed off the one central hallway. The two front rooms overlook the front balcony and the action of main street. *Directions*: Jamestown's Main Street intersects both Highways 108 and 49 on the east and west end of town.

THE NATIONAL HOTEL   *New*
Innkeepers: Pamela & Stephen Willey
77 Main Street, P.O. Box 502
Jamestown, CA 95327
Tel: (209) 984-3446 Fax: (209) 984-5620
11 bedrooms, 5 with private bathrooms
Double: $65–$80
Open all year
Credit cards: all major
Children under 10 accepted by prior arrangement

Located in a residential area south of the old Gold Rush town of Julian, is a miniature southern mansion, painted white with four stately columns accenting the front of the house. The style especially appealed to Alan whose family, many years ago, used to own a plantation, while the tranquil setting appealed to Mary. The large wooded lot is perfect for weddings and bridal party planning is her specialty. Inside, the home is simple, but very pleasant. The living room opens onto a sunlit dining room with a wall of windows looking out to a sloping forest of trees. The dining room is where Mary hosts small bridal receptions and also where each morning guests are served a full, homemade breakfast on family china and silver. Downstairs there is one bedroom wallpapered in muted shades of tan and dusty pink with a handsome Louis XVI antique bed. This is the French Quarter Room where feather masks and Mardi Gras memorabilia set the New Orleans theme. Upstairs, two bedrooms are nicely decorated in pastel blues and pinks, while the Honeymoon Suite has recently been redecorated in burgundy and tapestry. Also recently redecorated, the East Room is described by Mary as "subdued Victorian," decorated in blues and whites to complement the colors in the bath. *Directions:* From Julian head south on Highway 78. Turn left on Pine Hills Road, then right at the second street which is Blue Jay Drive. (Total driving distance from Julian is about 4 miles.)

THE JULIAN WHITE HOUSE
Innkeepers: Mary & Alan Marvin
3014 Blue Jay Drive, P.O. Box 824
Julian, CA 92036
Tel: (619) 765-1764 or (800) 948-4687 Fax: none
4 bedrooms with private bathrooms
Double: $90–$135
Open all year
Credit cards: MC, VS
Inappropriate for children under 5

Just a block off main street on Julian's hillside sits a lovely property, open for just a few years, that already boasts a very loyal clientele. It is not surprising when you see the accommodation: guestrooms are lovely, with handsome country furnishings complemented by beautiful wallpapers and coordinating fabrics. The Yellow Bellflower, for example, is decorated in tones of soft blues and yellow, with a beautiful blue arch or faience hung over the bed, materials of a subtle pinstripe and blue check, and a multi-colored quilt draped at the foot of the bed. There is nothing country-cute in the decor—rather, rooms are spacious and subtle in their elegance. Cottage guestrooms all enjoy private entrances, tucked in a garden setting, along a wandering path and central courtyard. All rooms are equipped with TV, VCR (complimentary video library), all but one have a fireplace, and half have whirlpool tubs. Bathrooms are spacious, modern, and wonderfully appointed. At the top of the property, the handsome lodge offers more standard rooms in terms of size and price, a lovely large public room with high vaulted ceilings and river-stone fireplace, a dining room, and an upstairs board or conference room. Room prices include a full breakfast and evening hors d'oeuvres. In the intimacy of the lovely dining room a delicious menu is offered three evenings per week. *Directions*: Washington Street crosses Main Street at the north end of town.

ORCHARD HILL COUNTRY INN
Innkeepers: Pat & Darrell Straube
2502 Washington Street, P.O. Box 425
Julian, CA 92036-0425
Tel: (619) 765-1700 or (800) 716-7242
Fax: (619) 765-0290 E-mail: pending
22 bedrooms with private bathrooms
Double: $130–$155
Closed two weeks in January
Credit cards: all major
Children accepted over 12

From the street The La Jolla Bed & Breakfast Inn is a nondescript building with a pale-peach stucco wash, but behind its façade is a surprising oasis of luxury. The inn is located a few blocks from the heart of La Jolla's elegant shopping district as well as its lovely beach and directly across the street from public tennis courts. The owners describe their decor as "elegant cottage style": beautiful furnishings, lovely fabrics, handsome prints, and splendid antiques have been carefully selected to suit the mood of each room. From the Bird Rock, the smallest and least expensive room, charmingly decorated in Laura Ashley blue-and-white pinstripes and dainty flowered prints, to the spacious and elegant Holiday room with its canopied four-poster bed, dramatic fireplace, and color scheme of white on white with beige accents, each room is unique and inviting. Fresh fruit, sherry, and flowers are placed in each guestroom. Ten rooms are located in the historic house and six in the annex. On sunny days pass through the arched doorway and laze in the back yard at tables set on a brick patio bordered by grass and flowers. Breakfast is served in the dining area, on the patio, the sun deck, or in your bedroom. *Directions:* From San Diego take Route 5 and exit right on La Jolla Village Drive. Turn left on Torrey Pines Road and proceed 2½ miles to Prospect Place. Turn right, drive nine blocks, then turn left on Draper Avenue.

THE LA JOLLA BED & BREAKFAST INN
Innkeeper: Marilouise Micuda
7753 Draper Avenue
La Jolla, CA 92037
Tel: (619) 456-2066 or (800) 582-2466
Fax: (619) 456-1510
16 bedrooms, 15 with private bathrooms
Double: $100–$225
Open all year
Credit cards: MC, VS
Children accepted over 12

Doing justice to La Jolla is the romantic La Valencia Hotel: subtle-pink adobe-like walls, thick Spanish-tiled roof, and a characterful tower domed with blue-and-gold mosaics set the stage for this special hotel. There is a captivating, old-world charm from the moment you stroll under the colonnade, alongside the palm-shaded garden restaurant, and through the front door. The hotel dates back to the 1920s: thankfully the essence and dream of the original hotel have been faithfully preserved—and even bettered. The reception parlor opens onto a dramatic long parlor whose soft-buff-colored walls, wrought-iron chandeliers, subdued lighting, blue-and-yellow tiled planter, luscious displays of fresh flowers, and painted ceiling are dramatized at the end of the room by a wall of glass framing the sea. All of the guestrooms are individually decorated in a traditional style of furnishings and fabrics. The most expensive rooms are those with a view of the ocean, but even the less expensive rooms (such as those next to the garden) are lovely. One of my favorites, room 813 overlooking the front street, is especially spacious and has the added bonus of a kitchenette. On one of the lower terraces there is a lovely pool enhanced by perfectly tended gardens and nearby a "secret gate" allows guests to stroll from the hotel grounds down the road to La Jolla's beautiful little coves. *Directions:* Exit Highway 5 north at Ardath Road (5 south at La Jolla Village), travel to Torrey Pines Road and right on Prospect Street.

LA VALENCIA HOTEL
Director: Michael J. Ullman
1132 Prospect Street
La Jolla, CA 92037
Tel: (619) 454-0771 Fax: (619) 456-3921
100 bedrooms with private bathrooms
Double: $150–$725 (breakfast not included)
Open all year
Credit cards: all major
Children accepted

Eiler's Inn, although on a busy highway, has been carefully designed so that the guestrooms do not face the traffic, but front onto a central courtyard where the only sound is that of the gurgling fountain. This inner brick-paved patio, filled with colorfully blooming plants and potted greenery, is the heart of the inn where guests gather in the evening for wine and cheeses and again in the morning for a wonderful buffet breakfast. If the weather is chilly, guests congregate around the blazing fire in the front lounge. Henk and Annette Wirtz, from Germany, were the previous owners of the inn but, sadly, Henk Wirtz recently passed away, so the tradition of welcome and camaraderie is now being continued by his son, Nico, and the resident managers. There is a true European ambiance and a mood of warmth and informal friendliness at Eiler's Inn. The bedrooms all differ in decor and were recently refurbished, with the majority receiving new carpets and new spreads to deck the beds. The rooms are pleasant, but on the cozy side in terms of size and beachside-casual in their appointments, many with rattan and wicker predominating. However, guests seem happy with both the hotel and its proximity to the beach, just a two-minute walk down the hill. *Directions*: On the coastal Highway 1, just south of the town center between Cleo and St Anna streets. (There is limited parking.)

*EILER'S INN   **New***
Owner: Nico Wirtz
Innkeepers: Cynthia & Norman Wright
741 South Coast Highway
Laguna Beach, CA 92651
Tel: (714) 494-3004 Fax: (714) 497-2215
12 bedrooms with private bathrooms
Double: $85–$195
Open all year
Credit cards: all major
Inappropriate for children

The Laguna House is located a few blocks up from the beach and south of the heart of town. Convenient and cute, Laguna House offers guests either overnight or comfortable long-term accommodation. Taking advantage of a few quiet days, resident innkeeper, Jean Willard, greeted us with a smile and a drop of paint on her nose—she was spring-cleaning, which involved painting walls and washing carpets while a gardener was adding to the bounty of bordering flowers. Jean takes great pride in the property and she is soley responsible for its operation and upkeep. If you are here on a long-term stay she will provide fresh towels but not necessarily daily maid service. Rooms are in a clustering of cottages and open onto a central brick courtyard with a pretty fountain. The beach-cottage atmosphere is carried out with fresh prints against the whitewashed walls, bleached pine, wicker, and plantation shutters. Down comforters adorn the beds and all suites have spotless, well equipped kitchenettes, color TVs, and phones. The Glennyre is a two-bedroom suite with glimpses of the ocean and the third-floor Catalina suite enjoys its own small rooftop deck and ocean views. The cottage at the front of the property is set under beams and enjoys a cozy fireplace. A barbecue is available for guests' use, and beach towels are offered for days on the sand. *Directions*: Exit Highway 5 or Highway 405 at Laguna Canyon Road and travel it to Laguna Beach. Catalina Street runs parallel to and just a few blocks up from the South Coast Highway between Legion and Park.

LAGUNA HOUSE
Innkeeper: Jean Willard
539 Catalina Street
Laguna Beach, CA 92651
Tel: (714) 497-9061 Fax: (714) 455-9641
9 bedrooms with private bathrooms
Double: $125–$185, weekly rates available
Open all year
Credit cards: all major
Children welcome

It was quite a change in careers when Lee left her job at Capital Records and moved with her husband, Johan, from Pacific Palisades to Lake Arrowhead. They bought a Cape-Cod-style home tucked in the trees in a residential area above the lake. Happily Johan, who was born in Holland, is a talented craftsman and through his major renovations, followed by Lee's creative decorating, what was once a simple little cottage has been transformed into an appealing bed and breakfast. You cannot miss the house: a wonderful old-fashioned buggy sits in front, leading the way to the soft-blue house with white trim and a cheerful front door painted bright red. You enter into a small living room which leads into the dining room and beyond to the prettiest room downstairs, a sun room wrapped in windows with comfy sofa and chairs slip-covered in a cheerful English floral print. French doors open onto a large deck, the perfect spot to relax and enjoy a view through the trees to the lake. Upstairs are three guestrooms. My favorite is the Brougham Room, charmingly decorated in pastels and whites and with a window seat from which to enjoy the view through the trees to the lake. Lee's warmth of welcome makes all guests want to return. *Directions:* From the Rim Forest Road, take Highway 173 signposted to Lake Arrowhead. Turn right at the stop sign when you reach the village. Continue for about 2 miles and turn right on Emerald Drive.

THE CARRIAGE HOUSE
Innkeepers: Lee & Johan Karstens
472 Emerald Drive
Lake Arrowhead, CA 92352
Tel: (909) 336-1400 or (800) 526-5070
3 bedrooms with private bathrooms
Double: $95–$125
Open all year
Credit cards: all major
Children accepted over 12

The Château du Lac, perched on the hillside above the crystal-blue water of Lake Arrowhead. Jody and Oscar Wilson were lucky to find a home serenely set amongst the trees overlooking Lake Arrowhead that was large enough to provide six guestrooms, yet small enough to maintain a homelike ambiance. Although of new construction, the effect is a pleasing adaptation of a Victorian style with pretty light-brown wood façade accented by crisp white trim and accents of French-blue shingles, but there is none of the Victorian gloom inside: the spacious living areas all open on to one another. The "prize" is the stunning dining room with French windows opening to a romantic deck which stretches around the house and provides a beautiful vista through the trees to the lake. The furnishings in the individually decorated bedrooms are mostly new, but achieve a French-country look. All of the bedrooms have private bath and the Wilsons have recently converted two guestrooms on the lower level into a suite. Jody is a gourmet cook and was a professional caterer in Los Angeles, so guests are certainly well tended in the food department. *Directions*: From the Rim Forest Road take road 173 signposted to Lake Arrowhead. When you reach the village, turn right at the first stop light and continue for about 3 miles. Turn right at Hospital Road and the Château du Lac is the first house on your right.

CHÂTEAU DU LAC
Innkeepers: Jody & Oscar Wilson
911 Hospital Road
Lake Arrowhead, CA 92352
Tel: (909) 337-6488 or (800) 601-8722
Fax: (909) 337-6746
5 bedrooms with private bathrooms
Double: $135–$240
Open all year
Credit cards: all major
Children accepted over 14

Although Eagle's Landing is a bed and breakfast, it is run so professionally that guests have the feeling that they are in a miniature hotel. There are four guestrooms with private bath and, although each varies in decor, they all maintain a comfy-homey ambiance and are all meticulously kept—everything "neat as a pin." One of the bedrooms, the Lake View Suite, is enormous, with its own fireplace and a spacious private deck with a view of the lake. However, my favorite room is the cozy Woods Room, tucked amongst the trees with its own little terrace and entrance. The living room has a large fireplace in the corner and a splendid long wooden trestle table, big enough for all the guests to gather and share their day's adventures. Just off the dining room is a cozy nook where guests can enjoy breakfast. Speaking of breakfast, Dorothy prides herself on treating her guests to a special brunch on Sunday mornings, a hearty start for exploring the lake which is located a short walk from Eagle's Landing. Since this is a private lake, public access is available only in the town of Arrowhead (about a five-minute drive away). *Directions:* Turn north from Highway 18 following signs for Blue Jay. Before you reach the lake, the road splits. Turn left on North Bay and watch for Cedarwood on your left—Eagle's Landing is on the corner of North Bay and Cedarwood.

EAGLE'S LANDING
Innkeepers: Dorothy & Jack Stone
27406 Cedarwood
Lake Arrowhead, CA 92352
M.A.: P.O. Box 1510, Blue Jay, CA 92317
Tel: (909) 336-2642
4 bedrooms with private bathrooms
Double: $95–$185
Open all year
Credit cards: all major
Children accepted over 16

The Saddleback Inn is tucked into its own wooded oasis just a short stroll from Lake Arrowhead Village. Although the inn dates back almost 70 years when it was built in the style of an English tavern by two sisters from the Midwest, there is nothing "dated" about this small inn. Its present owners have completely renovated every nook and cranny, creating a slick, very sophisticated hotel. Luckily, they have kept the old-world look with the use of a few antiques plus many reproductions in the decor. The reception area is located in the main lodge which exudes a Victorian mood in its cozy bar and dining room. The original staircase leads off the lobby to ten guestrooms, some quite small but all attractive. Scattered throughout the 3½ acres are small cottages connected by pathways which house the remaining guestrooms. All of the rooms are decorated with Laura Ashley fabrics and wallpapers, and most have a Jacuzzi tub in the bathroom—a wonderful respite after a day of hiking or sightseeing. The Saddleback Inn appears more "slick" than "homey," but behind its commercial façade is the warmth of the manager, Liza Colton, who creates the ambiance of a small inn. This hotel is an especially suitable choice when traveling with children, as a pretty beach is within walking distance. *Directions:* From Highway 173 take the Lake Arrowhead turnoff. Drive 2 miles and the hotel is on the left at the entrance to Lake Arrowhead Village.

SADDLEBACK INN
Innkeeper: Liza Colton
300 S. State Highway 173
P.O. Box 1890
Lake Arrowhead, CA 92352
Tel: (714) 336-3571 Fax: (909) 337-4277
10 rooms, 24 cottages, with private bathrooms
Double: $100–$395 (breakfast not included)
Open all year
Credit cards: all major
Children accepted

Lakeport, located on the banks of Clear Lake, is usually thought of as a playground for water enthusiasts, but tucked in among the weekend cottages there are many old Victorian homes. One of these, whose history dates back to the time of the Civil War, is the Forbestown Inn, a pretty clapboard house with an old-fashioned front porch heavily draped with wisteria. Upon entering, you find a hallway leading to a cozy living room with a cheerful dining area to one side with a wall of windows opening to one of the nicest features of the house—a lovely back garden with a towering redwood tree shading a generously sized hot tub and swimming pool. There are two guestrooms downstairs which share a very spacious bathroom with a claw-foot tub. Upstairs are two more bedrooms tucked under the eaves. These are a bit smaller than the rooms downstairs, but they share a lounge area at the top of the stairs which makes them more commodious. My favorite is an upstairs room nicely decorated with color-coordinating fabric and wallpaper in soft blues and peach tones and with its own private bathroom. Nancy and Jack have converted the adjacent carriage house into a private suite with private bath, hot tub and its own living room. Jack is a gourmet cook and treats guests to a bountiful breakfast each morning. *Directions:* Located one block west of Main Street, between 8th and 9th.

FORBESTOWN INN
Innkeepers: Nancy & Jack Dunne
825 Forbes Street
Lakeport (Clearlake), CA 95453
Tel: (707) 263-7858 Fax: (707) 263-7878
4 bedrooms, 1 with private bathroom
Double: $79–$150
Open all year
Credit cards: all major
Children accepted over 12

Glendeven is a charming New-England-style farmhouse built in 1867 by Isaiah Stevens for his bride, Rebecca. Today, this beautiful clapboard home, elegant in its simplicity, is owned by Jan (pronounced Yan), who hails from Holland, and his wife Janet who purchased the property in 1977 and created one of the most delightful inns on the Mendocino coast. Over the years they have expanded the inn to include a two-bedroom suite in the adjacent Barn House and four lovely guestrooms in Stevenscroft, a gabled, barn-sided building in the garden (most rooms have wood-burning fireplaces). Both Jan and Janet are very talented designers whose eye for proportion, style, and color are apparent in every detail. After enjoying a country breakfast in their room, guests usually stroll across to the gallery in Barn House, where they find furniture made by Jan and contemporary artwork and fine crafts chosen by Janet, an interior decorator. Across the highway a path leads through parkland to end at cliffs high above the ocean. Glendeven is just above Van Damme State Park with its scenic walking paths. *Directions*: Glendeven is located on the east side of Highway 1, south of Mendocino.

GLENDEVEN
Owners: Janet & Jan deVries
8221 North Highway 1
Little River, CA 95456
Tel: (707) 937-0083 or (800) 822-4536
Fax: (707) 937-6108
9 bedrooms, 1 suite, with private bathrooms
Double: $160–$240
Open all year
Credit cards: MC, VS
Children accepted in specific rooms

Nestled in the hills of Beverly Hills in a neighborhood of exclusive real estate, the Hotel Bel-Air is exceptional—elegant and sophisticated, but unpretentious and extending a truly warm welcome. An awning-covered walkway leading to the hotel's reception area gives you your first glimpse of the lush 12 acres transected by babbling streams. Furnishings are gorgeous, with handsome antiques and dramatic flower arrangements. The one- or two-story buildings nestling in the greenery are painted in a soft pastel wash with white doors, creating a peaceful and soothing effect. There is an elegant interior dining room and a terrace for dining under the shade of umbrellas and trees. Light meals are also available poolside as is a summertime grill. The setting is quiet, with the sound of fountains and a running stream breaking the natural silence. Most of the beautifully decorated guestrooms enjoy handsome tiled floors warmed by lovely Oriental carpets, and a welcome tea service and a personalized card are left as a welcome to incoming guests. Service is ever-present but subtle, with the wishes of guests seemingly anticipated, and nothing is too much of a problem or effort on the part of the staff. In my research I have seen some of the world's finest hotels and the Bel-Air made such an impression, it is one I am determined to return to as others do—on vacation! *Directions*: Take Sunset Boulevard west off Highway 405 and then turn north on Stone Canyon Road for about 1 mile. The hotel is found on the left just past the intersection of Tortuosa Way

HOTEL BEL-AIR   *New*
General Manager: Mr. Frank Bowling, V.P.
701 Stone Canyon Road, Los Angeles, CA 90077
Tel: (310) 472-1211 or (800) 648-4097
Fax: (310) 476-5890
92 bedrooms with private bathrooms
Double: $325–$435 Suite: $525–$2,500
Open all year
Credit cards: all major
Children accepted

On the northern edge of the campus of the University of Southern California is a small bed and breakfast whose name reflects its address. Sequestered behind a tall hedge and electronic gates which seal off the driveway at night, the guestrooms of the Inn at 657 are converted from apartment units. Luxurious in space, each unit, whether it has one bedroom or two, enjoys a living room, kitchen, and bathroom, with decor more in keeping with a private residence rather than a cutesy bed and breakfast—it is almost as if the tenant has stepped out and let you use his *pied à terre* for the evening. The decor profits from some international pieces—a Turkish rug, hand-painted Japanese silks, and the innkeeper's own elegant furnishings are souvenirs of Patsy's travels. Patsy left a law career to pursue her dream of operating a bed and breakfast—she loves flowers, entertaining, cooking, and making use of her silver. She plays hostess to an interesting array of guests attracted by the diversity of offerings of the university and the city. Breakfast is a feast and frequently proves to be a stimulating gathering of guests, often here on long stays, attracted by the comfort and size of the accommodation and proximity to the university. Units are private, with their own entrance that opens onto a private stairway, patio area, or garden. The grounds are immaculate and beautifully maintained. *Directions:* The inn is located one block west of Figueroa Street on 23rd Street.

INN AT 657
Innkeeper: Patsy Carter
657 West Twenty-Third Street
Los Angeles, CA 90007
Tel & fax: (213) 741-2200 or Tel: (800) 347-7512
6 bedrooms with private bathrooms
Double: $110
Open all year
Credit cards: none accepted
Children welcome

Elegant in its simplicity, Le Montrose is not an inn, but offers great value and exceptional accommodation in a safe neighborhood on the edge of Beverly Hills just up from the design center. Converted from an apartment complex, Le Montrose has a nondescript concrete square façade which belies the charm of the interior. Guest suites, all with a sunken living room, are described as corporate suites and come with welcome baskets of fruit, twice-daily maid service, color televisions equipped with VCRs, state-of-the-art multi-line phones, private e-mail, faxes, gas fireplaces, great mattresses, excellent lighting, and comfortable sitting areas. The decor in the rooms is handsomely elegant—tones of browns, beiges, golds, and blacks are used in the furnishings against the soft hues of the subtly elegant wallpapers and the classically framed art. The intimate, private library restaurant serves fine cuisine in a quiet ambiance or will provide room service. A small but well equipped fitness center is available to guests at no charge, lighted tennis courts are found on one level of the rooftop, and on a lower level a lovely large pool looks out to the rooftops of Los Angeles. *Directions*: Located one block east of Beverly Hills. Take a long journey east on Sunset Boulevard off the I-405, turn right on Hammond Street, just past Doheny. Or from I-10 take La Cienega north, turn east on Sunset Boulevard (past Santa Monica Boulevard), then turn left on Hammond.

LE MONTROSE SUITE HOTEL   New
General Manager: John Douponce
900 Hammond Street
West Hollywood, CA 90069
Tel: (310) 855-1115 or (800) 776-0666
Fax: (310) 657-9192
128 suites with private bathrooms
Double: $175–$475
Open all year
Credit cards: all major
Children accepted

On a quiet shaded street of Los Olivos sits a distinguished, subtly elegant hotel, traditional in its ambiance. Beautiful in decor and lavish in its comfort, the Grand Hotel is most definitely "grand" yet intimate in its number of guestrooms. With just 21 rooms, but staffed as if it had 50, the hotel gives guests personal and gracious attention. Accommodations are a good value when compared to the tariffs charged in neighboring Santa Barbara and the price includes a complimentary bottle of local wine and a Continental breakfast served to the privacy of your room. Each of the guestrooms, whether upstairs from the main lobby or in an attractive annex across the street, features a western or classic impressionist artist whose work is beautifully presented and featured throughout the room. Wood moldings, brass fixtures, and French armoires create a romantic turn-of-the-century ambiance. Guestroom amenities include a mini refrigerator, television, fireplace, beds topped with plump down comforters, and, in selected rooms, a Jacuzzi tub. A lovely heated swimming pool and Jacuzzi are a welcome treat for summer travelers. The Grand Hotel Los Olivos is a full-service hotel with an excellent restaurant with the ambiance of a quiet country lodge. *Directions:* South from San Francisco on Highway 101, take Highway 154 approximately 2 miles to Grand Avenue in Los Olivos.

THE GRAND HOTEL
Director: Ken Mortensen
2860 Grand Avenue
P.O. Box 526
Los Olivos, CA 93441
Tel: (805) 688-7788 Fax: (805) 688-1942
21 rooms with private bathrooms
Double: $160–$325
Open all year
Credit cards: all major
Children accepted

The bland roadside exterior with its 50s' motel sign is all that is left of the earlier version of this motel. Behind the façade is a simple, attractive entry dressed with fresh flowers opening onto the back central courtyard. The manicured back garden is beautifully landscaped and flows to a tiled patio which extends out to a glass-enclosed bay window alcove set with tables overlooking the ocean. A single-story wing of rooms sits right on the beach. Decorated in a simple, fresh look with wicker furniture, the beachfront rooms open onto a deck whose glass wall topped by a driftwood banister tempts one to climb right over and onto the sand. Other rooms are found in the building that fronts the Pacific Coast Highway, either on the first floor overlooking the lush interior courtyard or on the second floor enjoying views of the courtyard garden and glimpses of blue water. Some rooms are equipped with kitchenettes, some with gas fireplaces, and thoughtful touches such as bathroom amenities, in-room coffee makers, a soda and snack concession just off the courtyard, and colorful beach towels piled high behind the reception desk are indicators of the caring owners. For more than 40 years guests have been charmed by the ocean setting of this roadside motel, but under the ownership of Richard and Joan Page, the motel has taken on a special charm. *Directions*: Located south of town, on the Pacific Coast Highway between Cross Creek and Carbon Canyon Roads.

CASA MALIBU   New
Innkeepers: Joan & Richard Page
22752 Pacific Coast Highway
Malibu, CA 90265
Tel: (310) 456-2219 Fax: (310) 456-5418
21 bedrooms with private bathrooms
Double: $99–$199
Open all year
Credit cards: all major (no checks)
Children accepted

Newly constructed, the Malibu Beach Inn resembles the type of small hotel you would find on the Mediterranean, washed in a soft peach, detailed with green awnings and door trim, white doors, and tile roof. Guestrooms at the back of the inn open up to magnificent ocean views and the sound of surf. The entrance sits opposite the parking lot and an attractive fountain set amongst a small ring of palm trees. The public area is open and lovely, handsome handpainted tiles are found throughout, a fountain cascades, a fireplace dresses a sitting area, and an arched doorway opens out to a tiled deck set with tables. Standard rooms are a good value—at the heart of Santa Monica, the same ocean view would carry a price tag of $400. All first-floor rooms have two-person Jacuzzis on the outside deck. One suite is found on each floor, enjoying a larger deck, Jacuzzi, and fireplace. Simple, clean decor is similar throughout, with bamboo furniture and motel-floral prints, and rooms have every amenity such as fully stocked wet bars. I liked room 318, a "Pier Room," which has a corner view of the beach and pier and a nice corner deck, and, as with all third-floor rooms, enjoys a vaulted beamed ceiling and a gas fireplace. Room 310, a standard third-floor room, is also lovely. Robes are offered in third-floor rooms, suites, and first-floor Jacuzzi rooms. *Directions*: South of Malibu on the Pacific Coast Highway with Carbon Canyon Road as the closest cross street.

MALIBU BEACH INN   New
General Manager: Brian Bescoby
22878 Pacific Coast Highway
Malibu, CA 90265
Tel: (310) 456-6444 Fax: (310) 456-1499
47 bedrooms with private bathrooms
Double: $160–$295
Open all year
Credit cards: all major
Children accepted

Set on 92 acres of meadow, woodland, and creek, Victorian Gardens, dating back to 1904, is a lovely two-story, four-bedroom classic Victorian. Decoration is respectful of the Victorian period and yet the furnishings are an artistic arrangement of both traditional and contemporary, with Pauline and Luciano's family heirlooms and treasures on display. The kitchen, where breakfast is sometimes served, is definitely the "heart of the home" and Luciano's domain, a wonderful room warmed by a large open fireplace which Luciano also uses for cooking. Dinner, by reservation only and also open to non-guests, is an elegant presentation of seven courses featuring Italian regional dishes, with specially selected wines to complement the fixed menu which changes daily. Victorian Gardens has four guestrooms, two sharing a hall bath and two with private bath. The Master Bedroom (private bath) enjoys a sweeping view of meadow and the surrounding foothills; the Poppy Bedroom (shared bath) has an intimate reading nook and a small side window draped in hand-embroidered lace; the Golden Bedroom (shared bath) is an inviting front corner room with a lovely nook enticing you to settle and enjoy glimpses of the distant ocean; and the handsome Northwest Bedroom (private bath) is blessed with wonderful views and the most lavish bathroom. *Directions*: From San Francisco take 101 north to 128 west until it ends on Highway 1 then turn south. Travel 5 miles to Elk and then 8 miles to Victorian Gardens. The inn is signposted.

VICTORIAN GARDENS   New
Innkeepers: Pauline & Luciano Zamboni
14409 South Highway 1
Manchester, CA 95459
Tel: (707) 882-3606 Fax: none
4 bedrooms, 2 with private bathrooms
Double: $125–$185
Open all year
Credit cards: all major
Children accepted over 12

An elevated wooden walkway trimmed by flowers and bordered by lawn leads to the front door and porch of the Hogin House Bed & Breakfast, a dear, soft-yellow clapboard house trimmed in white and green. The passage beyond the small front entry leads through the kitchen adorned heavily with country knickknacks and on into the living room with its informal clustering of chairs and sofas in front of the handsome riverstone fireplace. The four guestrooms are found on the second floor under the eaves. The Front Room is spacious, with two double beds and a private bathroom with shower, The Blue Room has a queen bed decked with a lovely old quilt and a bathroom with shower, and steps down to a little sitting room enclosed by a wall of windows which then steps up to another guestroom, The Hideaway, cozy with an iron bed (double), which shares a hallway bathroom. Grandma's Room is a cute room which shares The Hideaway's bathroom. Guests breakfast together either in the dining room or at tables set on the porch, enjoying raisin bran cereal, a bounty of fresh fruit, and an assortment of home-baked muffins and breads accompanied by a wonderful variety of homemade jams. *Directions*: From Mount Shasta travel Highway 89 east for 10 miles. Take a left turn on Columbero and continue ¾ mile to Lawndale Court. Turn right and Hogin House is the second house on the left.

HOGIN HOUSE BED & BREAKFAST   **New**
Innkeepers: Angie & Richard Toreson
424 Lawndale Court
P.O. Box 550
McCloud, CA 96057
Tel & fax: (916) 964-2882
4 bedrooms, 2 with private bathrooms
Double: $60–$90
Open all year
Credit cards: all major
Children accepted

The McCloud Guest House has a wonderful setting—in its own pretty little park, surrounded by green lawn and trees, while in the distance is Mount Shasta, northern California's 14,162-foot giant. The inn is not pretentious, but most attractive in its simplicity. Built entirely of wood, the square building is wrapped with a spacious verandah whose supporting columns reach up to a steeply pitched roof from which little dormer windows peek out into the trees. Built in 1907, the inn was originally the home of J. H. Queal, the president of the McCloud River Lumber Company. After extensive renovations, it reopened as a restaurant on the ground level with five bedrooms upstairs. As you enter the foyer, the massive stone fireplace and wood-paneled walls set the country-lodge feeling. Upstairs, the guests have their own private parlor highlighted with an ornate pool table from the Hearst collection. The original master bedroom is decorated with flowered wallpaper in soft shades of mauve and pink set off by white wicker chairs. Each of the other guestrooms has its own color scheme. Most have antique white iron beds, but one has a four-poster bed which looks quite handsome against a dark plaid wallpaper. *Directions:* Drive north on Highway 5, then east on Highway 89 for 12 miles to McCloud. Before the village turn left on Colombero Drive.

McCLOUD GUEST HOUSE
Owners: Pat & Dennis Abreu
Innkeepers: Patti & Bill Leigh
606 West Colombero Drive
P.O. Box 1510, McCloud, CA 96057
Tel: (916) 964-3160 Fax: none
5 bedrooms with private bathrooms
Double: $85–$105
Closed Mondays & Tuesdays
Credit cards: MC, VS
Inappropriate for children

With great determination, expenditure, and hard work, Lee and Marilyn Ogden renovated a long-abandoned historic building at the heart of the mountain town of McCloud and now the McCloud Hotel with its pretty yellow façade proudly dominates Main Street. Inside, the high beamed ceiling and informal grouping of sofas and chairs set before a large fire give the feeling of a mountain lodge. Although the exterior of the hotel was in relatively good shape and required only cosmetic repairs, guestrooms benefit from the complete renovation and modernization of the interior. At the top of a wide, handsome staircase is an inviting upstairs parlor with a large-screen television and access to the front expanse of porch. Rooms on the first floor facing Main Street are a wonderful value with a nice-size room, washbasin, toilet, and private bathroom. Rooms on the first and second floors at the back of the inn have four-poster beds and an additional but small sitting area. Four suites enjoy big Jacuzzi tubs, three of which are found in the room proper. The decor is similar in theme throughout, with the use of country patterns, old trunks, and washstands to house in-room washbasins. Breakfast and afternoon tea are served at tables set in the lobby and guests staying in the suites have the extra option of having breakfast delivered to the room. *Directions*: From Interstate 5 take the McCloud-Reno Exit and travel east on Highway 89 10 miles. Turn left on Colombero Avenue and follow it into town, cross the tracks, and turn right on Main Street.

McCLOUD HOTEL   New
Innkeepers: Marilyn & Lee Ogden
408 Main Street, P.O. Box 730
McCloud, CA 96057
Tel: (916) 964-2822 or (800) 964-2823
Fax: (916) 964-2844
17 bedrooms with private bathrooms
Double: $68–$130
Open all year   Credit cards: all major
Children accepted in first-floor rooms only

The Blue Heron Inn is not the typical Mendocino Victorian, but a simple, New England-style house, painted white with blue trim. A white picket fence encloses the garden to each side, completing the adorable cottage look. The ground floor is a delightful restaurant (The Moose Café) where daily specials (usually fish fresh from the ocean and pasta dishes) are posted on the board and complemented by a short menu card. Enjoy a Caesar salad for lunch and cioppino for dinner. In the morning a breakfast with croissants or coffee cake and freshly squeezed orange juice is served here. Upstairs, you find three completely delightful bedrooms, each simply furnished with country antiques containing a lovely queen-sized bed made with the most attractive linens. Sunset Room (in cool greens) captures distant ocean views across the rooftops and shares a modern bathroom with the adjacent Bay Room which offers a tempting peek of the ocean from its window. The Blue Heron Room offers equally delightful decor, more space and a pristine en-suite shower room. *Directions:* Follow Highway 1 north into Mendocino. Turn left at Jackson Street, follow Jackson Street to Kasten Street, and turn right.

BLUE HERON INN
Innkeeper: Linda Friedman
390 Kasten Street
Mendocino, CA 95460
Tel: (707) 937-4323 Fax: none
3 bedrooms, 1 with private bathroom
Double: $80–$95
Open all year
Credit cards: none accepted
Inappropriate for children

The Headlands Inn is an especially attractive inn located within walking distance of all the pretty shops and fun little restaurants in Mendocino. This New England-style home, dating from 1868, is a three-story, salt-box Victorian with a bay window in front and gables peeking out from the steep roof. A picket fence encloses the front yard which is usually a bloom with flowers in a cheerful English garden. When you enter either Sharon or David will probably be there to greet you. Afternoon tea and cookies is served in the restful upstairs parlor. While all the bedrooms are particularly attractive, with antique furniture, feather beds, and down comforters, I especially enjoyed Strauss with its large bay window and view across the garden to the bay and Wilson with its private verandah with a table and chairs strategically placed to enjoy the distant ocean view. There are wood-burning fireplaces in five of the bedrooms and an old-fashioned wood-burning parlor stove in another. One of the rooms is a little cottage which opens directly onto the street. Whatever room you are in, a bountiful full breakfast is brought to you on a tray decorated with fresh flowers from the garden—breakfast at The Headlands is a special treat. *Directions:* From San Francisco drive north on Highway 101. Just past Cloverdale, turn left on Highway 128 west to Highway 1, and north to Mendocino.

THE HEADLANDS INN
Innkeepers: Sharon & David Hyman
Howard & Albion Streets, P.O. Box 132
Mendocino, CA 95460
Tel: (707) 937-4431 or (800) 354-4431
Fax: none
6 bedrooms with private bathrooms
Double: $100–$200
Open all year
Credit cards: all major
Children accepted over 12

The Joshua Grindle Inn, located just a short walk from the center of Mendocino, is surrounded by a 2-acre plot of land. A white picket fence encloses the front yard of this most attractive white clapboard farmhouse which, although architecturally simple, has hints of the Victorian era in the fancy woodwork on the verandah. In the 1879 farmhouse you find the guest lounge, a sedate room with old paintings and portraits on the walls, a fireplace, white lace curtains, a trunk for a coffee table, and an antique pump organ tucked in the corner. The light, airy guestrooms have a New-England country ambiance enhanced by the owner's early-American antiques and some have their own fireplace. Of the five guestrooms in the main building two overlook the town of Mendocino and the distant ocean, and all their bathrooms were recently remodeled with luxurious enhancements such as marble counters, whirlpool and deep soak tubs. A natural-wood cottage just behind the house contains two additional bedrooms, and very popular, are those tucked romantically into the age-weathered watertower in the rear garden. Especially attractive is Watertower II, a sunny, cozy room on the second floor where the ocean can be glimpsed through the trees. All of the bedrooms are spotlessly maintained, immaculately decorated, have well lighted, comfortably arranged sitting areas, and private bathrooms. *Directions:* Go north on Highway 1 through town, left on Little Lake Road.

JOSHUA GRINDLE INN
Innkeepers: Arlene & Jim Moorehead
44800 Little Lake Road
P.O. Box 647, Mendocino, CA 95460
Tel: (707) 937-4143 or (800) 474-6353
Fax: none E-mail: joshgrin@mcn.org
10 bedrooms with private bathrooms
Double: $90–$180
Open all year
Credit cards: all major
Children accepted over 10

Most of our selections for Mendocino feature the coastal splendor, but although not next to the ocean, the Mendocino Farmhouse has its own special qualities. It is located at the end of a narrow lane which weaves through a beautiful redwood glen, crosses a small creek, and then opens into a lovely meadow. There, amidst beds of flowers, next to a little duck pond and surrounded by a white picket fence, you will find an appealing tan farmhouse with white trim. Although it appears to be quite old, in reality the inn was newly constructed in 1976. Inside, the decor is fresh and pretty, with antique accents giving it an eclectic style. The breakfast tables capture the sunshine in a many-windowed niche overlooking the flower garden, or dining outside under redwoods is an option in good weather. A large family kitchen is located off the living room. Upstairs there are three bedrooms, each sparkling clean and with its own bathroom. Our favorite rooms are Cedar and Pine, found in the converted barn surrounded by its own little garden. Each is rustic in its mood with either cedar or bleached-pine paneling, a sitting area, and a large wood-burning fireplace. *Directions:* Just south of Mendocino, turn right off Highway 1 on Comptche-Ukiah Road. Go 1½ miles and turn left on Olson Lane—the Mendocino Farmhouse is at the end of the road.

MENDOCINO FARMHOUSE
Innkeepers: Margie & Bud Kamb
Olson Lane, P.O. Box 247
Mendocino, CA 95460
Tel: (707) 937-0241 Fax: (707) 937-2932
E-mail: mkamb@mcn.org
5 bedrooms with private bathrooms
Double: $85–$115
Open all year
Credit cards: MC, VS
Children accepted

At first glance The Stanford Inn by the Sea appears to be more like a motel than a country inn, but this is definitely untrue. Joan and Jeff Stanford have created a cozy, sophisticated little hotel within an attractive, but not unusual, two-story, natural-wood building. The inn is located at the crest of a grassy meadow where a few llamas graze in a paddock. The building is cleverly constructed so that every room has a view, either from a private deck or patio. Each of the guestrooms, many with four-poster beds, has been transformed into a snug little hideaway, with country antiques, color television (movies can be rented), telephone, posies of flowers, and either a wood-burning fireplace or stove—with plenty of wood to keep you warm on nippy nights. Everything is fresh and pretty and immaculately clean. The entire operation seems extremely professional and yet has a very personal touch. Each room has a complimentary bottle of Mendocino vintage wine. A wonderful bonus is the glass-enclosed sauna and "greenhouse" pool where guests can enjoy a swim even on blustery days. Plans are going ahead to add five two-bedroom suites and a dining room which will alleviate the breakfast-time congestion in the small living room. *Directions:* A quarter of a mile south of the village of Mendocino at the intersection of Highway 1 and Comptche-Ukiah Road.

THE STANFORD INN BY THE SEA
Innkeepers: Joan & Jeff Stanford
Highway 1 and Comptche-Ukiah Road
Mendocino, CA 95460
Tel: (707) 937-5615 or (800) 331-8884
Fax: (707) 937-0305
E-mail: stanford@stanfordinn.com
30 bedrooms with private bathrooms
Double: $175–$385
Open all year
Credit cards: all major
Children accepted

Ann and Gene Swett converted their family home into what continues to be one of the very nicest country inns in California. Their home is a most attractive Tudor-style house shaded by giant oak trees in an acre of wooded gardens full of colorful begonias, fuchsias, rhododendrons, and lush ferns in a quiet Monterey suburb. Everything is beautifully tended, giving the grounds a parklike appearance. The inside of the house is an oasis of gentility and tranquillity where everything is done with the comfort of the guest in mind. Most of the bedrooms in the main house, cottage, and carriage house have fireplaces, and all are beautifully decorated and thoughtfully appointed. The Library stands out as a particularly memorable bedroom with its book-lined walls, cozy fireplace, and private balcony overlooking the garden. A refrigerator is kept stocked with complimentary beverages, and juices and hot beverages are always available. In the evening the Swetts join their guests for wine and cheese in the living room. They are especially gracious hosts, adding great warmth and professionalism to their little inn. Breakfast is served at the long oak table in the dining room or brought to your room on a tray. *Directions:* Traveling south on Highway 1, exit at Soledad/Munras, cross Munras Avenue, go right on Pacific Street: Martin Street is on the left in a little over half a mile.

OLD MONTEREY INN
Owners: Ann & Gene Swett
Innkeeper: Patti Kreider
500 Martin Street, Monterey, CA 93940
Tel: (408) 375-8284 or (800) 350-2344
Fax: (408) 375-6730
E-mail: omi.oldmontereyinn.com
10 bedrooms with private bathrooms
Double: $170–$240
Open all year
Credit cards: MC, VS
Inappropriate for children

As an alternative to a bed and breakfast we recommend the Spindrift Inn, a lovely hotel with a great location overlooking the Monterey Bay. Just down the street from the fabulous Monterey Bay Aquarium, its rooms overlook either the bustle of Cannery Row or the serenity of the bay. We stayed in a front room overlooking Cannery Row and were pleasantly surprised to find that the deep-set windows and heavy drapes blocked out the noise of late-night revelers. Guestrooms on the bay side enjoy wonderful water views and corner rooms are spacious and enjoy a lovely window seat. The Spindrift Inn offers 42 bedrooms, each handsomely decorated with rich country fabrics, all with wood-burning fireplaces, beds topped with down comforters, and bathrooms finished in marble and brass. The feeling is European and the amenities are first class. A Continental breakfast of Danish or croissants and a selection of fruit is served on a silver tray in the room and in the evening a buffet of wine and cheese is offered in the front lobby. Service is cordial. There is almost always someone at the front desk in the lobby to assist with information or reservations, but shifts change regularly. This is a hotel, efficient, attractive, and comfortable, with a premier location. *Directions:* Take the Pacific Grove, Del Monte exit off Highway 1. Follow signs to Cannery Row and the Aquarium. The Spindrift is located right on Cannery Row.

SPINDRIFT INN
Director: Randy Venard
652 Cannery Row
Monterey, CA 93940
Tel: (408) 646-8900 Fax: (408) 646-5342
42 bedrooms with private bathrooms
Double: $189–$409
Open all year
Credit cards: all major
Children accepted

Karen (Brown) Herbert and her husband, Rick, have built their own romantic English-manor-style hideaway, Seal Cove Inn. Located just half an hour's drive south of San Francisco, the inn is bordered by towering, windswept cypress trees and looks out over fields of wild flowers and acres of parkland to the ocean. You enter through a spacious entrance hall into an elegantly comfortable living room with a large fireplace centered between French doors. Adjoining the living room is a dining room, and next to that, a small conference room—all with park and ocean views. Antiques are used throughout: grandfather clocks, cradles filled with flowers, handsome tables, antique beds, sideboards, trunks, etc. Each of the large bedrooms has a wood-burning fireplace, comfortable reading chairs, television, VCR, hot towel rack, and a refrigerator stocked with complimentary soft drinks and wine. Best yet, each of the bedrooms has a view of the distant ocean and doors opening either to a private balcony or onto the terrace. From the inn you can walk to a secluded stretch of beach or stroll through the forest along a path that traces the ocean bluffs. Karen has already had the pleasure of welcoming many guests to Seal Cove Inn who are also readers of her travel guides. *Directions:* From San Francisco take Highway 1 south to Moss Beach (about 20 miles). Turn west on Cypress (at the Moss Beach Distillery sign). Seal Cove Inn is one block off the road on the right.

SEAL COVE INN
Innkeepers: Karen & Rick Herbert
221 Cypress Avenue
Moss Beach, CA 94038
Tel: (415) 728-4114 Fax: (415) 728-4116
E-mail: sealcove@coastside.net
10 bedrooms with private bathrooms
Double: $165–$250
Closed Christmas
Credit cards: all major
Children accepted in garden-level rooms

The Pelican Inn, nestled among pine trees, jasmine, and honeysuckle, is a wonderful re-creation of a cozy English tavern with a few attractive guestrooms tucked upstairs. Wide wood-planked floors, an appealing small bar (with dart board), low-beamed ceilings, a giant fireplace with priest hole (secret hiding place), a cozy little guest lounge, and a dining room with trestle tables complete the first-floor scene. Besides the large indoor dining room, there is also a trellised patio where guests can have snacks or dine (in the evenings the candlelit tables are set with linens). Lunch features such English treats as succulent bangers and mash and fish and chips; dinner includes prime rib, rack of lamb, etc. Upstairs there are seven cozy bedrooms where the English motif is carried out with heavily draped half-tester beds, Oriental carpets, a decanter of sherry, and fresh flowers. Rooms are small but cozy and reminiscent of a wonderful old English inn. The location of the Pelican Inn is fabulous: only a few minutes' drive from the giant redwood grove at Muir Woods and a short walk to the ocean. Note: Reservations are needed six months in advance for weekends. Also know that the pub attracts hundreds of people on weekends and noise from the revelers can persist well into the late night. *Directions:* From Highway 101 take the Stinson Beach/Highway 1 turnoff. At the Arco station, go left for 5 miles on Highway 1 to Muir Beach. Pelican Inn is on the left.

PELICAN INN
Innkeeper: Katrinka McKay
10 Pacific Way
Muir Beach, CA 94965-9729
Tel: (415) 383-6000 Fax: (415) 383-3424
7 bedrooms with private bathrooms
Double: $148–$170
Open all year
Credit cards: MC, VS
Children accepted

As the gold boom passed, Murphys was left to sleep under its locust and elm trees until tourists discovered its beauty and slower pace of life. A few old stone buildings survive, one of which contains the Old Timers' Museum filled with pioneer and Gold Rush regalia. The Dunbar House, 1880, is a handsome inn with a wrap-around porch where guests can sit and sip Gold-Country wine or enjoy a refreshing glass of lemonade. Bob and Barbara's pride in their small inn is apparent—they have lavished their time and attention on making it extremely comfortable. Each of the four cozy guestrooms has a fireplace and a small refrigerator with ice and a complimentary bottle of wine. The Sequoia room has a queen-size bed and a claw-foot tub set before a wood stove. The Cedar room, just off the downstairs parlor, is a suite offering a luxurious Jacuzzi. Upstairs are two additional pretty bedrooms. Each room also provides a TV with VCR hidden away in an armoire. While you are out at dinner your bed will be turned down and chocolates placed on your pillow. Breakfast, served in the dining room by the fire, in the century-old garden, or in the privacy of your room, includes juice spritzer, fresh fruit, muffins, turnovers, an egg dish, and a hot beverage. An appetizer buffet is offered in the afternoon. *Directions:* From San Francisco take Highway 580 to Highway 99 north to Highway 4 east, then drive through Angels Camp towards Arnold. Murphys is 9 miles east of Angels Camp.

DUNBAR HOUSE, 1880
Innkeepers: Barbara & Bob Costa
271 Jones Street, P.O. Box 1375
Murphys, CA 95247
Tel: (209) 728-2897 Fax: (209) 728-1451
4 bedrooms with private bathrooms
Double: $115–$155
Open all year
Credit cards: all major
Children accepted over 10

Located just off the main street of Murphy's, the Redbud Inn runs the length of a short side street. The reception, small public sitting area, and side breakfast room, sparsely decorated in reproduction antiques, shout of newness. There are 11 guestrooms in the main house—Mae's Room on the first floor provides wheelchair access while the others are found at the top of a lovely staircase. From the Anniversary Suite, Room 2, which is spacious and elegant with its bay window overlooking a side street, private balcony, enormous spa tub, and romantic king bed draped in French ribbon and silk flowers, to the rooms at the back which benefit from the shade of a mature sycamore tree, the rooms all have lovely modern private baths, are individual in decor, and vary in size and floor plan. I particularly liked Blue Doris, room 7, with its shaded side balcony and country elegance in a decor of blue gingham, chintz, and white wicker, and the Sycamore, room 9, whose queen bed topped with a cozy burgundy quilt and cream-colored duvet is set on a lovely pine floor. Across from the main house, more spacious accommodation is offered in the Garden House, a two-bedroom, two-bath apartment equipped with a full kitchen. The Redbud Inn thrives under the unique efforts of a wife and husband, daughter and son-in-law team of innkeepers—truly a family affair. Breakfast is an offering of a hot entree accompanied by a buffet selection of juice and fruits. *Directions:* From San Francisco take Highway 580 to Highway 99 north to Highway 4 east, then drive through Angels Camp towards Arnold. Murphys is 9 miles east of Angels Camp.

*THE REDBUD INN   **New***
Innkeeper: Pamela Hatch
402 Main Street
Murphys, CA 95247
Tel: (209) 728-8533 or (800) 827-8533 Fax: (209) 728-9123
11 bedrooms, 1 apartment, with private bathrooms
Double: $90–$255 Open all year
Credit cards: MC, VS
Children accepted in apartment & Ope's Cabin

With 600 acres of vineyards as its backdrop, the Oak Knoll Inn has one of the most idyllic settings in the Napa Valley. You find the entry and prettily decorated front sitting room in the original stone farmhouse. An additional building was later added to each side to house guestrooms, each with a private entrance opening onto a wrap-around deck overlooking the vineyards. Breakfast is a feast served on winter mornings in front of the stone fireplace and on warm mornings outside on the deck where you can often watch the graceful hot-air balloons as they drift silently over the vineyards in the early-morning sunshine. The guestrooms are luxurious in their size, magnified further by the high vaulted ceilings. My favorite, number 6 (a corner room at the end of the house), has an arched window which towers to the height of the ceiling and offers a splendid view of the vineyards. Each bedroom enjoys a king-sized brass bed, a sitting area before a fireplace, and thick stone walls which provide efficient insulation. The bedrooms are being individually redecorated with lovely, richly-hued fabrics in a traditional style. The Oak Knoll Inn provides the perfect end to a perfect day of sightseeing. After sampling Napa Valley's many vineyards, you can sit poolside with a glass of wine and enjoy the quiet and beauty of a backdrop of vineyards and the valley's gorgeous hills. *Directions:* Go north on Highway 29 through Napa, then right on Oak Knoll Avenue, which has a left-right-zig-zag across Big Ranch Road.

OAK KNOLL INN
Innkeepers: Barbara Passino & John Kuhlmann
2200 E. Oak Knoll Avenue
Napa, CA 94558
Tel: (707) 255-2200 Fax: (707) 255-2296
4 bedrooms with private bathrooms
Double: $225–$285
Open all year
Credit cards: MC, VS
Inappropriate for children

La Residence is an inn that has grown around The Mansion, a beautiful Gothic-revival home built in the 1870s as a farmhouse to accommodate the large family of Harry Parker, a riverboat pilot from New Orleans. In later years additions more Victorian in style changed the appearance of the home. Nine rooms are housed in the original mansion and are dramatic in their decor which blends well with the grand feeling of the home. Rooms vary from cozy, top-floor rooms tucked under slanted ceilings to spacious and elegant accommodations with fireplaces on the first floor. The 11 rooms in the newly constructed Cabernet Hall, shingled and built in the style of a French barn, are beautifully designed and commodious, each enjoying a private bath, fireplace, and French doors opening onto a patio or balcony. These bedrooms are handsomely decorated with pine antiques imported from France and England and Laura Ashley prints. Breakfast is served in the Cabernet Hall's lovely dining room with tables set before a blazing fire. Between The Mansion and Cabernet Hall are a heated swimming pool and Jacuzzi spa. The excellence of the inn reflects the expertise and talents contributed by the partners who share in the management. *Directions:* Take Highway 29 through Napa. Take the first right turn after the Salvador intersection onto a frontage road (no name) which winds back south to the inn.

LA RESIDENCE
Innkeepers: David Jackson & Craig Claussen
4066 Saint Helena Highway
Napa, CA 94558
Tel: (707) 253-0337 Fax: (707) 253-0382
20 bedrooms, 18 with private bathrooms
Double: $165–$235
Open all year
Credit cards: all major
Children accepted

Chuck and Elaine Matroni are always ready to serve, spoil, pamper, and welcome guests to their three-story, soft-blue Victorian home, tiered on a hillside above gardens and lawn cascading down to the babbling Deer Creek. The parlors and dining room are quite formal with their Victorian furnishings and Oriental accents. The country kitchen at the back seems to be the nucleus of the home, where guests gather while observing the innkeepers prepare their gourmet, multi-course breakfast which is served either in the dining room or outside on the verandah. Deer Creek has five guestrooms, each named for the women who have owned the home over the past 136 years. Sheryl's Room is a cheerful front corner room whose iron bed is set on an Oriental carpet which warms the old wooden floorboards. Lela's Room boasts a dramatic four-poster bed and a claw-foot tub framed in an alcove, romantically draped with lace curtains. Winifred's Room features a canopied bed, an in-room claw-foot tub, and a private deck. Ida's Room's antique oak furniture is lovely against a floral backdrop and the trundle bed accompanying the white and brass day bed comfortably accommodates an additional person. Elaine's Room enjoys a lace-draped bed, a large Roman tub, and a private patio overlooking the grounds and the creek. *Directions*: Exit Highway 20/49 at Broad Street, traveling south across the creek. Turn left on Nevada Street. The inn is located just up the street on the right.

DEER CREEK INN   New
Innkeepers: Elaine & Chuck Matroni
116 Nevada Street, Nevada City, CA 95959
Tel: (916) 265-0363 or (800) 655-0363
Fax: (916) 265-0980
5 bedrooms with private bathrooms
Double: $90–$140
Open all year
Credit cards: MC, VS
Children over 13

This lovely Victorian at the top of Broad Street, childhood home of 19th-century opera star Emma Nevada, is very pretty and feminine with a soft-peach façade trimmed in white set behind a white picket fence bounded by roses. Guestrooms open off public areas that are central to the inn. The first guestroom off the entrance, Nightingale's Bower, was formerly the parlor and enjoys a bay window, antique pot-bellied stove, and elegant Italian bedding. Mignon's Boudoir is luxurious in size but quite cozy with its French country decor and Laura Ashley prints. A claw-foot tub in the bathroom is painted blue to cleverly match the decor and a sink is housed in a beautiful antique cabinet. Ruth Ann Riese's favorite is the regal Empress's Chamber with its wealth of light streaming through a wall of windows and bath with Jacuzzi tub. At the top of the stairs are three additional lovely rooms—Mockingbird's Nest overlooking the front garden, Palmer's Loft whose ceilings and walls are still in the handsome bead boarding original to the house, and Emma's Hideaway, a secluded room set under a steeply pitched roof. Public areas are also very attractive, with lots of windows and glorious light. Breakfast may be taken in the formal dining room, on the back deck under the shade of a 140-year-old cherry tree, or in the Sun Room with its interesting tower ceiling. *Directions*: Take the Broad Street exit off Highway 49 and travel up the hill, through the heart of town, when the road splits, continue on Broad Street to the right.

EMMA NEVADA HOUSE   *New*
Innkeeper: Ruth Ann Riese
528 E Broad Street, Nevada City, CA 95959
Tel: (916) 265-4415 or (800) 916-4416 (Emma)
Fax: (916) 265-4415 E-mail: emmanev@oro.net
6 bedrooms with private bathrooms
Double: $100–$150
Open all year
Credit cards: all major
Children accepted over 10

Located up a narrow stairway, the U.S. Hotel Bed & Breakfast is found entirely on the second floor of a wonderful old brick building that houses shops on the street level. Guestrooms, appealing in their individual decor, come off either side of a long hallway as does an inviting public room where guests can gather to play games, watch television, or play the piano. At the end of the hallway the kitchen with its one dining-room table is where a breakfast buffet is served. At the top of the stairs, the two most requested rooms are The Empire Room, boasting the only king bed in the house draped attractively with a ceiling canopy and decorated in greens, whites, and a rose floral, and The Broad Street Room with its queen bed and rustic decor. Both guestrooms have large private bathrooms with lovely old claw-foot tubs and each overlook the activity of Broad Street. The spacious Pine Room easily accommodates two queen beds and is pleasing in its decor, with light-pine furnishing and blue-and-white prints and floral against a backdrop of weathered old brick walls. The Garden Room is very pretty and feminine with pink-and-white prints and lace against a delicate pink-striped wallpaper, while The Emerald Room with its two queen beds is perfect for a family. The U.S. Hotel, owned and managed by a lovely young couple, is years removed from the rowdier days when it was a very popular bordello and later an old boarding house. *Directions*: Take the Broad Street exit off Highway 49, turn left to the intersection of Broad and Pine.

U.S. HOTEL BED & BREAKAST   *New*
Innkeepers: Renee & Jim Salyards
233-B Broad Street, Nevada City, CA 95959
Tel: (916) 265-7999 or (800) 525-4525
Fax: (916) 265-7990
7 bedrooms with private bathrooms
Double: $85 & $95
Open all year
Credit cards: all major
Children accepted

It was fun to discover The Doryman's Inn, a sophisticated, elaborately decorated small hotel next to the Newport Beach pier. In fact it sits just across the street, next to the old wooden wharf, where the fishermen still go to sea every day (as they have for 100 years) in their brightly painted dories, returning to sell their catch from the back of the boats. For beach buffs, the sand stretches for miles to the entrance to Balboa harbor. The hotel entry is quite discreet: just a tiny hall where an elevator takes you up to the reception area—the inn is located above the 21 Ocean Front restaurant, a dining establishment famous for its seafood. When you step off the elevator you are cordially greeted by managed staff and then immersed in the romantic ambiance of the Victorian era with elaborate paneling, reproduction gas lamps, dark wallpaper, and busy floral carpeting. The bedrooms open off the long hallway which is lit with skylights and graced by baskets of hanging ferns. Each of the bedrooms is elaborately decorated with splendid antique beds, fireplaces, and Italian-marble sunken bathtubs. No expense was spared— and it shows. In the morning a light breakfast of fresh pastries, seasonal fruits, yogurts, and assorted cheeses is served buffet-style in the small dining room or out on the patio. *Directions:* Take Highway 5 west to 55 south toward Newport Beach and follow the signs to the Newport pier: the hotel is across the street.

DORYMAN'S INN
Owners: Fi Laing & Michael D. Palitz
2102 West Ocean Front
Newport Beach, CA 92663
Tel & fax: (714) 675-7300
10 bedrooms with private bathrooms
Double: $135–$275
Open all year
Credit cards: all major
Children accepted over 5

Heavy iron gates swing open magically, allowing you to enter a world far removed from the neon signs that line the main street of Oakhurst, a town just to the south of Yosemite National Park. You enter through the château's heavy doors, cross a cool, flagged limestone foyer, and step down into a stunning living room opening onto a circular tower room where a grand piano sits center stage beneath a whimsically frescoed ceiling. Doors open to reveal a sunny breakfast room and a tiny chapel. A spiraling stone staircase leads up to the individually decorated bedrooms named for herbs and flowers: Saffron has an enormous ebony bed and black-marble fireplace, Lavender is sunny in bright blues and yellows, and Elderberry is cool in blue and white. Each of the splendid bedrooms has a wood-burning fireplace (placed at just the right height to see it from the bed), goose-down duvet, hidden CD player, luxurious bathroom with a deep soaking tub (many large enough for two), the finest toiletries, thick towels, and the softest of robes. In the evening, just walk across the garden, by the swimming pool, to the Elderberry House Restaurant (closed Tuesday in winter) where the château's owner, Erna Kubin-Clanin, presents a spectacular fixed-price six-course dinner. *Directions:* From the center of Oakhurst take Highway 41 toward Fresno. As the road climbs the hill, turn right at the medical complex and in through the wrought-iron gates.

CHÂTEAU DU SUREAU
Innkeeper: Erna Kubin-Clanin
48688 Victoria Lane, P.O. Box 2413
Oakhurst CA 93644
Tel: (209) 683-6800 Fax: (209) 683-0800
9 bedrooms with private bathrooms
Double: $310–$410, 10% service charge
Open all year
Credit cards: MC, VS
Inappropriate for children

Occidental is a dear country town nestled between the rugged Sonoma coast and the vineyards of the Russian River valley. The Inn at Occidental, a block up from Main Street, dates from 1867 and was refurbished as an inn in 1988. From the wrap-around porch you enter the living room whose intimate and elegant furnishings are set in front of an inviting wood-burning fireplace. The dining room where breakfast is served adjoins the living room. Breakfast offerings include freshly baked pastries and seasonal fruit which precede such tempting delights as orange-thyme pancakes. Beautiful fir floors accented with lovely Oriental carpets are found throughout the public rooms of the inn. The decor of each guestroom is taken from the colors in the original art displayed in the room and feather beds topped with European down comforters assure the guest of a wonderful night's sleep. Recently remodeled, each of the inn's eight rooms now boasts its own appealing amenities such as a romantic fireplace, hot tub in a private garden oasis, or luxurious Jacuzzi tub. Conference facilities are available in a downstairs room with antique pine furnishings and stone fireplace. I can wax eloquent about how lovely the inn is, and yet, the key element that makes this inn so very special and your stay memorable, is its owner, Jack. *Directions:* One hour north of San Francisco, take Highway 101 to Highway 116 west to Sebastopol then the Bodega Highway west for 6 miles toward Bodega Bay to the Bohemian Highway and on to Occidental.

THE INN AT OCCIDENTAL
Owner/Innkeeper: Jack Bullard
Assistant Innkeeper: Dee Wickham
3657 Church Street, Occidental, CA 95465
Tel: (707) 874-1047 Fax: (707) 874-1078
E-mail: innkeeper@occidental.com
8 bedrooms with private bathrooms
Double: $95–$195
Open all year Credit cards: all major
Inappropriate for children

The Inn at Shallow Creek Farm, a simple farmhouse enjoying the quiet and peace of a rural setting just a few miles off Highway 5, offers travelers a shady respite from the never-ending band of asphalt. Mary and Kurt have decorated their fruit-farm inn with family furnishings and mementos, creating a welcoming and pleasingly informal atmosphere, with leather sofas in front of the fireplace comfortably worn by years of guests. Breakfast, which not surprisingly features lots of fresh fruit, is often served in the formal dining room or at tables set on the back sun porch. Just off the living room is the Penfield Suite, a large restful room whose windows are dressed with a soft-yellow printed fabric and a sitting area which enjoys the morning sun (this has the only private bathroom in the main house). The other two guestrooms in the main house share a bathroom at the top of the landing, are cozy, set under the different angles and eaves of the old roof line, and have views out to the garden. Off to the side of the farmhouse is a free-standing cottage with its own fully stocked kitchen, separate living room, bedroom, and bathroom. The paneling in the living room is original to the cottage and its furnishings are basic and simple. *Directions*: Take the Chico-Orland exit from Interstate 5. Go west 2.5 miles then turn right on Road DD. Go half a mile, cross the low bridge, and turn right into the next driveway on the right.

INN AT SHALLOW CREEK FARM   New
Innkeepers: Mary & Kurt Glaeseman
4712 Road DD
Orland, CA 95963
Tel: (916) 865-4093 or (800) 865-4093 Fax: none
4 bedrooms, 2 with private bathrooms
Double: $55–$75
Open all year
Credit cards: MC, VS
Inappropriate for children

Sandwiched between the busier resorts of Monterey and Carmel, Pacific Grove has managed to avoid much of their more touristy ambiance and retains the air of being an inviting Victorian summer retreat. The Gosby House is a perfect place to retreat to, with certainly a lot more fun and frolic than in days gone by when it was the summer home of a stern Methodist family. While the decor is decidedly Victorian in flavor, it has been done with such whimsy and fun that all formal stuffiness has been dispelled: a glass-fronted cabinet in the dining room is filled with antique dolls and teddy bears are posed rakishly on each bed. The bedrooms are scattered upstairs and down, some have garden entrances and several occupy an adjacent clapboard house tucked behind the pretty garden. Over half the bedrooms have fireplaces and all but two have luxuriously appointed bathrooms. Each room is appealingly decorated in soft colors and many benefit from the romantic touch of antique beds. Before you venture out for dinner, enjoy hors d'oeuvres, wine, and sherry in the living room. When you return, your bed will be turned down and a rose and chocolates placed on your pillow—such a sweet way to end the day. *Directions:* Take Highway 1 to Highway 68 west to Pacific Grove. Continue on Forest Avenue to Lighthouse Avenue, turn left, and go three blocks to the inn.

GOSBY HOUSE
Owners: Sally & Roger Post
Innkeeper: Tess Arthur
643 Lighthouse Avenue
Pacific Grove, CA 93950
Tel: (408) 375-1287 Fax: (415) 775-2465
22 bedrooms, 20 with private bathrooms
Double: $85–$150
Open all year
Credit cards: all major
Children accepted in annex rooms

The Green Gables Inn is sensationally positioned overlooking Monterey Bay. This romantic, half-timbered, Queen Anne-style mansion with many interesting dormers is as inviting inside as out. The living room and dining room have comfortable arrangements of sofas and chairs placed to maximize your enjoyment of the view. Upstairs many of the bedrooms, set under steeply slanting beamed ceilings with romantic diamond-paned casement windows, offer ocean views. While the Garret room does not have an ocean view, it is the coziest of hideaways. All but one of the upstairs bedrooms share bathrooms. The ground-floor suite has a sitting room and fireplace. The more modern rooms in the adjacent carriage house all have fireplaces, sitting areas, and private bathrooms. While a guest at The Green Gables Inn you will certainly not perish from hunger or thirst— beverages are available all day, goodies are readily at hand in the cookie jar, and wine and hors d'oeuvres appear in the evening. Breakfast, too, is no disappointment: a hearty buffet of fruit, homemade breads, and a hot egg dish. *Directions:* From Highway 1 take the Pacific Grove-Del Monte exit. As you go through the tunnel, Del Monte becomes Lighthouse Avenue which you follow into Pacific Grove. Go right one block and you are on Ocean View Boulevard—the inn is on the corner at Fifth Street.

THE GREEN GABLES INN
Owners: Sally & Roger Post
Innkeeper: Emily Frew
104 Fifth Street
Pacific Grove, CA 93950
Tel: (408) 375-2095 Fax: (408) 375-5437
11 bedrooms, 7 with private bathrooms
Double: $100–$160
Open all year
Credit cards: all major
Children accepted

The Casa Cody, a moderately priced hotel in the heart of Palm Springs, although quite simple, stands out like a gem from its neighbors. The one-story inn has three U-shaped garden courtyards, two with their own swimming pool. There is a nostalgic, old-fashioned comfort to this pink-stuccoed building with turquoise trim. Once owned by Wild Bill Cody's niece, the Casa Cody (the oldest continuously functioning hotel in Palm Springs) had fallen into a state of hopeless-looking disrepair until bought by Therese Hayes (who is French) and Frank Tysen (who is Dutch). After hard work, lots of imagination, and much love, the hotel once again blossomed into an appealing small hotel with a nice choice of accommodations—ranging from a standard double to a spacious two-bedroom, two-bath suite. Many of the rooms have the added bonus of kitchenettes and fireplaces. The interior decor exudes a fresh, clean "Santa Fe" look with a southwest color scheme and handmade furniture. This friendly, comfortable inn is a remarkable value, especially the reasonably priced studio units such as 1, 2, 3, and 4 that have both fireplaces and well-equipped kitchens. However, my very favorite is the 1920s doll-house-like, one-bedroom cottage (with kitchen) tucked in under the trees in the corner of the property. *Directions:* Drive south through Palm Springs on Palm Canyon Drive. Turn right on Tahquitz-McCallum Road, then left on Cahuilla Road.

CASA CODY
Owners: Therese Hayes & Frank Tysen
Innkeepers: Therese Hayes & Elissa Goforth
175 South Cahuilla Road
Palm Springs, CA 92262
Tel: (619) 320-9346 Fax: (619) 325-8610
17 rooms with private bathrooms
Double: $79–$199
Open all year
Credit cards: all major
Children accepted mid-week

Stopping to chat with a delightful couple lounging by the pool, I was amazed to learn that this was their 36th season of vacationing at the Desert Hills Hotel. Actually, after a tour of the hotel I was not surprised to find the majority of guests return each year. Along with the scent of flowers, a gentle, friendly ambiance permeates the air, enhanced by the charming graciousness of your hostess, Joanne Petty, who built the hotel with her husband in 1956. The location is excellent—an easy walk to the heart of Old Palm Springs and yet snuggled up against the rugged San Jacinto mountains. The hotel does not have an antique ambiance, but rather a timeless theme of restful, pleasing pastel desert colors. The spotlessly tidy guestrooms (most with kitchenettes) are attractive, with liberal use of rattan furniture, comfortable chairs, excellent lighting, and quality mattresses. The rooms face a lush lawn and well-tended gardens surrounding a pretty pool. From the outside the one-story Desert Hills looks like most of the other hotels of similar vintage on the street—you only realize its specialness when you see that every detail shows loving care. The Desert Hills is not a flashy, trendy hotel that would appeal to those looking for action, but rather the old-fashioned kind of tranquil oasis where you can settle in for an extended time, relaxing by the pool, hearing the wind whisper through the palm trees, and feeling like a friend of the family. *Directions:* Turn west off Palm Canyon on Arenas and go six blocks—the hotel is on the northwest corner of Arenas.

DESERT HILLS HOTEL
Innkeeper: Joanne Petty
601 West Arenas Road, Palm Springs, CA 92262
Tel: (619) 325-2777 or (800) 350-2527
Fax: (619) 325-6423
14 bedrooms with private bathrooms
Double: $83–$170
Open all year
Credit cards: MC, VS
Inappropriate for children

As you enter the large wrought-iron gates of the Ingleside Inn, you have the impression of being the guest on a private estate. This is not surprising, since the Ingleside Inn was once the home of the Humphrey Birge family, manufacturers of the Pierce Arrow automobile. Although the hotel is located in the heart of Palm Springs it is an oasis of tranquillity. The parklike grounds are surrounded by a high adobe wall and the San Jacinto Mountains rise steeply behind the hotel, forming a dramatic backdrop. A pretty pool and gazebo highlight the front lawn. Some of the guestrooms open off an inner courtyard, while others are nestled in nearby cottages. Each room is individually decorated with antiques. All have whirlpool tubs, coffee makers, and refrigerators stocked with complimentary light snacks and juices. Many rooms have the added bonus of wood-burning fireplaces. Breakfast is served either on the verandah, poolside, or on your private patio. The owner of Ingleside Inn, Melvyn Haber, also owns one of the famous restaurants in Palm Springs, appropriately called "Melvyn's," which is located next to the lobby. In the evening the restaurant traffic intrudes somewhat upon the solitude, but it is wonderfully convenient to have such an excellent restaurant so close at hand. *Directions:* Drive through Palm Springs south on Palm Canyon Drive and turn right on Ramon Road.

INGLESIDE INN
Innkeeper: Roger Probst
200 West Ramon Road
Palm Springs, CA 92264
Tel: (619) 325-0046 or (800) 772-6655
Fax: (619) 325-0710
30 bedrooms with private bathrooms
Double: $95–$600
Open all year
Credit cards: all major
Children accepted over 16

Most of the newcomers to Palm Springs are slick, trendy resorts trying to outdo each other in money spent on glitzy glamour. However, the magic of the desert can best be captured on balmy, starlit nights from the bougainvillea-shrouded patios of intimate hotels with the laid-back style and grace of yesterday. A rare example of such perfection is the Korakia Pensione, a Moorish-style villa built in 1924 by Scottish artist Gordon Coutts, just four blocks from the heart of the Palm Springs. The derelict building had immediate appeal to Doug Smith who spent four years on a tiny Greek island running a bar and restaurant, catering to the rich and famous yacht set. Doug (an architect specializing in restoring historic buildings) saw the great potential of the Korakia, which reminded him of the sun-drenched houses of the Mediterranean. After several years of love and labor, his dream of a jewel of a small hotel materialized. With a backdrop of the San Jacinto Mountains, this little inn has the flavor of Europe mingled with the romance of the Greek islands: whitewashed walls, Oriental carpets, handmade furniture, lovely natural fabrics, antiques, Moroccan fountains, fragrant fruit trees, and a pool surrounded by gardens create a stunning ambiance. There are 12 bedrooms, but there will be more: Doug has purchased the property across the street and will soon offer additional rooms—reflecting, I am sure, his same faultless taste. *Directions:* Turn west off Palm Canyon on Arenas, go four blocks, turn south on Patencio Road.

KORAKIA PENSIONE
Innkeeper: G. Doug Smith
257 South Patencio Road
Palm Springs, CA 92262
Tel: (619) 864-6411 Fax: none
12 bedrooms with private bathrooms
Double: $79–$169
Closed August
Credit cards: none
Children accepted over 16

The Villa Royale is a romantic desert oasis. From the moment you enter this charming small hotel, you step into a magical world reflecting the essence of Spain: softly splashing fountains, walls draped in bougainvillea, decorative mosaic tile work, secluded little nooks, columned arcades, overhanging tiled roofs, and meandering paths. The guestrooms too are very special. Not only do many have their own wood-burning fireplaces and private spas, but each accommodation represents a country, so you can choose your room to complement your mood, with such options in decor as Irish, English, Moorish, Swiss, Italian, German, Spanish, Dutch, or Greek. There are 3½ walled acres in which the rooms are cleverly arranged for maximum privacy around secluded interior courtyards. Even the least expensive rooms, although small, have style and charm. The main courtyard has a swimming pool with a nearby terrace where tables are set for lunch or snacks. In the evening, dinner is served outside or in a romantic dining room reminiscent of the French countryside. The Villa Royale is located on the edge of Old Palm Springs. *Directions:* Drive south through Palm Springs on Palm Canyon Drive and just a couple of blocks after the road makes a bend to the left and becomes East Palm Canyon Drive, turn left on Indian Trail.

VILLA ROYALE
Innkeeper: Robert Lee
1620 Indian Trail
Palm Springs, CA 92264
Tel: (619) 327-2314 Fax: (619) 322-3794
E-mail: vroyale@earthlink.net
33 bedrooms with private bathrooms
Double: $75–$250
Open all year
Credit cards: all major
Inappropriate for children

When the last of Janet Marangi's four children left the nest, she fulfilled her dream of opening a small bed and breakfast. Just two blocks from the colorful center of South Pasadena, she found an 1895 Victorian-style farmhouse, built by a settler from Indiana for his family. The house is painted a pretty buttercup-yellow, accented by white trim. A white picket fence and old-fashioned swinging gate enclose a perfectly groomed front lawn. Ninety-four rose bushes line the fence and border the path leading to the spacious front porch. Janet's goal was to instill a totally comfortable, homey ambiance, re-creating happy memories of visits to grandmother's house. She has succeeded. The furnishings are mostly pieces lovingly collected over the years by Janet while antique-browsing. The living room is painted a rich green which sets off the white wicker furniture and rich floral fabrics. The five bedrooms are appealingly decorated, each representing an artistic period. The Eighteenth-Century English is a sunny, cheerful room with windows on three sides, king-sized bed, old-fashioned rose-patterned wallpaper, antique desk, dressing table, and white lace curtains. *Directions*: Fifteen minutes from downtown Los Angeles. Take Highway 110 (the Pasadena Freeway) and exit at the Orange Grove off-ramp. Turn right on Orange Grove, go two blocks, and turn left on Magnolia.

THE ARTISTS' INN
Owner: Janet Marangi
Innkeepers: Leah & Scott Roberts
1038 Magnolia Street
South Pasadena, CA 91030
Tel: (818) 799-5668 or (888) 799-5668
Fax: (818) 799-3678
5 bedrooms with private bathrooms
Double: $100–$125
Open all year
Credit cards: all major
Children accepted

Built in the 1880s for the renowned carpet-cleaner family, this is a lovely three-story home with dormer windows and wrap-around porch set on a lush lawn shaded by mature trees just 12 minutes from downtown Los Angeles. On one side of the entry you find the cozy library decorated in dark greens and plaids which looks out onto the swimming pool, and on the other side, through French doors, is the formal living room with its piano and sofas set in front of the fireplace. Central to the living room, the hand-carved wood fireplace opens up at the back so that it also warms the adjacent breakfast room. Just beyond the dining room it is fun to peek into the butler's pantry whose tin roof is original to the home and whose shelves display a lovely collection of Christmas Spode. The Novell Room on the second floor has lovely old wooden floors, twin beds, and private bath. The third floor boasts three romantic accommodations tucked under the eaves. Thoughtful amenities like a communal refrigerator stocked with complimentary refreshments, cookies, and brownies as well as in-room touches such as large fluffy towels, robes, fresh flowers, and a basket of fruit make you feel very welcome and cared for. *Directions*: From either the 134, 210, or 110 freeways, take the Orange Grove Avenue exit. The Bissell House is located on Pasadena's historical Millionaires' Row on the southwest corner of Orange Grove and Columbia. The entrance is on Columbia.

THE BISSELL HOUSE   New
Innkeepers: Russ, Leonore & Ivis Butcher
201 Orange Grove Avenue
South Pasadena, CA 91030
Tel: (818) 441-3535 Fax: (818) 441-3671
4 bedrooms with private bathrooms
Double: $100–$150
Open all year
Credit cards: all major
Inappropriate for children

Petaluma is a charming agricultural town situated on the Petaluma River which feeds into the San Francisco Bay. On a pretty residential street, the Cavanagh Inn is within walking distance of the historic downtown area with its multitude of antique shops and the river. Accommodations are in two neighboring neo-classic Victorian homes sharing a lawn shaded by a large Magnolia tree and enclosed by a white picket fence. The main home was built in 1902 as a family residence and the cottage was added on in 1912 to accommodate the sisters. The main home is lovely, handsome, and rich, with all-redwood floors and walls. Just off the entry is the library and parlor with chairs set in front of an open fireplace and a back dining room which opens onto the back porch and garden. Climb a beautiful staircase to reach a stunning, octagonal redwood-paneled landing. Four guestrooms open onto the landing where you can select from a library of books or find a forgotten item in the thoughtfully provided "basket of remembers." The guestrooms in the house are very comfortable and homey and all have a private bath or shower. The three rooms in the cottage enjoy a welcoming sun porch, are smaller, more calico than Victorian in decor, and two of the rooms share a bath. A gourmet breakfast is offered to all in the dining room of the main house or on the back porch in pretty weather. *Directions:* Traveling Highway 101 north, take Petaluma Boulevard South: follow it to Western Avenue. Turn left, go two blocks to Keller, and make another left on Keller.

CAVANAGH INN
Innkeepers: Jeanne & Ray Farris
10 Keller Street
Petaluma, CA 94952
Tel: (707) 765-4657 Fax: (707) 769-0466
7 bedrooms, 5 with private bathrooms
Double: $75–$125
Open all year
Credit cards: all major
Inappropriate for children

People simply driving by the Inn at Playa del Rey would probably not be drawn inside by the inn's exterior and location on a very busy road. However, this newly constructed Cape Cod-style inn backs onto the Ballona Wetlands, a 350-acre bird sanctuary, and was beautifully designed to complement rather than compete with the setting and natural surroundings. Large picture windows frame a panorama of grassy expanse of wetlands and distant ocean. A narrow channel banded by an inviting bike path weaves a passage through the wetlands, often navigated by tall-masted boats charting a course to the ocean. The decor is light and airy, with pine furnishings matched with lovely fabrics and attractive wallpapers. The guestrooms are each individual in style and floor plan, and maximize any opportunity to incorporate views. The choice rooms are of course those at the back of the inn with unobstructed views of the wetlands. Those at the front are less expensive and enjoy the morning light while dual-glazed and shuttered windows minimize the noise of traffic. Public areas include a front, central outdoor courtyard and a lovely breakfast room and living room running the length of the back of the building, banked by handsome French doors. *Directions:* Exit off the San Diego Freeway (405) onto the Marina Freeway (90) and travel west toward Marina del Rey. The freeway ends at a stoplight at Culver Blvd. Turn left and proceed west 2 miles to the inn.

INN AT PLAYA DEL REY
Owner: Susan Zolla
Innkeepers: Carol Detrick & Donna Donnelly
435 Culver Boulevard
Playa del Rey, CA 90293
Tel: (310) 574-1920 Fax: (310) 574-9920
E-mail: playainn@aol.com
22 bedrooms with private bathrooms
Double: $95–$225
Open all year
Credit cards: all major
Children accepted

The East Brother Light Station, sitting snugly on its own tiny island, dates back to 1873 when it was built to guide ships through a 2-mile-wide strait connecting San Francisco and San Pablo Bays. Adjoining the tower beacon, a small house with gingerbread trim was built for the lightkeepers and their families. This nostalgic lighthouse was doomed for destruction until a group of concerned citizens banded together in 1979, raised the funds, and rescued it. As a boy, one of the saviors, Walter Fanning, spent many happy hours at the East Brother Light Station, where his grandfather was the lighthouse keeper. Today, a few lucky guests enjoy the island in far more commodious circumstances than the keepers of old. Guests are brought by boat in the afternoon, treated to a champagne tour and delicious four-course dinner with wines, then lulled to sleep by the sound of a foghorn. There are four guestrooms, not large or luxurious, but pleasantly decorated with antiques and all with a view of the bay. The innkeepers, Lore and John, live on the island, prepare the meals, and graciously tend to the needs of their guests. Because all the water is caught from the rain and is limited, only guests staying more than one night may use the showers. *Directions:* The East Brother Light Station, located in San Pablo Bay, is reached by boat. When you call for reservations, ask for further information.

EAST BROTHER LIGHT STATION
Owner: US Coast Guard
Innkeepers: Lore Hogan & John Barnett
117 Park Place, Point Richmond, CA 94801
Tel: (510) 233-2385 Fax: (510) 232-5325
4 bedrooms, 2 with private bathrooms
Double: $295*
*Includes breakfast & dinner with wine
Open all year, Thursday to Sunday
Credit cards: all major
Inappropriate for children, unless the entire inn is
  booked by a private party

The known history of the Rancho Santa Fe property dates back to 1845 when an 8,842-acre land grant was given to Juan Maria Osuna. In 1906 the Santa Fe Railroad purchased the land grant, changed the name to Rancho Santa Fe, and planted about three million eucalyptus seedlings with the idea of growing wood for railroad ties. The project failed: the wood was not appropriate, so the railroad decided instead to develop a planned community and built a lovely Spanish-style guesthouse for prospective home buyers. This became the nucleus for what is now the Inn at Rancho Santa Fe and houses the lounge, dining rooms, offices, and a few of the guestrooms. The lounge is extremely appealing, like a cozy living room in a private home, with a large fireplace, comfortable seating, impressive floral arrangements, and a roaring fire. The dining rooms are more "hotel-like" in ambiance. The bedrooms, most tucked away in cottages scattered throughout the property, are attractively decorated with traditional fabrics and furnishings and many have fireplaces. The grounds are lovely, filled with flowers and shaded by fragrant eucalyptus trees. The inn's greatest asset is the Royce family, who own the hotel and give what first appears to be a slick commercial resort the warmth and friendliness of a small inn. *Directions:* From San Diego go north for 25 miles on Highway 5, take the Lomas Santa Fe Drive turnoff, and travel 4-1/5 miles to the inn.

INN AT RANCHO SANTA FE
Innkeeper: Duncan Royce Hadden
Linea del Cielo at Paseo Delicias
P.O. Box 869, Rancho Santa Fe, CA 92067
Tel: (619) 756-1131 Fax: (619) 759-1604
75 bedrooms with private bathrooms
Double: $95–$500 (breakfast not included)
Open all year
Credit cards: all major
Children accepted

Inland from the Del Mar racetrack, tucked into the foothills, you find an exclusive and quietly elegant resort, Rancho Valencia. The sports aficionado will love it here with the multi-tiered tennis courts and privileges at three distinguished private golf clubs, while the romantic will simply settle into one of the 21 individual casitas and hide away in the luxury of its accommodation. The casitas house 43 sumptuous suites, each with its own wet bar, fireplace, vaulted ceiling with overhead fans, spacious bathroom, dressing room, and private garden terrace. The feeling of the complex is Mediterranean, with warm, soft-peach-stucco buildings, doors and windows trimmed in an attractive forest-green, and roofs decked with rich terra-cotta tiles. Lovely garden paths bordered by an abundance of colorful flowers weave through the property and lead to the central lodge whose handsome pine and wicker furnishings set on terra-cotta floors, large open wood-burning fireplaces, and bountiful flower arrangements beckon you indoors. Central to the lodge is a lovely courtyard patio with a soothing fountain, set with tables amidst terra-cotta pots overflowing with flowering plants. On the far side of the lodge is a restaurant whose lovely expanse of window overlooks the tennis courts and surrounding valley—dining here is an epicurean delight. *Directions*: From the Interstate 5 in Del Mar, take the Via de la Valle Road east to San Dieguito Road and follow signs to the resort.

RANCHO VALENCIA RESORT
Director: Michael Ullman
5921 Valencia Circle, P.O. Box 9126
Rancho Santa Fe, CA 92067
Tel: (619) 756-1123 Fax: (619) 756-0165
E-mail: rvr@aol.com
43 suites with private bathrooms
Double: $360–$3,000 (breakfast not included)
Open all year
Credit cards: all major
Children accepted

Tiffany House is a pretty soft-blue Victorian set back behind a white picket fence. Off the front porch the lovely entry serves as the reception and is also central to most of the public rooms. From the formal parlor decorated in 1850s' furniture and rich hues of dark blue, you can climb the stair to the three guestrooms in the main house. The Victorian Rose Room is dressed in colors of greens, mauves, and blacks, reminiscent of the Victorian period, and a claw-foot tub is staged dramatically in the alcove of the turret with distant but unobstructed views of Mount Lassen. Off the landing to the right is the attractive, light, and airy Oak Room whose colors of red, white, and blue complement the nostalgic Americana theme. The Oak Room, hung with 12 signed Wallace Nutting prints, has an inviting sitting area tucked under the eaves and overlooks the peaceful back garden. The Tierra Room is a pretty and restful room with its white iron bed and delicate blue-and-white prints all set under the delightful angles and eaves of the roofline. Accessed off the back garden patio with its own private entrance is Lavinia's Cottage, light, airy, and spacious, with lovely pine walls, a romantic high iron bed, an in-room sunken Jacuzzi, and a sitting area in a large corner of the room blessed with an expanse of paned windows through which you can glimpse Mount Lassen. *Directions*: From Interstate 5 travel west on Lake Boulevard for 4/5 mile to Market Street. Go south on Market to Benton Drive then west on Benton Drive for 1/5 mile to Barbara Road.

TIFFANY HOUSE   New
Innkeepers: Susan & Brady Stewart
1510 Barbara Road, Redding, CA 96003
Tel: (916) 244-3225 Fax: none
E-mail: tiffanyhse@aol.com
4 bedrooms with private bathrooms
Double: $75–$125
Open all year
Credit cards: all major
Inappropriate for children

If you want to be in the heart of historic Saint Helena, close to enticing shops and only steps from some of Napa Valley's finest restaurants, the Inn at Southbridge is a perfect choice. The Inn at Southbridge is an upscale, sophisticated small hotel with charm. There is no pretense that this is an antique building: instead, the well-known architect, William Turnbull, Jr., unabashedly blends the latest enhancements available in modern construction with a traditional, timeless design. The building is new (the hotel opened in November 1995) and features large, extremely well soundproofed rooms which are decorated in a most pleasing, restful style. The decor throughout is refreshingly simple— only the configuration and the color scheme of pastel greens and soft yellows vary from room to room. All of the fabrics and linens are of the finest quality, and perfectly color-coordinated. The wooden furniture (which looks like light cherry) has a simplicity and purity reminiscent of Shaker design. Each of the guestrooms has its own fireplace. The Inn at Southbridge is affiliated with the world-class resort, Meadowood (also in our guide), and guests have access to Meadowood's swimming pool and fitness center for $15 and $25 per couple per day. (Golf and tennis are also available at Meadowood for a fee.) *Directions:* Take highway 29 north from Napa (highway 29 becomes Main street as it passes through Saint Helena). The Inn at Southbridge is located at the south end of town, on the east side of Main Street, just beyond Tra Vigne restaurant.

INN AT SOUTHBRIDGE
Innkeeper: Kristina Schoell
1020 Main Street, Saint Helena, CA 94574
Tel: (707) 967-9400 or (800) 520-6800
Fax: (707) 967-9486
21 bedrooms with private bathrooms
Double: $195–$325
Open all year
Credit cards: all major
Children accepted

On 256 sprawling acres, Meadowood, an attractive complex of sand-gray gabled wooden buildings with crisp white trim, is a resort community in a secluded, quiet valley sheltered by towering Ponderosa pines and Douglas firs. Wooded areas open up to a nine-hotel golf course, two croquet courts, and seven tennis courts. Centrally located, the clubhouse, a rambling, three-story structure overlooking the golf course, houses the country-elegant Restaurant at Meadowood, the less formal Grill, golf shop, conference facilities, and the inviting reception lodge with a wonderful fieldstone fireplace. There are 13 guestrooms in the Croquet Lodge which overlooks the perfectly manicured croquet lawn. Other bedrooms are found in clusters of lodges scattered about the property. The atmosphere, relaxed, informal, and unpretentious, is accurately described as "California casual." Although expensive, the accommodations are luxuriously appointed and attractively furnished, reflecting an incredible attention to detail. Concern for a guest's comfort and satisfaction is foremost and service is carried out with a friendly and professional flair. Meadowood is a luxurious resort with every amenity, including a full-service, state-of-the-art health spa and a most caring staff. *Directions:* From Saint Helena take Pope Street east from Highway 29 to the Silverado Trail. Cross the Silverado Trail, jog to the left and then right on Howell Mountain Road following Meadowood signs.

MEADOWOOD NAPA VALLEY
Director: Jorg Lippuner
900 Meadowood Lane
Saint Helena, CA 94574
Tel: (707) 963-3646 Fax: (707) 963-3532
85 bedrooms with private bathrooms
Double from $345 to $570 (breakfast not included)
Open all year
Credit cards: all major
Children accepted, under 12 free

With an entry tucked off a small shopping arcade on Saint Helena's delightful main street, the Hotel Saint Helena affords an ideal location for those who want to stay within walking distance of shops and a wide range of interesting restaurants. The attractive lobby, decorated in rich tones of burgundy, mauve, and brown, sets an inviting ambiance that is carried through to the decor in the bedrooms. A few steps up off the lobby is an extremely cozy wine bar whose intimate tables are set against rose-colored walls and dressed with pink cloths. Here you can sample by the glass fine Napa Valley wines and accompany your tasting with tempting appetizers or cheese plates. In addition, the wine bar serves a large selection of imported beers, coffees, and teas. A Continental breakfast of croissants, cereal, fresh fruit, and hot beverages is also served in the wine bar and on sunny days you can carry a tray out into the lovely garden courtyard. The hotel's 17 bedrooms and one suite are located up a narrow flight of stairs decorated with attractive prints on the walls. While the guestrooms are on the small side, most have private bathrooms and all are delightfully decorated and furnished with Victorian antiques including some brass headboards and bent-willow furniture. Members of the Martin family share innkeeping duties in the course of the week and Adam Roberts is there to welcome and offer assistance on a daily basis. *Directions:* Located on the west side of Main Street in downtown Saint Helena.

HOTEL SAINT HELENA
Innkeeper: Elisabeth Martin
1309 Main Street
Saint Helena, CA 94574
Tel: (707) 963-4388 Fax: (707) 963-5402
18 bedrooms, 14 with private bathrooms
Double: $130–$250
Open all year
Credit cards: all major
Children accepted

Just off Highway 29 at the corner of El Bonita, on the outskirts of Saint Helena, the Vineyard Country Inn backs onto an expanse of vineyards. Newly constructed to resemble a French country manor, the attention to detail and the quality of appointments is impressive. Handsome slate roofs dotted by whimsical brick chimneys top the inn's complex of buildings. A path winds from the main building which houses the lobby and attractive breakfast room past the enclosed pool and Jacuzzi, through patches of flowering garden to the guestrooms. Accommodations are all suites which enjoy a sitting area in front of a wood-burning fireplace, a game table or work area, and then a bedroom furnished with either a four-poster king bed or two queen sleigh beds. The decor is clean and elegant in its simplicity. Bathrooms are lovely in their tile and wallpaper and are beautifully fresh and modern. Under beamed ceilings, the downstairs rooms (with the exception of two) open onto patios and under vaulted ceilings, all the upstairs rooms open onto private decks. The Vineyard Country Inn offers guestrooms that are spacious and priced well in comparison to other luxury accommodation offered in the valley. A bountiful breakfast buffet is offered in the mornings. *Directions:* Just on the south approach to Saint Helena, traveling Highway 29, the Vineyard Country Inn is located on the left-hand side at the intersection of El Bonita.

VINEYARD COUNTRY INN
Owners: Michael & Mary Ann Pietro
Innkeepers: Gene & Ida Lubberstedt
201 Main Street
Saint Helena, CA 94574
Tel: (707) 963-1000 Fax: (707) 963-1794
21 suites with private bathrooms
Suite: $145–$195
Open all year
Credit cards: all major
Children accepted

The Wine Country Inn is a complex of buildings built of wood and stone, fashioned after the inns of New England, settled on a low hillside and surrounded by acres of vineyards. The inn has twenty-four rooms which have been oriented to enjoy the tranquil and scenic setting: fourteen rooms are housed in the main building, six in the Brandy Barn, and four in the Hastings House. Many of the rooms have private patios, balconies, and fireplaces. Each room, unique in its appeal and character, has its own bath and is individually decorated with country furnishings. Many of the quilts were handmade by the owner. The setting is peaceful, the mood relaxing, and the staff knowledgeable and friendly. Public areas include a lovely lobby which opens onto a large expanse of deck and a pool (now heated all year) on the terraced hillside bounded by a patio and colorful gardens. Room tariffs include a wonderful breakfast and an offering of wine and appetizers in the afternoon. *Directions:* Two miles north of Saint Helena on Highway 29 turn right onto Lodi Lane. The Wine Country Inn is in a quarter of a mile on the left.

THE WINE COUNTRY INN
Innkeeper: Jim Smith
1152 Lodi Lane
Saint Helena, CA 94574
Tel: (707) 963-7077 Fax: (707) 963-9018
E-mail: countryin.aol.com
24 bedrooms with private bathrooms
Double: $120–$250
Open all year
Credit cards: all major
Inappropriate for children

This guide supposedly features small hotels with charm, so how could we even remotely consider including a resort hotel? Especially one with over 700 rooms! The reason is quite simple: there is just nothing else in California to compare with the marvelously whimsical Hotel del Coronado. If you are looking for a secluded hideaway or subdued elegance, this is definitely not your cup of tea. But if you want a hotel with boundless action, plenty of pizzazz, fabulous architecture, and an incredible creamy-white sandy beach, the Hotel del Coronado is tops. Its history dates back to 1887 when Elisha Babcock and H. L. Story purchased Coronado Island. They reserved the prime 33 acres of real estate for their extravagant venture, then sold off the remainder of the land to finance the building of one of the world's largest wooden structures. Within a year, their dream came true. The Hotel del Coronado, a white Victorian, gingerbread-hotel—a fantasy of turrets, wrap-around porches, funny little towers, and perky gables—was ready to open. Over the years, two modern wings have been added, but the original old hotel remains much as it was over a hundred years ago (except of course for a computer game arcade and a virtual shopping paradise discreetly tunneled beneath the building). If you want a modern beach-front room, opt for the new section, but if you value nostalgia, ask to be in the original building (be well aware that some of the rooms are very small). *Directions:* Take Highway 5 to the Coronado Bridge. Turn left on Orange Avenue.

HOTEL DEL CORONADO
Manager: Dean Nelson
1500 Orange Avenue
Coronado, CA 92118
Tel: (619) 435-6611 Fax: (619) 522-8262
700 bedrooms with private bathrooms
Double: $149–$1,275 (breakfast not included)
Open all year
Credit cards: all major
Children accepted

It is a joy to visit the Inn at the Opera and see how with imagination, excellent taste, and (of course) money, a mediocre hotel can be converted into a real gem. Stepping into the intimate lobby is like walking into a lovely home. Comfortable chairs slipcovered in muted green, a superb carpet with a rose design, an antique cabinet, potted palms, soft lighting, and beautiful floral bouquets add to the mood of quiet elegance. From the reception area a hallway leads to one of San Francisco's most appealing small restaurants and cocktail lounge. Here, in the Act IV lounge, the ambiance changes from light and airy to cozy and romantic. Dark paisley-like print wallpaper, rich paneling, subdued lighting, leather upholstered chairs, green plants, beautiful flower arrangements, a baby grand piano playing softly, and the open fireplace create the perfect rendezvous. The guestrooms maintain the same tasteful decor promised by the public rooms. Most have traditional furnishings in dark woods which contrast pleasantly with pastel walls, carpeting, and drapes. The least expensive rooms are quite small, but even these have terry-cloth robes in the armoire, a small refrigerator, microwave oven, two-line telephone with data ports and voice mail, and chocolates on the pillow. *Directions:* As the name implies, the Inn at the Opera is located in the heart of the city's Performing Arts Complex—a perfect hotel choice for patrons of the opera, ballet, and symphony.

INN AT THE OPERA
Innkeeper: Thomas R. Noonan
333 Fulton Avenue
San Francisco, CA 94102
Tel: (415) 863-8400 Fax: (415) 861-0821
Tel: (800) 325-2708 or (800) 423-9610 (in CA)
48 bedrooms with private bathrooms
Double: $140–$280
Open all year
Credit cards: all major
Children accepted

The Inn at Union Square has an absolutely perfect location, smack in the heart of San Francisco—just steps from Union Square, the theaters, and shopping. But it is not just its strategic position that makes this inn so appealing: it is a winner in every respect. The charm is apparent from the moment you enter into the cozy lobby which looks more like the entryway of a country home than a lobby in a commercial hotel. An elevator takes guests to the upper floors. As you step off the elevator, each floor has its own little sitting area where chairs are grouped comfortably around a fireplace and where complimentary tea is served each afternoon from 4 to 6 pm with sandwiches and cakes, followed in the early evening from 6 to 8 pm by wine and hors d'oeuvres. Newspapers are left outside each door in the morning. Guests can either go to the lounge (the same one where tea and wine are served) for Continental breakfast or else they can have a tray brought to their room. The decor in each of the rooms is most attractive, with a traditional mood created by the use of beautiful fabrics and fine furniture. Some of the rooms have their own fireplaces and the penthouse suite has a Jacuzzi tub. Every room, from the least expensive small room to the deluxe suites, is spotlessly maintained and appealing. *Directions*: Located one block off Union Square on Post Street.

THE INN AT UNION SQUARE
Owners: Nan & Norman Rosenblatt
Innkeeper: Brooks Bayly
440 Post Street
San Francisco, CA 94102
Tel: (415) 397-3510 Fax: (415) 989-0529
E-mail: inn@unionsquare.com
30 bedrooms with private bathrooms
Double: $130–$300
Open all year
Credit cards: all major
Children accepted

The Marina Inn is not a typical country inn: in fact, it is a large, four-story building whose boxy exterior is made more lively by tiers of bay windows. But as soon as you enter, the successful effort to achieve the warmth of a homey inn is immediately apparent. The lobby is small and intimate, with light-pine furniture, a pair of handsome upholstered chairs, green potted plants, and off-white walls. The staff is friendly and eager to be helpful. An elevator leads upstairs to the bedrooms, each similar in decor with two-poster country beds, pastel-print wallpaper, comfortable chairs, light-pine armoires, and forest-green carpeting. In addition to being pleasantly decorated, the rooms offer all the amenities of a proper hotel: television in each room, comfortable queen-sized beds, direct-dial telephones, and modern bathrooms with toiletries and marble sinks. On the second floor a sitting room is provided where in the morning a buffet Continental breakfast is served and in the afternoon complimentary sherry. One of the nicest merits of this hotel is its excellent price—a real value for such a spiffy place. Other pluses: Cribs are provided for babies and children under five are free of charge. The hotel is located just a brisk walk from Fisherman's Wharf, Ghirardelli Square, and the Saint Francis Yacht Club. *Directions:* Take Van Ness Avenue north to Lombard Street. Turn left and go three blocks to Octavia.

MARINA INN
Innkeeper: Suzie Baum
3110 Octavia
San Francisco, CA 94123
Tel: (415) 928-1000 Fax: (415) 928-5909
40 bedrooms with private bathrooms
Double: $55–$95
Open all year
Credit cards: all major
Children accepted

The Petite Auberge is a lovely little hotel on Bush Street sitting next to its sister "Four Sisters" hotel, the White Swan. Whereas the White Swan has an English flavor, the Petite Auberge is like a romantic French country inn snuggled at the heart of the city, just steps from the famous theater district and exclusive shopping and fine dining. The façade is most appealing—a narrow, four-story building with a double column of bay windows bordered by narrow windows decorated with flowerboxes. An antique carousel horse, burnished woods, and soft pastel colors give a warm welcome to the cozy entry. Each guestroom is attractively decorated with delicate colors, all have private baths, and many have fireplaces. Downstairs there is a suite with a private outside entrance and deck. Wine and tea are available every afternoon for those guests who want a quiet moment after a busy day. A delicious breakfast is served buffet style in the delightful breakfast room with its French marketplace mural and sliding glass doors giving onto a pretty patio where you can sit in pleasant weather. Breakfast includes a selection of teas and coffee, homemade breads, fruit, a hot dish, cereals, and pastries. *Directions:* Take Van Ness Avenue north to Bush Street. Turn right on Bush and go approximately 1 mile. The inn is between Taylor and Mason.

PETITE AUBERGE
Owners: Sally & Roger Post
Innkeeper: Brian Larsen
863 Bush Street
San Francisco, CA 94108
Tel: (415) 928-6000 Fax: (415) 775-2465
26 bedrooms with private bathrooms
Double: $110–$220
Open all year
Credit cards: all major
Children accepted

The Sherman House is an oasis of luxury and provides San Francisco with some of its most exceptional accommodation and personalized and attentive service. This French Italianate three-story mansion was built in 1876 for Leander Sherman, founder of the Sherman Clay Music Company and host to a number of famous musicians who performed within its walls. A soaring, three-story music hall is now a stunning salon for hotel guests. The main house contains 11 rooms or suites, while the carriage house, set in the middle of the gardens designed by Thomas Church, offers three spectacular suites. Armoires, mirrors, desks, chairs, paintings, and chandeliers have been carefully selected for each room. Each room, although grand in decor is not necessarily grand in size, has a grand canopy bed, sumptuously draped in luxurious fabrics with feather-down mattresses, and a magnificent private bath finished in black granite with the exception of one in Chinese slate. The restaurant is open only to hotel residents and is spectacular when compared to any of the world's finest restaurants. The chef shops every day to obtain only the freshest and finest ingredients and plans his menu accordingly. *Directions:* From the south, take Highway 101 to Fell Street, bear left onto Fell for one block, then turn right on Webster. After about 35 blocks turn left off Webster onto Green Street. The Sherman House will be in the middle of the block on the right-hand side.

SHERMAN HOUSE
Owner: Manou Mobedshahi
Manager: Christine Berlin
2160 Green Street
San Francisco, CA 94123
Tel: (415) 563-3600 Fax: (415) 563-1882
14 bedrooms with private bathrooms
Double: $295–$825 (breakfast not included)
Open all year
Credit cards: all major
Children accepted

The Spencer House does not look like a hotel and there is no sign in front of the beautiful old Victorian to give any clue that guests are solicited. Yet within this stately, immaculately maintained mansion is one of San Francisco's most personalized, delightful places to stay. The owners, Barbara and Jack Chambers, have converted a woefully neglected charmer back to its original glory—the attention to detail and the amount of love, labor, and money that must have gone into the project is astounding: the floors gleam again as when first installed, Lincresta Walton wall coverings have been restored to their original perfection, the living room and bedrooms have been padded and "papered" with beautiful fabric to soften any distracting noises, the kitchen looks straight out of *Gourmet*, the original gas lights are still operable. Barbara took advantage of Jack being a commercial airline pilot and flew to London to pick out all of the exquisite fabrics and many of the gorgeous antiques used throughout. It is like being in a private home with each guestroom exuding its own personality, but all, even the smallest, are most inviting. One of the greatest assets of the inn is Barbara, a superb hostess and a fabulous cook. Breakfast is always a memorable, gourmet event and dramatically presented using the finest china and silver. *Directions:* From the south, take Highway 101 to Fell Street. Turn left off Fell onto Baker then three blocks on to Haight.

SPENCER HOUSE
Innkeepers: Barbara & Jack Chambers
1080 Haight Street at Baker
San Francisco, CA 94117
Tel: (415) 626-9205 Fax: (415) 626-9230
6 bedrooms with private bathrooms
Double: $105–$175
Open all year
Credit cards: all major
Children accepted over 16

For those familiar with San Francisco, Union Street is always a favorite place to dine, shop, and play. The several blocks of Union Street which stretch out at the foot of exclusive Pacific Heights offer charming restaurants and pretty boutiques in quaint Victorian houses. Right in the heart of this attractive area, snuggled into a pretty, off-white Victorian house, is The Union Street Inn. Steps on the left side of the building lead up to the front door which opens into a small reception foyer. To the left is an old-fashioned parlor, comfortably furnished with antiques. Doors from the parlor lead out to the most special feature of the inn—an exceptionally attractive, English-style garden where a brick path meanders through a medley of shrubs, flowers, and shade trees. At the end of the garden, behind a white picket fence, is a cute cottage that has been converted into a guest suite. In the house itself are five more guestrooms, each individually decorated in a traditional style. My favorite is the English Garden Room which has its own small deck overlooking the garden. All of the rooms have a welcome basket of fresh fruit. Continuing the mood of hospitality, wine and hors d'oeuvres are set out for guests each afternoon, and in the morning a full breakfast is served. Your hosts are Jane Bertorelli, who is English, and David Coyle, who is Irish. They oversee every detail of the inn and personally welcome guests. *Directions:* Take Van Ness north and turn west on Union Street. The inn is located on the left between Fillmore and Steiner.

THE UNION STREET INN
Owners: Jane Bertorelli & David Coyle
2229 Union Street
San Francisco, CA 94123
Tel: (415) 346-0424 Fax: (415) 922-8046
6 rooms with private bathrooms
Double: $125–$225
Open all year
Credit cards: all major
Children accepted

The Washington Square Inn has a great location in the North Beach area, facing historic Washington Square. Within easy strolling distance is a wealth of wonderful little places to eat and a bit farther, but an interesting walk through Chinatown, are the theaters and shops of the Union Square area. From the moment you enter, the ambiance of the French countryside surrounds you—an antique dining table, mellowed with age and surrounded by country chairs, stretches in front of large windows framed with tie-back drapes. A superb armoire, large gilt mirrors, baskets of flowers, and a fireplace with an antique wooden mantel add to the country appeal. In the afternoon guests have tea in front of the fire and in the morning an expanded Continental breakfast of juice, fruit, muffins, breads, croissants and hot and cold cereals, is served here (if guests prefer, breakfast will be brought to their room). Two staircases lead to the guestrooms, each individually decorated. From the simplest room with shared bathroom to the most luxurious suite, each of the rooms, dressed with beautiful coordinating fabrics, exudes a lovely country charm. A couple of rooms have cozy bay windows accented with inviting sitting nooks. Under new ownership, the Washington Square Inn will benefit from the current upgrades and improvements under way as this edition goes to press. The restaurant next door, Moose's, serves fine Italian cuisine. *Directions:* In North Beach, on Washington Square.

WASHINGTON SQUARE INN
Innkeeper: David A. Norwitt
1660 Stockton Street
San Francisco, CA 94133
Tel: (415) 981-4220 or (800) 388-0220
Fax: (415) 397-7242
15 bedrooms, 10 with private bathrooms
Double: $120–$195
Open all year
Credit cards: all major
Children accepted

The White Swan Inn, a small, London-style hotel with English-country decor, has a splendid location just steps from a wide selection of quaint restaurants and a five-minute walk from San Francisco's fabulous Union Square shopping and theater district. But the appeal of the White Swan is far greater than its setting: from the moment you enter, you will know immediately that this is not a standard commercial hotel. A small sitting area greets you, with a reception desk to your right, but the heart of the inn is down a flight of stairs where a spacious lounge awaits with one section set up with tables and chairs for breakfast—a hearty meal of coffee, muffins, a hot entree, juices, and cereals. Beyond the eating area is a pretty living room with a fireplace and comfortable lounge chairs. Next door is the library, cricket bat mounted on the wall, another cozy area for relaxing. Although the inn is in the center of the city, French doors open out from a conference room at the back onto a deck and small English-style garden. The bedrooms are beautifully decorated with pretty coordinating fabrics. Each room has a separate sitting area, fireplace (which can be turned on by a bedside switch), small refrigerator, wet bar, direct-dial telephone, and color television. This hotel is an absolute delight. *Directions:* Take Van Ness Avenue north, turn right on Bush and go approximately 1 mile. The inn is between Taylor and Mason.

WHITE SWAN INN
Owners: Sally & Roger Post
Innkeeper: Brian Larsen
845 Bush Street
San Francisco, CA 94108
Tel: (415) 775-1755 Fax: (415) 775-2465
26 bedrooms with private bathrooms
Double: $145–$250
Open all year
Credit cards: all major
Children accepted

The Gerstle Park Inn, a rambling wood-shingled home on 1½ acres, is a beautiful inn set in a residential district of San Rafael, caters mostly to businessmen, local families, and Sausalito's overflow. The inn carries an air of sophistication wonderfully complemented by a homey and welcoming ambiance. You enter the main house from the back garden into the entry which doubles as the reception. You can settle just off the entry in the formal living room or continue on to the enclosed wrap-around porch which serves as a very intimate and elegant breakfast room. Each guestroom is individual in its decor and appeal. On the ground floor the Grove Suite, the smallest room, has a double brass bed and enjoys a private smoking deck, while the Leonhard Suite is a spacious room with a handsome king bed and marvelous Jacuzzi tub. Upstairs, rooms range from the Redwood Suite, cozy and romantic with its pine-planked, low-angled ceiling and wooded views afforded by a row of windows tucked right at ceiling height, to the San Rafael Suite, spanning the length of one end of the building, with its twin beds and large deck facing the surrounding hills. All the rooms enjoy amenities and conveniences such as two-line telephones with voice mail, televisions, VCRs, hairdryers, and robes. For Judy and Jim Dowling, your gracious and talented hosts, running Gerstle Park Inn is a dream fulfilled. *Directions*: Exit Highway 101 at San Rafael Central exit. Go east on 3rd Street, then left on D Street, right on San Rafael Avenue, and left on Grove Street.

GERSTLE PARK INN   New
Innkeepers: Judy & Jim Dowling
34 Grove Street
San Rafael, CA 94901
Tel: (415) 721-7611 Fax: (415) 721-7600
10 bedrooms with private bathrooms
Double: $119–$179
Open all year
Credit cards: all major
Children accepted

The Cheshire Cat is comprised of two lovely beige and white Victorians sitting side by side near the center of Santa Barbara and connected by a tranquil bricked patio (where breakfast is served on all but grim days). Behind the patio a Jacuzzi is sheltered by a lacy white gazebo. In the foyer a grouping of *Alice in Wonderland* figurines placed on a small table beside the guest book immediately sets the whimsical theme of the inn: each of the rooms is named for an *Alice in Wonderland* character with the exception of two rooms—Jean's (named for the owner Chris's mother) and the Eberle Suite (named for the previous owners). Laura Ashley coordinated prints and wallpapers are used throughout with different color schemes, from plums and creams in the Mad Hatter Room to smoke-blue and cream in the Dormouse's Room. Each bedroom is different: some are dramatic with a large Jacuzzi bath in the bedroom, some have cozy bay windows, others an intimate private balcony. Two wonderful recently added suites, Tweedle Dum and Tweedle Dee, are located above the garage and enjoy the luxury of space, fireplace, Jacuzzi, and their own entrance off the back garden. Loving touches make each guest feel special: fresh flowers in the rooms, individual bottles of Baileys Cream, and delicious chocolates. *Directions:* Exit Highway 101 at Mission Street, go east on Mission Street for five blocks, right on State Street for three blocks, and right on Valerio.

THE CHESHIRE CAT
Owner: Christine Dunstan
Innkeepers: Jenny Martin & Tracey Miller
36 West Valerio Street
Santa Barbara, CA 93101
Tel: (805) 569-1610 Fax: (805) 682-1876
14 bedrooms with private bathrooms
Double: $135–$269
Closed Christmas
Credit cards: MC, VS
Children accepted over 8, mid-week

Set on 22 acres across from Santa Barbara's famous beach is a lovely resort, the Four Seasons Biltmore—hardly a country inn, but very representative of what Santa Barbara has to offer. The beautiful adobe complex's lovely old tiled roofs, wrought-iron fixtures, weathered beams, arched doorways, tiled floors, shuttered windows, secluded patios, lush expanse of lawn, and beautifully manicured gardens lend a Mediterranean warmth and an elegant ambiance that is both inviting and comfortable. If you enter the gorgeous lobby with its lovely tiled floors mirroring dramatic flower arrangements in the afternoon, you will be drawn to a lower lobby where a formal afternoon tea is served in front of a roaring fire. Lunch is a lazy affair on the outdoor patio under umbrellas with an unobstructed view across an expanse of lawn to the glistening blue Pacific. Indoors is the elegant La Marina restaurant whose roof opens up to the evening stars on warm summer nights. Accommodation is attractive—not luxurious, but comfortable. Most guestrooms are in buildings clustering around the pool, but there are 12 free-standing cottages lining the outer edge of the property and rail line which are very popular. The Biltmore is exceptional because of the quality of service and attention to detail. Guests of the Biltmore can use, for a nominal fee, the private club across the street with its pool and fitness facility. *Directions:* Four miles south of Santa Barbara exit Highway 101 at Olive Mill Road and travel half a mile to the ocean and Channel Drive.

FOUR SEASONS BILTMORE
General Manager: John Indrieri
1260 Channel Drive
Santa Barbara, CA 93108
Tel: (805) 969-2261 Fax: (805) 969-4682
234 rooms with private bathrooms
Double: $225–$1,700
Open all year
Credit cards: all major
Children accepted

Not a new inn to Santa Barbara, the Secret Garden, however, has realized its potential under the wonderful ownership of Christine of the long-recommended Cheshire Cat. This complex of cottages shaded by trees and banded by a beautiful garden, is lovely. With her sophisticated eye, Christine has not made dramatic changes, but rather subtle ones to the decor that surprisingly make a huge difference to the appeal and ambiance of the inn. The main building houses an inviting living room, a lovely country dining room, and two of the guest accommodations. The other guestrooms are extremely private, located in individual guest cottages with their own entrance—very romantic, peaceful, and restful. Each room has its own decor and special appeal, such as Hummingbird with a private deck and hot tub and Nightingale with a spacious living room and wonderful wood-burning fireplace. Central to the cottages at the back of the main house is a lovely, lush garden that surrounds a patio shaded by persimmon, avocado, and mock orange trees. On mornings blessed with sunshine, tables are set here for breakfast. Ensuring quiet, televisions are available only on request. *Directions*: From Highway 101 northbound, exit at Arrellaga Street; from Highway 101 southbound, exit at Mission Street, travel two blocks to Bath Street. Cross streets are Arrellaga and Mission.

THE SECRET GARDEN INN
Owner: Christine Dunstan
Innkeeper: Jack Greenwald
1908 Bath Street, Santa Barbara, CA 93101
Tel: (805) 687-2300 or (800) 676-1622
Fax: (805) 687-4576
E-mail: garden@silcom.com
10 bedrooms with private bathrooms
Double: $110–$195
Open all year
Credit cards: all major
Children accepted in Wood Thrush Cottage

The Simpson House Inn, a handsome, rosy-beige Victorian landmark with white and smoke-blue trim, is located on a quiet residential street only a five-minute walk from the main shopping attractions of State Street. The lush surrounding gardens of the inn include an acre of lawn banded by beautiful flower beds and mature shade trees. One of the most irresistible features of the inn is a cheerful back porch under an arbor of draping wisteria with white wicker chairs and comfy pillows: a perfect niche to enjoy the garden. In the main house the sitting room and dining room are quite formal. However, the formality disappears upstairs in the charming guest chambers, each individually decorated to suit different tastes—some are lacy and frilly, others have a more tailored look. Each room enjoys niceties such as terry-cloth robes, fresh flowers, bottled water, and sherry. Off the lawn in the back garden are three cottages which are beautifully decorated in rich fabrics and intimate with a Jacuzzi tub nestled right into a bay window. The barn also offers spacious accommodations, light and airy, whose pine furnishings are perfect against the exposed beams of the original barn. Although the Davies's presence is still felt, they now employ a very efficient and capable staff to oversee the duties of the inn. *Directions:* From downtown take Santa Barbara Street northeast toward the Mission, then turn left onto Arrellaga.

SIMPSON HOUSE INN
Owners: Linda & Glyn Davies
Manager: Dixie Adair Budke
121 East Arrellaga Street
Santa Barbara, CA 93101
Tel: (805) 963-7067 Fax: (805) 564-4811
14 bedrooms with private bathrooms
Double: $140–$300
Open all year
Credit cards: all major
Children accepted

The Tiffany Inn is an especially handsome old Victorian separated by a lawn from a rather busy street in Santa Barbara's residential area. Although the traffic in front is a bit distracting, the back garden is very charming and gives a quiet retreat for guests with an attractive, lattice-covered verandah set with prettily covered wicker chairs. If you are a fan of beautifully decorated Victorians, you will thoroughly enjoy a stay at the Tiffany Inn. Carol has done a lovely job of decorating, with romantic, old-fashioned antiques accented by well chosen, colorful fabrics. The living room with its grouping of sofas and chairs around a fireplace is just the perfect place to sit and relax while planning sightseeing adventures. Each comfortable bedchamber exudes its own charm and character and several have the added bonus of a cozy, log-burning fireplace. For those who crave privacy, one of the rooms has its own outside entrance and the added bonus of breakfast delivery each morning. Other guests enjoy a hearty breakfast of an entree, fresh fruits, muffins, and coffee served in the dining room or on sunny days in the peace and quiet of the lattice-covered porch in the back garden. *Directions:* Exit Highway 101 in Santa Barbara at Mission Street, drive east to De La Vina, turn right and the inn is on your right

TIFFANY INN
Innkeepers: Carol & Larry MacDonald
1323 De La Vina Street
Santa Barbara, CA 93101
Tel: (805) 963-2283 or (800) 999-5672
Fax: (805) 962-0994
7 bedrooms with private bathrooms
Double: $125–$200
Open all year
Credit cards: all major
Children accepted

The foundations of The Babbling Brook Inn date back to the 1790s when padres from the Santa Cruz Mission built a grist mill on the property, taking advantage of the small stream to grind corn. In the late 19th century a tannery powered by a huge water wheel was constructed. A rustic log cabin remains today as the "heart" of the inn with a living room where guests congregate around a roaring fire with tea and coffee and homemade cookies. The historic wheel was recently returned to the brook pond. Most of the guestrooms are in shingled chalets nestled in the garden surrounded by pines and redwoods and overlooking the idyllic little meandering brook. Each of the 12 guestrooms is decorated in European country style with an individual flair and has a private bathroom, telephone, radio with alarm, and television. Most have a cozy fireplace, private deck, and an outside entrance—four have deep, soaking, jet bathtubs. Helen King, who is the owner and manager, adds greatly to the warmth and charm of her appealing little inn. Helen, who has won many awards for her cooking, not only keeps guests well supplied with cookies, but also serves a delicious full breakfast each morning. *Directions:* From San Jose or San Francisco take Highway 17 to Santa Cruz. Turn north on Highway 1, then left on Laurel for one and a half blocks to the inn.

THE BABBLING BROOK INN
Innkeeper: Helen King
1025 Laurel Street
Santa Cruz, CA 95060
Tel: (408) 427-2437 or (800) 866-1131
Fax: (408) 427-2457
12 bedrooms with private bathrooms
Double: $85–$165
Open all year
Credit cards: all major
Children accepted over 12

The Channel Road Inn dates back to 1910 when Thomas McCall, a Scotsman who made a fortune in Texas oil and cattle, moved to California where he built an elaborate wood-shingled home for his family of six daughters. Although the house was large to begin with, a third story was later added, giving plenty of space for 14 guestrooms. The house has an interesting location: just on the fringe of the elegant suburb of Pacific Palisades yet on a busy street that leads through the somewhat honky-tonk neighborhood to the beach. But, oh what a beach! The wide, sandy stretch of the Santa Monica beach is a wonderful playground. The downstairs lounge and dining areas are sedately decorated, beautifully in keeping with the style of the home. The guestrooms, tucked throughout the large house, are all individually decorated and each has its own personality. My favorite rooms were number 1, one of the less expensive rooms but delightful with a fresh white-and-blue color scheme, and a more expensive room, number 11, with stripped-pine furniture looking so pretty against the dark-green carpet. Kathy can help you pick out a room when you make a reservation. *Directions:* From Highway 405 take 10 west, then Route 1 north about 2 miles. Turn right on West Channel Road.

CHANNEL ROAD INN
Owner: Susan Zolla
Innkeeper: Kathy Jensen
219 West Channel Road
Santa Monica, CA 90402
Tel: (310) 459-1920 Fax: (310) 454-9920
E-mail: channelinn@aol.com
14 bedrooms with private bathrooms
Double: $145–$225
Open all year
Credit cards: all major
Children accepted

With the opening in 1993 of Shutters on the Beach, a stunning, deluxe hotel emerged in the Los Angeles area. The property fronts directly onto the superb Santa Monica beach and although it is of new construction, the hotel has a delightfully nostalgic mood. The attractive, Cape Cod-like whisper-gray, wood-shingled building is enhanced by white gingerbread trim. I am not sure how it is accomplished, but there is an engaging, home-like ambiance throughout—perhaps it is the low ceiling, or the cozy groupings of plump, comfy sofas, or the fireplaces. The designer's goal was to create an inn where guests would feel that they were staying at a friend's beach house rather than a commercial hotel: the goal has certainly been achieved. My favorite rooms are in the two-story building that fronts the sea. A garden terrace (where white lounge chairs are grouped around an attractive swimming pool) spans a small street to connect the beach house with a more traditional-looking hotel section. All of the guestrooms are attractive: pastel blues, aquas, beiges, and peach colors accent a predominantly white color scheme. An uncluttered, simple yet elegant mood prevails, enhanced by fine linens and furniture of excellent quality. Every room has heavy wooden, white louvered shutters which give the hotel its name. *Directions*: Go west on Highway 10 (Santa Monica Expressway) to Santa Monica. Take the 4th Street exit south to Pico Boulevard.

SHUTTERS ON THE BEACH
Director: Klaus Mennekes
One Pico Boulevard
Santa Monica, CA 90405
Tel: (310) 458-0030
Fax: (310) 458-4589
198 bedrooms with private bathrooms
Double: $305–$2,450 (breakfast not included)
Open all year
Credit cards: all major
Children accepted

The Gables is a fine example of a bed and breakfast whose owners' love, dedication, and caring enhance the comfort and welcome and make it a very special place to stay. Judy and Mike selected The Gables, an aristocratic Victorian home on the outskirts of Santa Rosa, with a dream of opening a bed and breakfast. Although the Gables enjoys an expanse of 3 acres at the back, with a wonderful old barn that creaks with age, the home sits just off Petaluma Hill Road. A little traffic can be heard from the front guestrooms, but the rooms at the back overlooking the garden fully enjoy the quiet of the country meadow setting. The decor throughout the inn is in keeping with the grandeur of the home. Guestrooms are spacious and pretty with a country-Victorian theme. Accommodation is also offered in a dear side cottage which enjoys its own little sitting area, fireplace, kitchenette, Jacuzzi tub, and cozy upstairs sleeping loft. Judy is quite an accomplished cook and her casual afternoon tea features homemade cookies and brownies. Breakfasts are quite a repast with freshly squeezed juice, fruit, and a main course—a bounty that will take one right through to dinner. Mike is a talented craftsman and he is responsible for many of the fine finishes throughout the inn, most notably a wonderful birdcage, home to some beautiful finches, which sits on the inn's back deck. *Directions:* From San Francisco travel Highway 101 north to Sonoma County. Exit at Rohnert Park Expressway. Turn right off the exit ramp and travel 2½ miles, turning left on Petaluma Hill Road.

THE GABLES
Innkeepers: Judy & Mike Ogne
4257 Petaluma Hill Road
Santa Rosa, CA 95404
Tel: (707) 585-7777 Fax: (707) 584-5634
7 bedrooms with private bathrooms
Double: $103–$189
Open all year
Credit cards: all major
Children accepted in the cottage

Sausalito is a quaint waterfront town with fabulous views across the bay to San Francisco. Alongside the harbor runs one main street from which small roads spider-web up the steep hillside checkered with many Victorian houses. Among these is a lovely home, built in 1885, with marble fireplaces, stained-glass windows, wrought-iron grillwork, and lacy wood trim, which has been converted to a wonderful hotel. The dining room and a few of the guestrooms are in the original home, while the rest of the rooms are in a new building which terraces down the hill. Guestrooms in the original house have been refurbished in Victorian style with all the behind-the-scenes amenities added for modern comfort. The newer rooms are larger, enjoy bay views and each has its own style of decor. Casa Cabana has a southwest flavor; Misia's Lilac and Lace is all fancy with eyelet and laces; La Belle Provence is very pretty in its country-French style and colors; Summer House is light and airy with light woods and wicker furniture; Artist's Loft is most appealing with a cottagey New-England look and a tempting easel set center stage—to mention just a few! The restaurant, with its large glassed-in porch, and gorgeous views, is popular for dinner or Sunday brunch. *Directions:* By ferry from San Francisco or by car on Highway 101 across the Golden Gate Bridge to Alexander Avenue which becomes Bridgeway.

CASA MADRONA HOTEL
Innkeeper: John W. Mays
801 Bridgeway
Sausalito, CA 94965
Tel: (415) 332-0502 Fax: (415) 332-2537
E-mail: casa@abn.com
34 bedrooms with private bathrooms
Double: $105–$245
Open all year
Credit cards: all major
Children accepted

Just beyond Sausalito's yacht club and ferry dock, right on the water's edge, sits The Inn Above Tide, very cleverly converted to an inn from what was originally an apartment complex and then most recently an office building. All of its 30 rooms enjoy million-dollar views of the San Francisco Bay and skyline and all are appropriately stocked with binoculars. Twenty-four of the rooms have wonderful little decks whose partitioning wall is of glass, creating the illusion of being right on the water, almost boatside. The remaining six rooms, although without a deck, benefit from being a little more spacious. All the rooms are attractive, light, and airy so as not to compete with the view, many have fireplaces, and the decor plays on a nautical theme with porthole windows and blue-and-white prints with little fish. The two suites are both spectacular, spacious rooms with magnificent views of the city and private decks. The buffet in the Parlor is set in the evenings with an offering of wine and cheese, and mornings with a Continental breakfast. (Breakfast may also be enjoyed in the privacy of your guestroom.) If you want to use Sausalito as a base from which to explore San Francisco, you can easily journey back and forth by ferry, avoiding the hassle and cost of a car. *Directions*: From San Francisco cross the Golden Gate Bridge and exit on Alexander Avenue. Alexander becomes Bridgeway. Turn right toward the water after the first stop light, on El Portal.

THE INN ABOVE TIDE   **New**
Owner: William H. McDevitt
Manager: Verena Zürcher-Burgoon
30 El Portal, Sausalito, CA 94965
Tel: (415) 332-9535 Fax: (415) 332-6714
E-mail: inntide@ix.netcom.com
30 bedrooms with private bathrooms
Double: $195–$400
Open all year
Credit cards: all major
Children accepted

Located on the eastern outskirts of Shingletown near Mount Lassen National Park, Weston House offers a private oasis nestled on 5½ mountaintop acres with million-dollar views of meadows, valleys, and mountains stretching for miles below. The setting and views are breathtaking and the handsome complex of wood-shingled houses complement rather than compete with the setting. Running the length of the main house is a magnificent lap pool banded by an expanse of deck whose various levels afford intimate settings from which to enjoy the sweeping panorama. There are currently just four guestrooms: Rhys's Room and Vanessa's Room, named for Angela's children, share the tower wing. Rhys's Room, accessed off the pool deck, is on the ground floor and shares the Westons' own spectacular master bath. Climb the stair in the tower to Vanessa's Room, my favorite, with a lovely queen bed angled in the corner to maximize the view through the sliding glass door across the small private balcony to some fabulous views, and enjoying a bath and wood stove. Just up from the pool and off a meadow of glorious wildflowers are Helen's and Laura's rooms, very popular two rooms with guests. Note: As restaurant options are limited and quite a distance away, you might want to consider packing a picnic dinner. A full breakfast is offered. *Directions*: Take Shingletown Ridge Road (on the west side of town) off Highway 44 and then turn left on Red Rock Road. Signs encourage you along as the road winds, weaves, narrows, and changes from asphalt to loose gravel.

WESTON HOUSE   New
Innkeepers: Angela & Ivor Weston
Red Rock Road, P.O. Box 276
Shingletown, CA 96088
Tel: (916) 474-3738 Fax: (916) 244-1850
4 bedrooms, 3 with private bathrooms
Double: $85–$130
Open all year Credit cards: MC, VS
Inappropriate for children

The renovated El Dorado Hotel is located on the Spanish Plaza in the town of Sonoma. Built in 1843 by Salvador Vallejo, the stately El Dorado offers 26 rooms with private bath and balcony. It is owned by a corporation, but managed by an efficient, professional staff. The decor throughout the hotel is clean, fresh, and attractive with tile floors, cream-colored walls, and white trim. The entry just off the square serves as the reception and also as the passageway to the hotel's highly regarded Ristorante Piatti (specializing in regional Italian cuisine) and two retail shops (a women's clothing store and antique store). Most of the guestrooms are found by climbing the stairs from the reception area, although there are four rooms with enclosed patios located off the courtyard by the pool. The guestrooms are comfortable in size and identical in their decor with four-poster pewter beds, color television, sliding shuttered windows, and soft pastel colors. The quietest bedrooms are those overlooking the vine-covered interior courtyard, but since most rooms face the street, the choice of location cannot be confirmed in advance. *Directions:* The town of Sonoma is 60 miles to the north of San Francisco and 15 miles south of Santa Rosa. The El Dorado Hotel is located on the northwest corner of the town's main square.

EL DORADO HOTEL
Innkeeper: Jana Trout
405 First Street West
Sonoma, CA 95476
Tel: (707) 996-3030 or (800) 289-3031
Fax: (707) 996-3148
26 bedrooms with private bathrooms
Double: $85–$145
Open all year
Credit cards: all major
Children accepted

On a full hilltop acre above the town of Sonora, the attractive Barretta Gardens Inn, built around 1895, sits off the road in the shade of its own mature and lush landscaped garden. Barretta Gardens benefits from the enthusiasm, dedication, and graciousness of its new proprietors, Mike and Nancy Brandt, who have thoughtfully refurbished the inn to give it its present fresh and tastefully elegant appearance. Just off the formal Victorian living room is an appealing solarium, a plant-filled room set with white furniture, enclosed on each side by a wall of windows overlooking the outside foliage. On the other side of the living room with its an array of family pictures and a handsome grandfather clock is the dining room whose custom table is original to the home. Two guestrooms are found on the entry level. The Krystal room, with its wall of windows looking out to the Sonora hills, is dressed in greens and maroons and enjoys a large Jacuzzi for two and a private bath. Christy, off the living room with windows overlooking the front porch, is set under 10-foot-high ceilings and a crystal chandelier. Beautiful Italian beds have been converted to accommodate a queen mattress. Its private bath is across the hall. Upstairs, the Stephanie room is pretty in a wash of rose, while the Angelina room boasts Nancy's mother's brass king bed. A small parlor sits between the Angelina room and the pretty Gennylee room which together can be rented as a two-room suite or as a one-room suite with just the Gennylee room. *Directions*: Barretta Street is off business Highway 108.

BARRETTA GARDENS INN   New
Innkeepers: Mike & Nancy Brandt
700 South Barretta Street,Sonora, CA 95370
Tel: (209) 532-6039 or (800) 206-3333
Fax: (209) 532-8257
5 bedrooms with private bathrooms
Double: $95–$250
Open all year
Credit cards: MC, VS
Children accepted

The Casa del Mar, a Mediterranean-style home crowning a maze of lovely terraced gardens, is a pastel-peach, three-story stucco building with a red-tile roof. Refreshingly different from most California bed and breakfasts, there are no fussy frills to the decor of Casa del Mar: it has fresh white interior walls, furnishings of light pine and wicker, terra-cotta tiled floors, and colorful fabrics. For accent, the owner, Rick Klein, has selected bright and dramatic paintings and sculptures from local talent. The guestrooms are modest in size, with just enough space to accommodate a queen mattress set upon a custom-made wood platform and a corner chair or two. The closet is a functional alcove with a free-standing chest of drawers. Four guestrooms (Passion Flower, Shell, Hummingbird, and Heron) have subtle decorative touches to match their name and balconies where chairs are set for you to enjoy the view. Although spartan and a little worn, the decor is fitting for a beach and park setting. Just steps from the bed and breakfast is an entrance to the park which accesses hundreds of miles of trails, while two blocks down the road is the justifiably famous white sandy stretch of Stinson Beach. *Directions:* As you drive into town from the south, the first building on the right is a small firehouse. Turn right at the firehouse onto Belvedere Avenue: Casa del Mar is located 100 yards just up the street on the left.

CASA DEL MAR
Innkeeper: Rick Klein
37 Belvedere Avenue, P.O. Box 238
Stinson Beach, CA 94970
Tel: (415) 868-2124 or (800) 552-2124
Fax: (415) 868-2305
4 bedrooms with private bathrooms
Double: $125–$220
Open all year
Credit cards: all major
Children accepted over 6

Sutter Creek is a charming Gold Country town whose main street is bordered at either end by New England-style residences surrounded by green lawns and neatly clipped hedges. Occupying one of these attractive homes is The Foxes, an idyllic hideaway put together with great flair and taste by Min and Pete Fox. The symbol of the inn is the fox and the perky little fellow pops up everywhere, yet this is not an inn with a cutesy theme, but an unpretentious, sophisticated inn where everything has been done with exquisite flair. Four suites are found in the main house and three new suites have been added to the rear. The Honeymoon Suite is the largest, most elegant bedchamber where a large brick fireplace overlooks a magnificent bed and gorgeous Austrian armoire. Sparkling crystal chandeliers light the enormous bathroom. In the Foxes' Den a border of foxes, hunt prints, a hunting horn, leather-bound books, and leather chairs set before the fireplace give the room an inviting study feel. Each suite has a sitting area with a table to accommodate breakfast. Min and Pete discuss with you what you would like for breakfast and then it is brought to your room with silver service accompanied by a large pot of coffee or tea. The Foxes pamper guests. *Directions:* Sutter Creek straddles Highway 49, 4 miles north of Jackson. The Foxes is at the north end of Main Street.

THE FOXES
Innkeepers: Min & Pete Fox
77 Main Street, P.O. Box 159
Sutter Creek, CA 95685
Tel: (209) 267-5882 Fax: (209) 267-0712
7 suites with private bathrooms
Suite: $115–$145
Closed Christmas
Credit cards: all major
Inappropriate for children

Grey Gables Inn is a pretty, soft-gray-blue house detailed with a white trim sitting appealingly behind a stone fence within easy walking distance of the wonderful array of shops and restaurants in Sutter Creek. A red-brick pathway winds to the front entrance and weaves its way through a lovely back garden with fountains, vine-covered arbors, and a patchwork of flowers. Inside this newly constructed inn, the ambiance reflects the owners' heritage—Roger and Sue Garlick hail originally from the Cotswolds and they have brought a touch of the English countryside to the Mother Lode. Seven of the eight guestrooms are named for an English poet. Browning, Byron, Wordsworth, and Shelley are located on the main floor, just off the entry, while Keats, Brontë and Tennyson are found on the lower garden level. Garden-level rooms have fewer windows and, although described as cozy, are on the dark side. Secluded away on the top floor is the Victorian Suite. All the rooms are decorated with floral spreads that complement the decor in hues of greens, rose, and mauve. All rooms have fireplaces, most have garden views, and some enjoy claw-foot tubs. Guests settle in the formal dining room and parlor to enjoy a traditional afternoon tea with scones, refreshments with cakes and wine in the early evening, and a bountiful breakfast. *Directions*: Grey Gables Inn is located on the west side of Highway 49 on the north side of town.

GREY GABLES INN   **New**
Innkeepers: Sue & Roger Garlick
P.O. Box 1687, 161 Hanford Street
Sutter Creek, CA 95685
Tel: (209) 267-1039 or (800) 4739-9422
Fax: (209) 267-0998
E-mail: greygables@cdepot.net
8 bedrooms with private bathrooms
Double: $95–$135
Open all year Credit cards: all major
Inappropriate for children

The Cottage Inn, built as a resort in 1938, offers a number of story-book cottages nestled under the trees on the edge of Lake Tahoe. Parking is limited, so unfortunately the drive that weaves through the grounds is hampered by guests' cars. The lovely cottages, all with individual themes, capture the mountain-cabin atmosphere with their exposed knotty-pine walls, rich fabrics, Swedish pine furniture, and a variety of beds (brass, willow, or pine). The Fireplace Room has the added attraction of a wood-burning fireplace. The Pomin House, the original home on the property, contains a reception area, a breakfast room, and a large sitting room with games, books, local restaurant menus, and a small sitting area where wine and cheese are set out in the afternoons before the blazing log fire. In summer you can happily while away the hours sunning yourself on the dock and swimming in Lake Tahoe's cool, clear waters—the inn boasts its own private beach. The more energetic can take advantage of the lovely bicycle trail that passes in front of the inn and travels the lakeshore drive. Vikingsholm, Emerald Bay, and D.L. Bliss Park are a short car ride south. Ski resorts are between a five-minute and twenty-minute drive distant. *Directions*: From the Bay Area take Highway 80 to 89 Tahoe City exit, follow the river to Tahoe City, and continue south on 89 following West Lake Boulevard: the inn is 2 miles along on your left.

THE COTTAGE INN   New
Owners: Patti & Terry Giles
Innkeeper: Donna Nash
1690 West Lake Boulevard, P.O. Box 66
Tahoe City, CA 96145
Tel: (916) 581-4073 Fax: (916) 581-0226
15 bedrooms with private bathrooms
Double: $140–$210
Open all year
Credit cards: MC, VS
Inappropriate for children

Lake Tahoe is an exquisite, crystal-clear blue lake ringed by pines and backed by high mountains. The only outlet for this enormous body of water is the Truckee River, and standing on a broad river bend some 3 miles downstream is River Ranch. This lodge enjoys a marvelous river setting, and the circular bar with its picture windows and expanse of outdoor patio opening onto the river is particularly popular with the winter après-ski crowd and summertime rafters. On a recent visit, public areas were worn from the traffic of heavy winter boots, but the bedrooms were still attractive. All the guestrooms have phones, televisions, and river views. The very nicest have queen-size beds and private balconies, while one very inexpensive tiny room has bunk beds. Accommodation is comfortable but on busy days and nights the restaurant and patio tend to be crowded and noisy. In the mornings, a basic Continental breakfast of sweet rolls, muffins, and beverages is served in the bar. This is not a country inn, but rather a lodge-style hotel which serves as a convenient base from which to explore the area. The ski resorts of Squaw Valley and Alpine Meadows are close at hand for winter fun, with sightseeing, hiking, trout-fishing, and river-rafting as favorite summer pastimes. *Directions:* From the Bay Area take Highway 80 to the 89 Tahoe City exit and follow the river to River Ranch.

RIVER RANCH
Innkeeper: Peter Friedrichsen
2285 River Road, P.O. Box 197
Tahoe City, CA 96145
Tel: (916) 583-4264 or (800) 535-9900
Fax: (916) 583-7237
21 bedrooms with private bathrooms
Double: $75–$185
Open all year
Credit cards: all major
Children accepted

Newly constructed to resemble a mountain retreat, this handsome two-story wooden lodge backs right onto the West Shore of Lake Tahoe, offering guests a million-dollar view of lake and mountain. Public areas indoors are cozy and inviting, with antler chandeliers, high-vaulted ceilings, exposed beams, rich fabrics, and a dominating riverstone fireplace. All the public rooms frame the wonderful view with large picture windows and open onto a deck which runs the length of the lodge. With sailboats moored right off the deck in the lodge's own marina, the Sunnyside Lodge is popular with locals as well as with resident guests. A stair just off the entry winds up to the 23 guestrooms categorized as either lakeview, lakefront, or suite. I was unable to view a suite, but the standard rooms are all well appointed, a nice comfortable size, well lit, and equipped with modern baths. Off the upstairs landing a modest buffet of hors d'oeuvres is available in the afternoons and a Continental breakfast buffet is set out in the mornings. Also off the upstairs corridor is a large central patio set with lounge chairs. Be aware that since this is a lodge and a popular place to dine or spend an afternoon, public areas are designed to accommodate many, not just overnight guests. *Directions*: Take Highway 89 to Tahoe City and then travel south along West Lake Boulevard to the district of Sunnyside. The lodge is located 1-4/5 miles south of Tahoe City on the lakeside.

SUNNYSIDE RESTAURANT & LODGE   ***New***
Manager: Janet Patterson
1850 West Lake Blvd
P.O. Box 5969
Tahoe City, CA 96145
Tel: (916) 583-7200 Fax: (916) 583-2551
23 bedrooms with private bathrooms
Double: $110–$185
Open all year
Credit cards: all major
Children accepted

The Lost Whale, a gray-wash Cape-Cod house with blue trim set on the windswept coast of northern California, was designed by Susanne and Lee Miller who manage it with a refreshing, bountiful enthusiasm. The mood is set by the living room with its fir floors warmed by throw rugs, and comfortable sofas arranged to enjoy not only the fireplace but also the magnificent view across the garden, through the towering pine trees to the ocean. Five rooms capture this same glorious view while three overlook the quiet road that runs behind the inn. Whichever room you select you will find it decorated in a light, airy decor. Several rooms have an extra bed to accommodate a child and two have a sleeping loft. Whereas most inns discourage children, here at The Lost Whale they are made genuinely welcome. Relax on the deck or strategically placed chairs in a quiet corner of the garden and listen to the crashing waves and the distant barking of sea lions. Stroll down the cliff path to the little beach or pop into your car for the short drive up the road to Patrick's Point State Park which offers miles of beaches, walking paths along rocky headlands, and the opportunity to explore a re-created Indian village. The Lost Whale is a homey inn in a spectacular setting. *Directions:* North from Trinidad take the Seawood Drive exit, cross under the freeway, travel 1-1/8 mile north on Patrick's Point Drive. South from Oregon, exit at Patrick's Point Drive, continue south 1 mile.

THE LOST WHALE
Innkeepers: Susanne Lakin & Lee Miller
3452 Patrick's Point Drive
Trinidad, CA 95570
Tel: (707) 677-3425 Fax: (707) 677-0284
E-mail: lmiller@lost-whale-inn.com
8 bedrooms with private bathrooms
Double: $125–$155
Open all year
Credit cards: all major
Children accepted

The Trinidad Bay Bed & Breakfast is a Cape Cod-style home constructed in 1949, painted barn-red with crisp white trim, located just across the road from the Trinidad Memorial Lighthouse. Although neither the building nor the furnishings are old, this small inn is very inviting. You enter into a cheerful family room with a brick fireplace faced by a sofa and flanked by two wooden rockers. A table is set prettily for breakfast which consists of homemade jams, hot baked bread and muffins, and fresh fruit. Upstairs are two double rooms, each with an alcove in the dormer with views of the coast. Above the garage is a suite with the best view from its long strip of windows overlooking the harbor. The fourth room, a suite on the ground floor, has a wrap-around window, king-sized bed, a fireplace for cozy evenings, its own private entry, and a private area of the garden perfect for soaking up the magnificent view of ocean and rocky headland. Both suites enjoy the luxury of breakfast delivered to the room. There is nothing outstanding in the decor, but then there is no pretense: this is just a homelike inn, but immaculately clean with everything shining with a "just scrubbed" look. The best part of all is the location: overlooking Trinidad Bay, whose old wharf still looks like a proper wharf should and where the trails along the magnificent headlands still maintain their unspoiled splendor. *Directions:* Take the Trinidad exit west off Highway 101 to Trinidad Bay Memorial Lighthouse—the inn is across the street.

TRINIDAD BAY BED & BREAKFAST
Innkeepers: Carol & Paul Kirk
560 Edwards Street, P.O. Box 849
Trinidad, CA 95570
Tel: (707) 677-0840 Fax: none
4 bedrooms with private bathrooms
Double: $125–$155
Closed December & January
Credit cards: MC, VS
Children accepted

Immediately south of Santa Monica, Venice Beach is one of Los Angeles' most popular stretches of beach and its Oceanfront Walk draws a colorful crowd. Just a block from the bustle of Oceanfront Walk is a lovely residence offering bed and breakfast accommodation, the Venice Beach House. Sheltered behind its own fence and lovely gardens, the Beach House is inviting with a lived-in ambiance and comfort. You enter from the front porch into an open and pretty sitting room where iced tea and cookies are set out in the afternoons and a full breakfast is served each morning. Fresh flowers dress the room which is warmed on cooler days by a wood-burning fireplace. The welcome by the innkeeper is casual and relaxed, yet gracious and warm. The home has nine guestrooms of varying sizes, five of which enjoy a private bathroom, and are decorated like bedrooms in a private home. Just off the front room the Olympic Suite, which commemorates the 1932 Olympic games hosted by Venice Beach, is lovely, with a large bay window which seems to bring the garden into the room. Favorite rooms upstairs are the Abbott Kinney, small but cozy with its own porch and decorated in a tartan of blues and greens, and the Pier Suite which boasts an ocean view and a wood-burning fireplace. *Directions:* Exit the 405 at Washington Street and travel west to Speedway. The Venice Beach House is located off Speedway between 29th and 30th. Limited private parking is found on the north side of the inn.

VENICE BEACH HOUSE
Innkeepers: Phillip & Vivian Boesch
15 Thirtieth Avenue
Venice, CA 90291
Tel: (310) 823-1966 Fax: (310) 823-1842
9 bedrooms, 5 with private bathrooms
Double: $85–$165
Open all year
Credit cards: all major
Children accepted

Contra Costa County by and large comprises bedroom communities for San Francisco commuters. Walnut Creek is one of its more attractive towns, having the advantages of both freeways and the fast, high-tech Bay Area Rapid Transit trains to whisk you into San Francisco. Surprisingly, this urban enclave has a perfect hideaway inn for those who want to get away from San Francisco and yet cannot travel very far. The Mansion at Lakewood is a lovely Victorian estate sitting behind high, white, wrought-iron gates in a quiet residential neighborhood of ranch-style homes. Sharyn and Mike McCoy bought the Mansion as a dilapidated home and after extensive renovations opened it as a country inn, giving it a new lease on life with luxurious appointments and inviting decor. The bedrooms range from the cozy Attic Hideaway to the opulent Estate Suite where an extraordinary antique four-poster brass bed draped with lace and soft pink damask sits center stage. The suite's enormous bathroom has every luxurious amenity: Jacuzzi tub, extra large shower, his and hers vanities, oodles of soft towels and fluffy robes. A breakfast of hot, flaky, homemade croissants and fresh fruit is exquisitely presented. The former ballroom has been transformed into The Secret Garden tea room, offering tea luncheons in the style of English high tea. *Directions:* From Highway 680 take Ygnacio Valley Road north, turn right on Homestead and left on Hacienda: downtown Walnut Creek is just ¼ mile away.

THE SECRET GARDEN MANSION
Innkeepers: Sharyn & Mike McCoy
1056 Hacienda Drive
Walnut Creek, CA 94598
Tel: (510) 945-3600 Fax: (510) 945-3608
7 bedrooms with private bathrooms
Double: $135–$300
Open all year
Credit cards: all major
Children accepted over 13

The Ahwahnee with 123 bedrooms hardly qualifies for inclusion in a country inn guide. It is a large, bustling resort with a level of activity in its lobby that is comparable to that at many airports, yet it merits inclusion because it is the most individual of hotels, with all the sophistication of a grand European castle, surrounded by the awesome beauty of Yosemite Valley. The lofty vastness of the lounge dwarfs the sofas and chairs and its huge windows frame magnificent views of the outdoors. The dining room has to be the largest in the United States: it is gorgeous with its massive floor-to-ceiling windows framing towering granite walls, cascading waterfalls, and giant sugar pines. In contrast to the surrounding wilderness the dining room wears an air of sophistication in the evening when guests dress for dinner and flickering candlelight casts its magical spell. Bedrooms are in the main building or in little cottages in a nearby woodland grove. There is a small swimming pool just off the back patio and it is not unusual to see deer grazing on the lawn. This is undeniably a grand old hotel but if the price tag is a little rich for your blood, less expensive accommodations in Yosemite Valley are briefly outlined on pages 60 and 61. *Directions:* The Ahwahnee is located in Yosemite Valley just east of Yosemite Village.

THE AHWAHNEE
Innkeeper: Deborah S. Price
Yosemite National Park, CA 95389
Tel: (209) 372-1407 Fax: (209) 456-0542
Reservations: (209) 252-4848
E-mail: yosemitepark.com
123 bedrooms & cottages,
 all rooms with private bathrooms
Double: $215–$641 (breakfast not included)
Open all year
Credit cards: MC, VS
Children accepted

While the attractions of staying in Yosemite Valley cannot be denied, a more serene, country atmosphere pervades the Wawona Hotel, located within Yosemite Park about a 27-mile drive south of the valley. With its shaded verandahs overlooking broad, rolling lawns and a 9-hole golf course, the hotel presents a welcoming picture that invites one to while away the afternoon beside the pool, fondly referred to as the swimming tank. Bedrooms are in several scattered buildings and private bathrooms are at a premium. Bedrooms without private facilities use two blocks of men's and women's bathrooms, which can be situated a long walk from your bedroom. The hotel was refurbished in 1987 with a most attractive decor. This is the kind of wonderful old hotel that attracts lots of families. In the summer rangers give interpretive presentations on such topics as bears, climbing, and photography and there are carriage rides, wonderful Sunday brunches, Saturday-night barbecues, and barn dances. The Wawona now offers two bed-and-breakfast packages: Autumn Golf and Winter Romance, both very good value for money. *Directions:* Wawona is in Yosemite National Park, 27 miles south of Yosemite Valley on Highway 41.

WAWONA HOTEL
Innkeeper: Martha Moses
Yosemite National Park, CA 95389
Tel: (209) 375-6556 Fax: (209) 456-0542
Reservations: (209) 252-4848
E-mail: yosemitepark.com
105 bedrooms, 50 with private bathrooms
Double: $71–$98 (breakfast not included)
Closed mid-week January to Easter
Credit cards: MC, VS
Children accepted

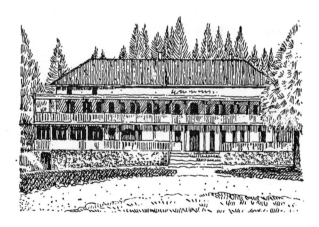

Located high above the Napa Valley, where the Yountville Cross Road meets the beautiful Silverado Trail, the Cross Roads Inn is a lovely home with redwood siding, large windows, and a multitude of decks from which to soak in and breathe the beauty of the wine country. The view, once your car negotiates the steep driveway, is truly breathtaking—a panorama of peaceful vineyards and the Mayacamas mountains as far as you can see. This contemporary home, which was built as an inn, is situated so that every one of its four suites can fully appreciate the commanding view. Their decor is light and airy, reminiscent of romantic children's books. The wine bar and Jacuzzi spa in each room, without the intrusion of phone or television, provide just the right accompaniments for a sybaritic getaway. A full breakfast, taking advantage of the many in-season fruits available to the area, is served in your spacious room or on the deck right outside. Your gracious innkeeper, Nancy Scott, is more than happy to arrange for dinner reservations, hot-air balloon rides, and other diversions. Twenty-three acres with hiking trails surround the inn where you can enjoy native flora and fauna. *Directions:* From Highway 29 north, turn right onto Madison Street into Yountville. Turn left up Yount Street and then right onto Yountville Cross Road to the Silverado Trail. Take another right turn and then a very quick left into the inn's driveway.

CROSS ROADS INN
Innkeepers: Nancy & Sam Scott
6380 Silverado Trail
Yountville, CA 94558
Tel: (707) 944-0646 Fax: none
4 suites with private bathrooms
Suite: $225–$250
Closed Christmas
Credit cards: MC, VS
Children accepted over 16

The location of the Maison Fleurie is superb—right in the heart of the quaint town of Yountville, within walking distance of great shopping and a selection of restaurants. The inn (with a look of the French countryside) is a romantic cluster of thick stone and brick buildings, entrancingly draped with ivy. From the moment you enter, the mood is conducive to a carefree holiday. You come into a parlor-like foyer with a corner fireplace, sofa, and chairs. When you begin to wonder if this is a hotel, you notice a discreet reception desk in the room beyond. To the right, a few steps lead down to an inviting lounge where two comfortable sofas (slip-covered with a pretty floral fabric) flank a brick fireplace. The price of the bedrooms depends upon size—the larger are more expensive. None are especially spacious, but all are appealingly decorated and well priced for value received. The friendly, well managed Maison Fleurie offers many extras: not only is a hearty breakfast served in the morning, but also wine and hors d'oeuvres in the late afternoon. Cold and hot drinks are available all day, along with cookies. The morning paper, bathrobes, turn-down service, and the complimentary use of bicycles are additional amenities. Tucked into the courtyards behind the inn are a swimming pool and a hot tub. *Directions:* Coming north from Napa on Highway 29, turn right into Yountville onto Washington Street. When the road splits, keep to the right onto Yount Street. You will see the inn on your left.

MAISON FLEURIE
Owners: Roger & Sally Post
Innkeeper: Roger Asbill
6529 Yount Street, Yountville, CA 94599
Tel: (707) 944-2056 Fax: (707) 944-9342
13 bedrooms with private bathrooms
Double: $110–$200
Open all year
Credit cards: all major
Children accepted

The Vintage Inn is a large hotel complex nestled between Highway 29 and the main street of Yountville. The 80 rooms are housed in an attractive mix of two-story green and blue, wood-sided and red-brick buildings which are connected by meandering paths. We recommend the Vintage Inn as an alternative to bed and breakfast accommodation, if you seek a bit more anonymity, privacy, and the full services of a luxury hotel. A concierge is present for assistance, a limited menu is offered poolside and through room service, and the stretch limousine parked at the front entry is available for hire. Guestrooms are very attractive in their decor, spacious, and comfortable, equipped with television, fireplace (duraflame logs), coffee maker, a complimentary bottle of wine, tub-shower with Jacuzzi jets, and terry-cloth robes. Turn-down service is offered each evening and appreciated touches such as a fresh supply of towels and bedside chocolates are thoughtfully provided. In the mornings, an appetizing champagne breakfast buffet of juice, hot beverages, fresh-baked pastries, cereals, yogurt, and fruit is set out in the front lobby and You can sit either inside or at tables on the patio. The Vintage Inn has a capable management team which extends a courteous welcome and strives to please. *Directions:* Take the Yountville exit off Highway 29, turn right at the bottom of the exit, then a quick left on Washington Street. The Vintage Inn is just off Washington Street beyond Vintage 1870.

VINTAGE INN
Innkeeper: Patti Larson
6541 Washington Street
Yountville, CA 94599
Tel: (707) 944-1112 Fax: (707) 944-1617
80 rooms with private bathrooms
Double: $175–$275
Open all year
Credit cards: all major
Children accepted

Key Map

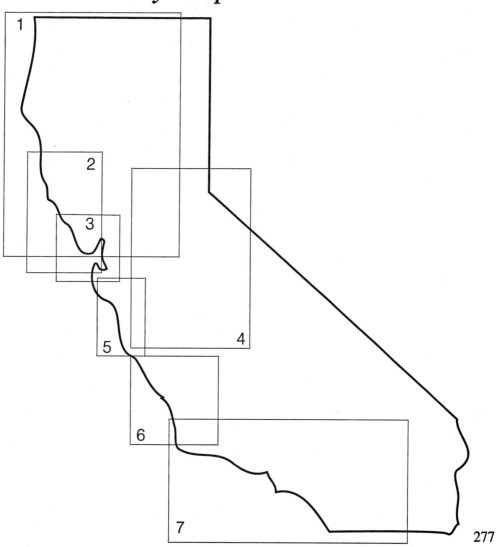

Map 1

OREGON

Crescent City

Yreka

Mt. Shasta

McCloud

Trinidad

299

Burney

Cassel

Eureka

101

Weaverville

Redding

Shingletown

Lassen Volcanic National Park

Ferndale

Scotia

Igo

Garberville

5

Drakesbad

Leggett

Ft. Bragg

Willits

Mendocino

Little River

101

Orland

Chico

Albion

128

Ukiah

Elk

Boonville

Manchester

Cloverdale

1

Geyserville

SACRAMENTO

Healdsburg

Gualala

116

Guerneville

Ft. Ross

Santa Rosa

Occidental

1

Petaluma

Inverness

San Rafael

Muir Beach

SAN FRANCISCO

P A C I F I C
O C E A N

● Places to Stay

○ Points of Reference

a	b	Quadrants
c	d	

279

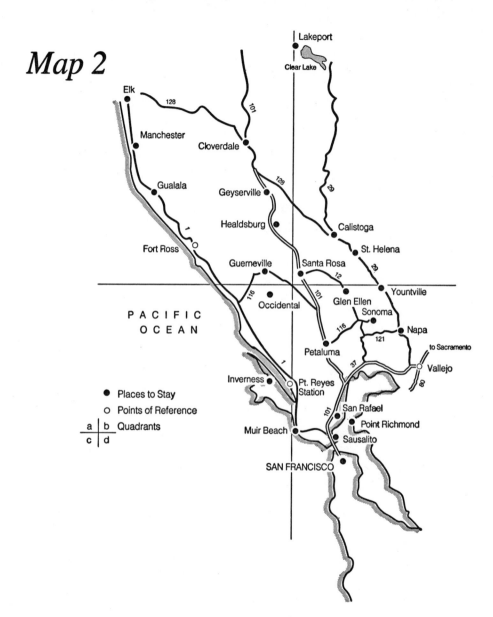

Map 2

Lakeport

Clear Lake

Elk

128

101

Manchester

Cloverdale

128

29

Gualala

Geyserville

Healdsburg

Calistoga

Fort Ross

St. Helena

1

29

Guerneville

Santa Rosa

Yountville

116

12

Occidental

101

Glen Ellen

Sonoma

PACIFIC
OCEAN

116

Napa

121

to Sacramento

Petaluma

Vallejo

1

37

80

Inverness

Pt. Reyes
Station

101

San Rafael

● Places to Stay

○ Points of Reference

Point Richmond

a	b
c	d

Quadrants

Muir Beach

Sausalito

SAN FRANCISCO

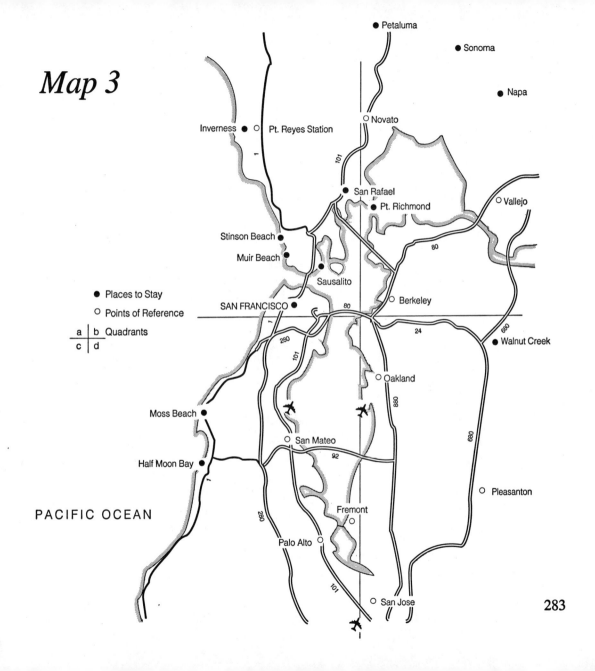

Map 3

Petaluma

Sonoma

Napa

Inverness ● ○ Pt. Reyes Station

○ Novato

101

● San Rafael
● Pt. Richmond

○ Vallejo

80

Stinson Beach ●

Muir Beach ●

Sausalito ●

● Places to Stay
○ Points of Reference

a	b	Quadrants
c	d	

SAN FRANCISCO ●

80

○ Berkeley

24

680

280

101

● Walnut Creek

○ Oakland

880

Moss Beach ●

○ San Mateo

92

680

Half Moon Bay ●

○ Pleasanton

1

PACIFIC OCEAN

280

Fremont
○

Palo Alto ○

101

○ San Jose

283

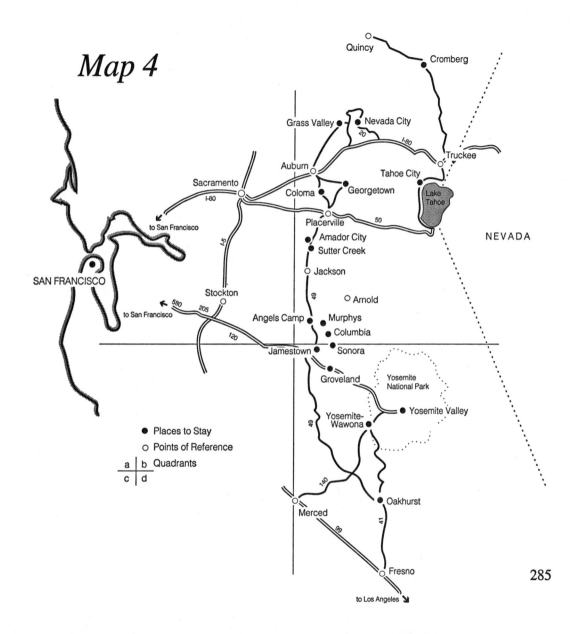

Map 4

Quincy

Cromberg

Grass Valley ● ● Nevada City

20

I-80

Truckee

Auburn

Sacramento

I-80

Coloma ● ● Georgetown

Tahoe City

Lake Tahoe

NEVADA

to San Francisco

I-5

Placerville

50

Amador City

Sutter Creek

Jackson

SAN FRANCISCO

Stockton

Arnold

49

to San Francisco

580 205

120

Angels Camp ● ● Murphys

● Columbia

Jamestown ● ● Sonora

Groveland

Yosemite National Park

Yosemite Valley

Yosemite-Wawona

● Places to Stay

○ Points of Reference

a	b
c	d

Quadrants

49

140

Oakhurst

Merced

99

41

Fresno

to Los Angeles

Map 5

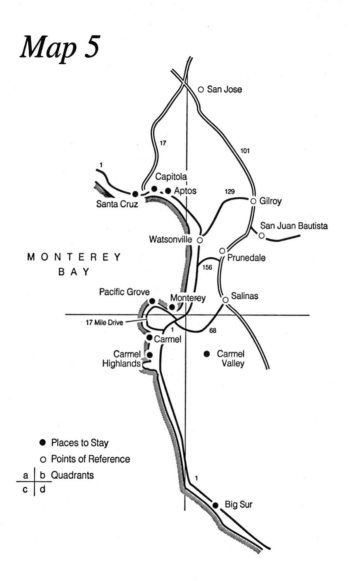

○ San Jose

17

101

1

Capitola
● Aptos

Santa Cruz

129

○ Gilroy

San Juan Bautista
○

Watsonville ○

MONTEREY
BAY

○ Prunedale

156

Pacific Grove

Monterey

○ Salinas

17 Mile Drive

1

68

● Carmel

Carmel
Highlands

● Carmel
Valley

● Places to Stay
○ Points of Reference

a	b
c	d

Quadrants

1

● Big Sur

287

Map 6

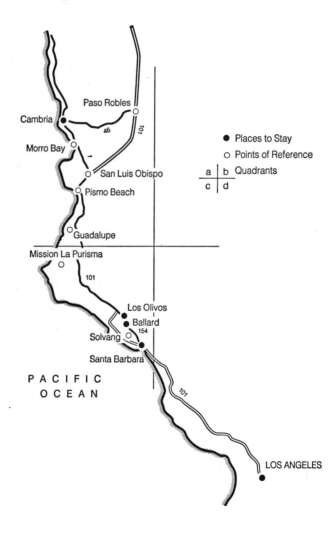

Paso Robles

Cambria

Morro Bay
46
101
1

San Luis Obispo

● Places to Stay
○ Points of Reference

a	b
c	d

Quadrants

Pismo Beach

Guadalupe

Mission La Purisma
101

Los Olivos
Ballard
154
Solvang

Santa Barbara

PACIFIC
OCEAN

101

LOS ANGELES

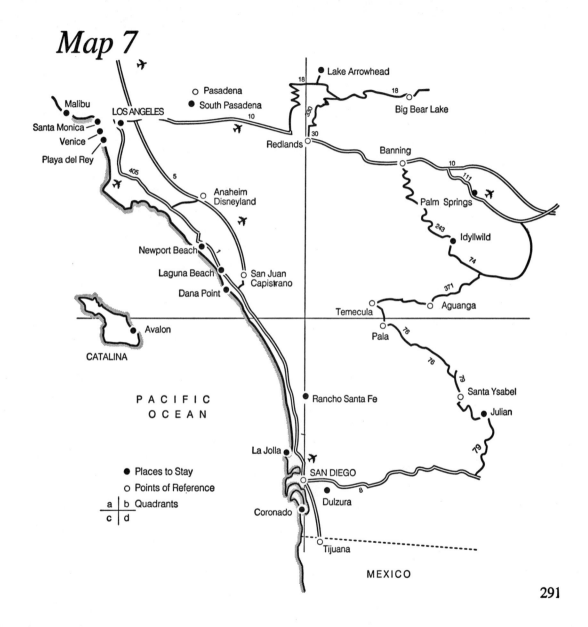

Map 7

Malibu

LOS ANGELES ✈

○ Pasadena
● South Pasadena

Santa Monica

Venice

Playa del Rey

18

● Lake Arrowhead

18
○ Big Bear Lake

330

10

405

5

30

Redlands ○

Banning
○

10

111

Palm Springs
● ✈

○ Anaheim
   Disneyland

✈

243

Idyllwild
○

Newport Beach 1

Laguna Beach

Dana Point

○ San Juan
   Capistrano

74

371

Temecula
○

○ Aguanga

○ Avalon

CATALINA

Pala
○

76

76

79

Santa Ysabel
○

Julian
●

P A C I F I C
O C E A N

● Rancho Santa Fe

79

La Jolla ●

✈

● Places to Stay

○ Points of Reference

a	b	Quadrants
c	d	

SAN DIEGO
○

8

● Dulzura

Coronado ●

○ Tijuana

M E X I C O

Index

Karen Brown presents

Karen Brown Travel Services
Providing all your travel needs

Book your air with us and our staff, trained by Karen Brown, is available to assist the individual traveler and the travel industry with:

- Special offerings on airline tickets and car rentals

- Personalized countryside mini-tours based on Karen Brown's Guides

- Reservations for hotels, inns and B&Bs in California and Europe, as featured in Karen Brown's Guides (subject to availability)

Quality, personal service, and great values

Call Karen Brown Travel Services today!
telephone: 1-800-782-2128
fax: 415-342-8292
e-mail: KBTRAVEL@aol.com
http://www.karenbrown.com

UNITED AIRLINES
is the preferred airline of Karen Brown's Guides and
Karen Brown Travel Services

UNITED AIRLINES

is the

Preferred Airline

of

Karen Brown's Guides

and

Karen Brown Travel Services

Thank You For Your Kind Words

"When I came back from Italy last year I ordered all the Karen Brown guides to be sent to me in Hong Kong since they offer the best advice one can obtain from a guide book. We based our travels on your book and had the most wonderful time, thank you! We enjoyed our trip immensely and are busy planning our next trip around your guide." Melanie Pong, Hong Kong

"We used your guide "France: Charming Bed & Breakfasts" as our sole source of information on accommodations in the rural areas of the country. Your advice proved to be golden. Congratulations to you for your wisdom in selecting and describing these wonderful hosts." Betty and Bob Kelsey, Charlottesville, VA, USA

"My husband and I recently returned from a two week vacation touring the south and west of Ireland using your book as our guide. We had a marvelous trip, in large part, because your book is so accurate, easy to read, and well organized. Thanks for helping to make our vacation so terrific." Sandy Mullaney, Mashfield, MA, USA

*"I've been using your book for over five years now. I live in Italy with my Italian husband and we use your book **always** for our vacations, weekend getaways, and business trips. You guys have found everything! I'm always guaranteed a wonderful trip when I'm lucky enough to get a room in a hotel mentioned in your guide. Thanks for a great book and making living in Italy more enjoyable!"* Nancy Barker, Milan, Italy

"Thank you for creating your guide. I had vague stirrings toward the Dordogne/Lot, but hadn't a clue of where to go or what to do. Then, I found your guide—I'm sure you've heard this before, but it was exactly what I needed." Bruce Barnes, Mt. Shasta, CA, USA

"We like that we can trust you to have carefully scouted out and tested the places you recommend and your additional comments and notes on things to see are very useful. And all of this so logically organized and easy to reference! Thanks again for the good materials you keep providing and updating for all of us who need such expert guidance. With an new trip in mind, I always look for Karen Brown's input first." Denny Dudley, Iowa City, IA, USA

"Thank you, Karen, for your insightful and accurate recommendations. Our trip would not have had nearly the impact without these wonderful experiences." Holly and Gary Campbell, Atlanta, GA, USA

Thank You For Your Kind Words

"Thank you for creating such a wonderful guide book, "Ireland: Charming Inns & Itineraries." I found your book to be most useful in my travels and I consider it to be my "bible" in recommending accommodations and sights to my clients. I have a travel business which specializes in places "off the beaten path" for which your books detail many excellent suggestions. Bravissima for such well-written and complete books." Sharon P. Sands, Roads Not Taken, Orlando, FL, USA

"We have used almost all of your books at one time or another and you have brought us many wonderful experiences." Pat and Bob Brown (no relation!), Portola Valley, CA USA

"Your guidebooks have served us, and friends, as an invaluable basis for enjoying the countryside of Europe. They have never steered us wrong; in fact, you so invariably "steer us right" that we are very big fans of Karen Brown's Guides. Thanks for such a fine, useful series of books." Maureen and Scott Holmberg, Atlanta, GA, USA

"This year my husband and I had the opportunity to tour the coastline of California from San Diego to San Francisco. It was a glorious trip and we had our first experience with staying at bed and breakfasts. We became familiar with your guidebook while at the J. Patrick Inn and found that it was our bible for the remainder of our trip. On our next trip we will certainly not leave home without your guidebook." Betty Caskey, Rockport, IN, USA

"We've used your Italian, English, German, and French guides and couldn't have been more pleased. Thanks for making our trips so great!" Susan M. Otstott, Dallas, TX, USA

"We absolutely love your guides. You're our most favorite travel book for France and Germany for the past ten years, plus. Thank you! Thank you!" Kim and Doug Wetmore, Foothill Ranch, CA, USA

"What a trip we had!!!! Your Charming Inns and Bed and Breakfast books were both just great. All I can say is that we have recommended your books to everybody, and will continue to do so. Thank you for writing your wonderful books, you made our trip." Suzi and Bryce Neff, West Hills, CA, USA

"My wife and I used your guide to Italy for our recent vacation there and want to thank you for your excellent advice. We would recommend your guides to anyone." Mitchell Reiss, New York, NY, USA

Seal Cove Inn

Located in the San Francisco Bay Area

Karen Brown Herbert (best known as author of the Karen Brown's guides) and her husband, Rick, have put 20 years of experience into reality and opened their own superb hideaway, Seal Cove Inn. Spectacularly set amongst wild flowers and bordered by towering cypress trees, Seal Cove Inn looks out to the distant ocean over acres of county park: an oasis where you can enjoy secluded beaches, explore tidepools, watch frolicking seals, and follow the tree-lined path that traces the windswept ocean bluffs. Country antiques, original watercolors, flower-laden cradles, rich fabrics, and the gentle ticking of grandfather clocks create the perfect ambiance for a foggy day in front of the crackling log fire. Each bedroom is its own haven with a cozy sitting area before a wood-burning fireplace and doors opening onto a private balcony or patio with views to the park and ocean. Moss Beach is a 35-minute drive south of San Francisco, 6 miles north of the picturesque town of Half Moon Bay, and a few minutes from Princeton harbor with its colorful fishing boats and restaurants. Seal Cove Inn makes a perfect base for whale-watching, salmon-fishing excursions, day trips to San Francisco, exploring the coast, or, best of all, just a romantic interlude by the sea, time to relax and be pampered. Karen and Rick look forward to the pleasure of welcoming you to their coastal hideaway.

Seal Cove Inn, 221 Cypress Avenue, Moss Beach, California 94038, USA
Tel: (415) 728-7325   Fax: (415) 728-4116   E-mail: sealcove@coastside.net

CLARE BROWN has many years of experience in the field of travel and has earned the designation of Certified Travel Consultant. Since 1969 she has specialized in planning itineraries to Europe using charming small hotels in the countryside for her clients. The focus of her job remains unchanged, but now her expertise is available to a larger audience—the readers of her daughter's country inn guides. Clare lives in Hillsborough, California, with her husband, Bill.

KAREN BROWN wrote her first travel guide in 1976. Her personalized travel series has grown to 12 titles and Karen and her small staff work diligently to keep all the guides updated. Karen, her husband, Rick, and their children, Alexandra and Richard, live on the coast south of San Francisco at their own country inn, Seal Cove Inn, in Moss Beach.

BARBARA TAPP, the talented artist who produces all of the hotel sketches and delightful illustrations in this guide, was raised in Australia where she studied in Sydney at the School of Interior Design. Although Barbara continues with freelance projects, she devotes much of her time to illustrating the Karen Brown guides. Barbara lives in Kensington, California, with her husband, Richard, their two sons, Jonothan and Alexander, and daughter, Georgia.

JANN POLLARD, the artist responsible for the beautiful painting on the cover of this guide, has studied art since childhood, and is well-known for her outstanding impressionistic-style watercolors which she has exhibited in numerous juried shows, winning many awards. Jann travels frequently to Europe (using Karen Brown's guides) where she loves to paint historical buildings. Jann lives in Burlingame, California, with her husband, Gene.

Order Form for 1997 Editions of Karen Brown's Guides

Please ask in your local bookstore for KAREN BROWN'S GUIDES. If the books you want are unavailable, you may order directly from the publisher. Books will be shipped immediately.

Austria: Charming Inns & Itineraries $17.95

California: Charming Inns & Itineraries $17.95

England: Charming Bed & Breakfasts $16.95

England, Wales & Scotland: Charming Hotels & Itineraries $17.95

France: Charming Bed & Breakfasts $16.95

France: Charming Inns & Itineraries $17.95

Germany: Charming Inns & Itineraries $17.95

Ireland: Charming Inns & Itineraries $17.95

Italy: Charming Bed & Breakfasts $16.95

Italy: Charming Inns & Itineraries $17.95

Spain: Charming Inns & Itineraries $17.95

Switzerland: Charming Inns & Itineraries $17.95

Name _____ Street _____

Town _____ State _____ Zip _____ Tel _____

Credit Card (MasterCard or Visa) _____ Exp _____

For additional information about Karen Brown's Guides visit our web site at karenbrown.com

For orders in the USA, add $4 for the first book and $1 for each additional book for shipment. California residents add 8.25% sales tax. Overseas orders add $10 per book for airmail shipment. Indicate number of copies of each title; fax or mail form with check or credit card information to:

KAREN BROWN'S GUIDES
Post Office Box 70, San Mateo, California 94401, USA
tel: (415) 342-9117   fax: (415) 342-9153   e-mail: karen@karenbrown.com